The Sensible Guide to Program Management Professional (PgMP)® Success

The Sensible Guide to Program Management Professional (PgMP)® Success

Including 420 Practice Exam Questions

Dr. Te Wu (PfMP®, PgMP®, PMP®, PMI-RMP®)

Estee Wu,
Contributor

CRC Press
Taylor & Francis Group
Boca Raton London New York

CRC Press is an imprint of the
Taylor & Francis Group, an **informa** business

AN AUERBACH BOOK

CRC Press
Boca Raton and London

First Edition published 2021
by CRC Press
6000 Broken Sound Parkway NW, Suite 300, Boca Raton, FL 33487-2742

and by CRC Press
2 Park Square, Milton Park, Abingdon, Oxon, OX14 4RN

© 2021 Taylor & Francis Group, LLC

CRC Press is an imprint of Taylor & Francis Group, LLC

The right of Te Wu to be identified as author of this work has been asserted by him in accordance with sections 77 and 78 of the Copyright, Designs and Patents Act 1988.

Library of Congress Cataloging-in-Publication Data
A catalog record has been requested for this book

ISBN: 978-1-032-03319-8 (hbk)
ISBN: 978-0-367-70237-3 (pbk)
ISBN: 978-1-003-14516-5 (ebk)

Typeset in Garamond
by KnowledgeWorks Global Ltd.

DEDICATION

This book was written during the COVID-19 pandemic, depressing, or worse distressing billions of lives around the world. We, the humanity, fought back valiantly, utilizing every arsenal available. This includes applying project and program management to develop vaccines, scale up the production, manage the logistics of distribution, and deliver the jabs into the arms of billions.

This book is dedicated to all ***project, program, and portfolio management professionals***, especially in (1) healthcare industries who have endless hours helping others, developing drugs, planning the massive logistical challenges of distributing the vaccines, and other vital roles, (2) educational sectors that had to rapidly adjust how the world learns, and (3) essential businesses that have kept us fed and warm during the darkest of hours. Thank you!

Contents

Preface

This book is designed for professionals taking the Program Management Professional (PgMP)® exam based on the *Standard for Program Management – 4th Edition* (PgM4 Standard). As a principle-based standard, the Project Management Institute (PMI) has shifted away from the traditional processes and knowledge areas. The impact on the exam is complicated. On the positive side, the PgMP exam has far less "memorization" than Project Management Professional (PMP). However, as an experience-based exam, the depth of understanding of program management knowledge and applications is much deeper, and passing the exam requires a significant amount of program management experience.

At the time of this book's publication, the number of PgMP professionals is just slightly over 3,000 active credential holders. This means that there is relatively little experience with the exam. Based on anecdotal evidence, discussions with various entities administering the exam, and PMO Advisory's experience of training professionals for the PgMP exam, this exam is likely the most difficult of the PMI certification exams. Therefore, to create an effective guide to help you, I took a fresh approach. In addition to providing exam tips, practice questions, and more sample deliverables, this book takes on a more Socratic approach of questions and answers. I hope through thinking and understanding the key challenges and issues, you will be more prepared for the experience-based questions that are prevalent on this exam.

Furthermore, this book does not claim to be an "all in one" guide. It is highly unrealistic for anyone interested in any of the PMI's certifications to go without a thorough understanding of its underlying standards, whether it is the *Project Management Body of Knowledge* (*PMBOK® Guide*), the *Standard for Portfolio Management*, or in this case, the *Standard for Program Management*. Therefore, this book should be viewed as a companion guide to the *Standard for Program Management – 4th Edition*. It augments the PgM4 Standard with additional clarifications, sample deliverables, and key questions and answers that every program professional needs to know.

In short, this book is designed for busy professionals like you whose responsibilities have taken them into the realm of coordinating, facilitating, managing, and leading programs. Program managers are leaders who are directly managing large amounts of project resources for your organization. This book primarily addresses three concerns:

1. What are the essential concepts, processes, and tools that form the foundation of today's program management?
2. Since program management is still an emerging profession with professionals often working in different ways, what does this mean for a "standard" exam? More specifically, how does that impact your ability to pass the PgMP exam?
3. What is the best way to prepare for the PgMP exam?

On the first concern, this book highlights the underlying rationale for program management: why it exists in organizations, why it is becoming ever more important, how to think like a portfolio manager (especially important since experience-based exam questions are difficult to predict) and what are the most important concepts, processes, and tools for this profession. This book attempts to simplify complex ideas and communicate them in plain English with relevant examples. The goal is not only to pass the PgMP exam, but also to serve as an essential guide to program managers.

On the second concern, this book differs from most other study guides by describing my experience as a program manager and addressing the most pressing questions for each performance domain in the *Standard for Program Management.*

To address the third concern, this book includes the following resources to help readers prepare for the exam:

1. *Content.* The content in this book is based on tried-and-true approaches from PMO Advisory, a premier PMI Authorized Training Partner that has achieved a 99% first time pass rate, sustained since 2016.
2. *Practice Questions and PgMP Exam Simulator.* This book contains 420 sample and practice questions. By registering this book at www.pmoadvisory.com/product-registration, recipients receive access to the PgMP Exam Simulator with access to these 420 questions for up to 30 days free.
3. *Support Group.* All registered users of this book will be invited to a moderated LinkedIn forum dedicated to users of this book and our products. Here, PMO Advisory will regularly monitor the questions and provide answers to your questions. It is my hope that others in the Group will also provide peer support.
4. *PgMP Exam Simulator.* Discount to PMO Advisory's PgMP Simulator with more questions, PgMP bootcamps, and other resources, you need to register this book at www.pmoadvisory.com/product-registration. Make sure you attach the receipt to receive 30 days of access. (If you do not have a receipt, you can still receive 10 days of access for free.)

Core Principles

This book is based on three core principles that underpin all materials in this book. These are designed to add tremendous value to you. This book assumes that you are intelligent, accomplished, and very busy. Therefore, where feasible this book will:

1. Use the simplest language possible to enable greater clarity
2. Provide the basic rationale to encourage deeper understanding
3. Refer to the *Standard of Program Management – 4th Edition*, henceforth referred to as the "Standard" or "PgM4 Standard", where this book cannot add significant value

The last principle assumes an obvious fact. All prospective program managers planning to take the PgMP exam should read and understand *The Standard of Program Management – 4th Edition*. The PMI made substantial improvements to this latest edition, and it is a worthy reference guide. I studied the 1st edition thoroughly back in 2010 when I prepared for the PgMP exam. I am pleasantly surprised at the improvements in the subsequent editions, especially the 4th edition, which had many refinements from the 3rd edition. While I may not necessarily agree with everything in the Standard, it is an excellent guide.

In this sense, this book should be viewed as a companion guide that advances the two concerns stated in the opening paragraph: highlighting of the core concepts and building the necessary mindset required for program professionals to pass the PgMP exam

Clarification: In common business language, the role of program management can be ambiguous. The term is commonly used in the industry by professionals managing large projects. In the government, defense, and education sectors, the term "program" and "program management" are often ubiquitous. Most of these endeavors are projects, not programs. In the Standard and in this program, program refers to a collection of highly related projects, subprograms, and other initiatives, and the success of the overall program depends on the contribution of all the program components. Program management is the art and discipline of managing large, complex, and often deeply entangled endeavors and organizations strive to achieve greater value and effectiveness by utilizing program management. Think of 1 + 1 + 1 > 3. How to best achieve these gains and successfully deliver the endeavor is the role of program managers.

Acknowledgments

Some of the materials in this book have been extracted or adapted from previous publications including *The Sensible Guide to Passing the PfMP Exam* (iExperi Press) and *Optimizing Project Management* (Taylor & Francis), from PMO Advisory's Program Management Professional (PgMP) training materials, and from blogs and articles that I have written over the years. These are reproduced with permission from Te Wu and PMO Advisory.

I would like to sincerely thank all our dedicated PgMP bootcamp customers who we had the honor of helping. Since we first offered the PgMP bootcamp in traditional classroom format in 2016, the world has changed and PMO Advisory has adapted to the new virtual and eLearning world. From your feedback over the years, we have progressively improved our content and delivery methods to achieve an over 99% first time pass rate. My gratitude also extends to our PgMP trainers, including Mike Otero, Charmagne Tellis, and Brian Williamson. Many of their nuggets of wisdom and insights are embedded in this book.

I am a fortunate person, and in my career, I had many great mentors who have helped me to reach new heights. Here, I like to thank the people that truly mattered: Janice O'Neill, my first manager after graduating from college; Ken Warren, who gave me the opportunity to start my first professional business (and shipped me overseas); Sarah Henry, who exposed me to better ways of empowering people and teams; Eamonn Maguire, who challenged me to think out of the box; Mike Cole, who constantly pushed me to do the right things; Richard Peterson, who encouraged me to teach and pave that way; Li-Chun Lin, who showed me that decency and care truly matter; and to many others who have guided and supported me.

I also want to thank extend my thanks to John Wyzalek and everyone at CRC Press/Taylor & Francis Group for their dedication and support. This includes providing editorial direction, guidance, and management of the book's development process. This is our second book together, and I am looking forward to many more.

Finally, I like to thank my family for their continuous love and support. A special thanks goes to my wonderful daughter, Estee Wu, who has spent the holiday season of 2020 helping me edit this book.

About the Author

Dr. Prof. Te Wu is the founder and CEO of PMO Advisory, one of the most specialized project management consulting and training firms. On consulting, the firm concentrates on strategic business execution, specializing in Project Management Office (PMO) and project management. On training, the firm is an authorized training partner of the Project Management Institute (PMI) and is one of the first organizations to offer PMI certification training in Portfolio Management Professional (PfMP®), Program Management Professional (PgMP®), Project Management Professional (PMP®), Risk Management Professional (PMI-RMP®), and Agile Certified Practitioner (PMI-ACP®) training. In addition, the firm also offers training in organization change management, PMO, business management, and strategic business execution. The firm is a socially progressive firm balancing the goals of profitability with social aims. Dr. Wu is also a professor at multiple universities including Montclair State University (second largest university in New Jersey) and China Europe International Business School (CEIBS is ranked number 5 among the top MBA programs in the world by the Financial Times in 2019). Previously, he also taught at Stevens Institute of Technology and Touro Graduate School of Business.

With over 25 years of experience of helping businesses to improve their strategy execution, Dr. Wu is one of the few in the world with these professional certifications: portfolio management (PfMP), program management (PgMP), project management (PMP), and risk management (PMI-RMP). He is also an award-winning project manager, earning Honorable Mention in 2015 Project of the Year by the PMI-NJ Chapter.

Dr. Wu holds a doctorate degree with a dual concentration in management and international business from Pace University, two master degrees in industrial engineering and MBA from Columbia University and University of Phoenix, and two bachelor degrees in chemical engineering and philosophy from Stevens Institute of Technology. Besides running PMO Advisory and teaching, he has served on Project Management Institute Global's Portfolio Management and Risk Management standard committees as a core member, and he is currently active on several task teams. At the chapter level, he is currently the Director of Symposium for PMI-NYC Chapter. In his spare time, he enjoys writing business articles and blogs, speaking at conferences especially when there are opportunities to expound on the value of project management, traveling to different corners of the world with his family, and just sitting back and reading good books and watching Netflix.

PfMP, PgMP, PMP, and PMI-RMP logos are registered marks of Project Management Institute Inc.

Organization of This Book

This book is presented in ten chapters. Each chapter is written so that they are largely independent, and you can easily jump from one section to another. Chapter 1 provides an overview of the PgMP exam, test-taking tips, context of program management, a framework to look at the abstract level of organization activities, and starts to develop the necessary mindset of program managers. Chapter 10 contains two full length practice exams. Chapters 2–8 are largely aligned with the Standard, and these chapters each contain four sections:

1. Overview of the performance domain
2. Key concepts and additional explanations (when applicable)
3. Additional example of program management application, such as tools and techniques
4. Twenty practice questions

Chapter 1: Introduction to Program Management Profession and Its Credential
The first part of this chapter discusses the PgMP certification qualification, certification application process, and some likely challenges. Then, the chapter presents a study plan and test-taking strategy designed to ease anxiety and aid in the test-taking process. Next, this chapter addresses the question of what are programs and program management and their relationship between project management, program management, portfolio management, business strategy, and organization. This chapter will also describe the mindset of program managers and how they should think.

Chapter 2: Understanding Program Management Performance Domains
PMI's current *Program Management Standard – 4th Edition* presents five performance domains including strategy alignment, benefits management, stakeholder engagement, governance, and program life cycle management. There are also three life cycle phases: definition, delivery, and closure.

Chapter 3: Understanding Program Strategy Alignment
Program strategy alignment is the first performance domain in the Standard, and it serves as a strong link between the program and the associated strategy. This chapter also clearly emphasizes the importance of programs as mechanisms to achieve organizational goals and objectives. This chapter will cover the important principles and key concepts.

Chapter 4: Understanding Program Benefits Management
Organizations should not undertake a program lightly as it is resource intensive and often risky. But programs are also enablers to achieve significant benefits for the sponsoring organization. This chapter explains the importance of benefits management and how program managers can successfully achieve the intended benefits.

Chapter 5: Understanding Program Stakeholder Engagement
Programs are large, and they involved many stakeholders. Program managers must carefully identify, evaluate, plan, and engage the multitude of stakeholders at the right time and in the most effective way to achieve the desired outcomes.

Chapter 6: Understanding Program Governance
Perhaps what best differentiates programs from projects is the emphasis on good governance, which is essential for decision-making, especially on highly contentious programs. In addition to covering the key principles and concepts, this chapter will discuss some practical examples of its application.

Chapter 7: Understanding Program Life Cycle Management
Similar to projects, programs are temporary endeavors, and they have a life cycle in which programs are first defined, then executed, and finally closed. As stated in Chapter 1, there are two possible program life cycle phases on the exam – one for the PgM4 Standard and another from the Examination Content Outline (ECO). This chapter will explain both and map the two different life cycles to each other.

Chapter 8: Understanding Program Activities
Embedded within the life cycle are a series of program activities. For those who appreciate the *Project Management Body of Knowledge*, a majority of these activities are highly similar with the *PMBOK® Guide*'s knowledge area. The book will use this opportunity to provide more details about these program activities.

Chapter 9: Program Management Skills
This chapter contains a full description of over 120 program management skills. For those who are preparing for the PgMP exam, it is important to understand and be able to articulate these common skills as many of them will appear on the exam.

Chapter 10: Full Practice Tests
This chapter contains two full-length exams with 170 questions each.

Additional Support by Registering This Book

Since the author of this book, Dr. Te Wu, is also the CEO of PMO Advisory, he has made arrangements for the readers of this book to receive additional support for the preparation of the exam. Registrants of this book will receive the following support free of charge:

1. Access to a special edition of the PgMP Exam Simulator with 420 exam questions in this book for up to 30 days. Readers can access the PgMP Exam Simulator via browser, and it is designed to work well with mobile devices too.
   a. For the original purchase of this book, by submitting a copy of the receipt, you will receive 30 days of access.
   b. For all other readers, you will receive 10 days of free access.
2. Digital copy of the PgMP Exam Aid as shown in Chapter 1, Figure 1.3.
3. Discounts to PMO Advisory's PgMP courses, offered in multiple modes including eLearning, Live Virtual, traditional classroom, and onsite.

To register the book, visit www.pmoadvisory.com/product-registration.

About Project Management Institute and Program Management Professional
About PMI
The Project Management Institute (PMI®) is currently the world's large project management professional organization dedicated to advancing the project management profession. According to the November/December 2020 issue of *PMI Today*, there are 627,346 members around the world. Its most popular certification is the Project Management Professional (PMP®) with over 1,038,000 credential holders.

PMI currently has eight active certifications in which PMI provides the active credential holder information (Table I.1).

By becoming a certified professional, you are joining a growing family of project professionals.

Table I.1 PMI® Certifications

#	Certification Name	Number of Active Credential Holders[a]
1	CAPM or Certified Associate in Project Management®	46,357
2	PMP or Project Management Professional®	1,038,797
3	PfMP or Portfolio Management Professional[SM]	896
4	PgMP or Program Management Professional®	3,002
5	PMI-RMP or Risk Management Professional®	6,309
6	PMI-SP or Scheduling Professional®	2,176
7	PMI-ACP or Agile Certified Professional®	36,839
8	PMI-PBA or Professionals in Business Analysis[SM]	4,188

[a]According to PMI Fact File in PMI Today, November/December 2020 issue.

About Program Management Professional (PgMP)

Based on the increasing demand of project professionals, the PMI developed the new PgMP certification and initiated the PgMP credential process in 2007. According to the Credential Library on January 1, 2021, there are 3,088 PgMPs. (This number differs from *PMI Today* likely because of the publication delays.) The PgMPs are distributed among 90 countries with the United States in the lead with 1,190 PgMPs. Of the PgMPs in the United States, California has the highest number (147), followed by Virginia (132), Texas (123), and New Jersey (68). See Tables I.2 and I.3 and Figures I.1 and I.2 for details.

Personal Note: The inclusion in the Certification Registry is voluntary. Therefore, not all credential holders are listed. Also, based on this registry, I am the 391th person in the world achieving and still holding the certification.

About the **Standard for Program Management – 4th Edition**

The *Standard for Program Management* (the "Standard" or the "PgM4 Standard") is PMI's latest update to refresh and to formalize the discipline of project program management. Currently in the 4th edition, the Standard is essential for you to carefully read and assimilate the principles and performance domains in this standard in order to pass the PgMP exam.

The PgM4 Standard is a principle-based standard in which the "how" of program management is largely absent. The benefit of a principle-based standard is the greater universality of applications. For aspiring Program Management Professionals, the latest standard is considerably shorter than the *PMBOK® Guide*. But lacking "hows" also makes the exam more difficult to study, as the exam is now based more on experience and less on "memorization" of processes, inputs, outputs,

Table I.2 Top 20 PgMPs Countries

#	Country	PgMP
1	United States	1,190
2	China, mainland	350
3	India	340
4	Canada	233
5	Saudi Arabia	140
6	Australia	111
7	United Arab Emirates	72
8	Singapore	51
9	United Kingdom	39
10	Germany	33
11	France	28
12	Ireland	27
13	Switzerland	25
14	Qatar	24
15	Pakistan	21
16	Hong Kong	20
17	Egypt	19
18	Italy	19
19	Jordan	18
20	Mexico	17

Table I.3   Top 20 PgMPs US States

#	State	PgMP
1	CA	147
2	VA	132
3	TX	123
4	NJ	68
5	FL	66
6	GA	56
7	IL	50
8	NC	48
9	MD	47
10	AZ	36
11	CO	34
12	PA	33
13	MA	29
14	MN	29
15	NY	28
16	MI	25
17	OH	24
18	WA	22
19	CT	18
20	IN	17

tools, and techniques. This book addresses this challenge by emphasizing the need to develop the right mindset, which enables test takers to ask the right questions and think critically as a PgMP.

In addition, to make this book truly easier for aspiring PgMPs, I have worked with PMI and received their permission to use the key concepts including the performance domains. This is a significant advantage to you, who will be spending many hours studying for the exam. Unlike other guides that may not have the intellectual property rights, this book will use these key terms exactly the same as how they would be used on exams. Not only will this save considerable effort, it will also reduce confusion.

Figure I.3 highlights the three important frameworks whose understanding is required for passing the PgMP exam.

Global Map of PgMP Credential Holders (n/i United States)

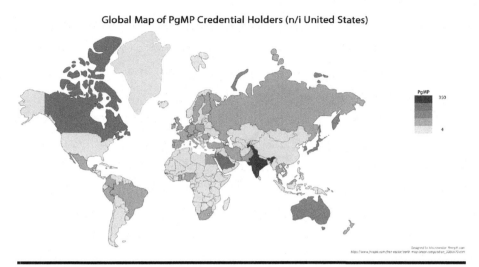

Figure I.1   Active PgMP credential holders, by country (not including the United States).

About Program Management Career

In many, if not most, organizations, program management is an evolutionary improvement above and beyond project management. Organically, as organizations grow, they start to tackle bigger, more complex, and more involved

United States Map of PgMP Credential Holders

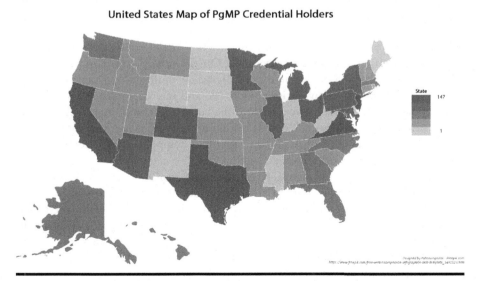

Figure I.2   Active PgMP credential holders in United States.

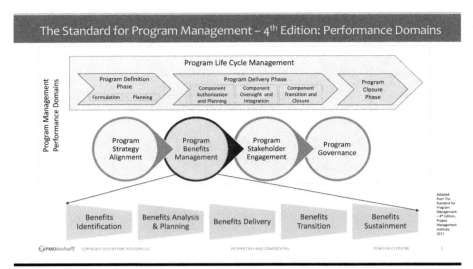

Figure I.3   Important program management frameworks (used with permission).

business initiatives. These initiatives often have many components. Programs can contain a combination of projects, subprograms, and other program-related work including operational activities. One of the main goals of the program is to manage them in a coordinated and integrated fashion to achieve additional efficiency.

Commonly in today's business world, programs have a broad range from "loose" to "tight" interconnectedness of components or centrality of goals. Loose programs are more like portfolios, which is a collection of related components but not necessarily interconnected components. A loose program may share or have dependencies or share similar resources, for example. On the other hand, a tight program is by definition very interconnected, typically across multiple considerations such as common business objectives, time, resources, and interdependencies. In a truly tight program, the failure or weakness of one component impacts gravely on the overall health of the program. PMI's definition of program is more leaning toward a tight program than a loosely connected group of components. See Section 1.3.3 for a clearer description of program.

Professionally, program managers are responsible to lead programs, which in most organizations require more responsibility and authority. Figure I.4 provides an idealized career path for project professionals. In my view, program management represents the highest level of the technical side of the project management discipline. Beyond program management, for example, portfolio managers are generally more business and executive oriented than applying technical leadership to execute business initiatives.

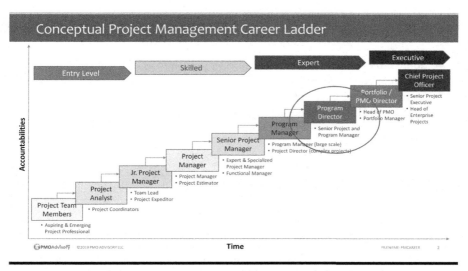

Figure I.4   Project management career ladder (used with permission).

Even though, for most people, program management is the next logical career advancement for project managers, there can be non-traditional paths leading to program management. For example, through my work in PMO Advisory with our customers and PMI, it is clear that at least two alternative paths exist:

1. Business executives who are not traditional project managers but have managed large initiatives for their organizations. Even though these executives are not necessarily trained in project management, they command the prerequisite knowledge of working with project managers.
2. Professionals in the government and other related sectors that may not have the traditional business project management role. For example, strategy alignment is likely to occur at the Director level with Congressional oversight. In those cases, program alignment responsibilities are largely involved in execution and not definition. Nonetheless, PMI recognizes these special circumstances and approve some of our customers for the PgMP certification.

Please note that one of the qualifications for the certification is having a minimum of four years of project management experience. In these alternate routes above, even though the professional may not have the formal project management title, their responsibilities still require the prerequisite project leadership experience. If your background falls into one of these areas or if you never had the "project manager" job title before, then please be extra diligent to explain why your prior experience is equivalent with the project manager role.

Abbreviations and Acronyms

Throughout this book, we used abbreviations and acronyms for three reasons:

- Some tables are dense and place a heavy premium on the spacing
- Some concepts and names are long and are used frequently
- Some acronyms have become a part of the natural language or are commonly used by PMI. Therefore, they may appear on exams as acronyms.

Abbreviation or Acronym	Description
ECO	Examination Content Outline
PfMP®	Portfolio Management Professional
PgMP®	Program Management Professional
PMBOK® Guide	A Guide to the Project Management Body of Knowledge
PMI®	Project Management Institute
PMIS	Program management information system
PMP®	Project Management Professional
Standard	The Standard for Program Management – 4th Edition

PgMP, PfMP, PMP, PMI, and PMBOK Guide are registered marks of Project Management Institute, Inc.

Chapter 1

Introduction to Program Management Profession and Its Credential

In this chapter, you will

- Learn the Program Management Professional (PgMP) qualification, process, and exam details
- Learn a tried and proven approach to studying for the exam
- Customize your own strategy and approach to passing the PgMP exam
- Learn a simplified framework for organization and how program management serves to advance organization strategies
- Learn to think like a program manager

1.1 About PgMP Certification

1.1.1 PgMP Certification Requirements

The bar of entry to become a PgMP is set intentionally high. It is designed for current program managers looking to advance their career by solidifying and proving their ability to coordinate, manage, and lead a program of multiple projects and other endeavors. PgMP can be seen as a distinctive differentiator among the professionals and in the eyes of employers. Attaining the certification indicates a command of the program management knowledge and skills and provides significantly greater credibility professionally.

To qualify for PgMP, applicants must have the qualifications as listed in Figure 1.1.

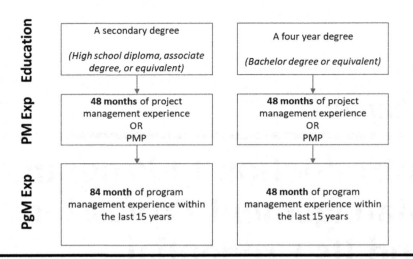

Figure 1.1   PgMP minimum qualifications.

To qualify for the certification, a professional MUST have 48 months of project management experience and up to 84 months of program management experience. Unlike Project Managemet Professional (PMP), there is no additional education requirement. However, even for advanced practitioners, it is imperative to read the Standard and this study guide carefully. Similar to PMP and PgMP, it is not sufficient to pass the exam based solely on work experience. The purpose of PgMP exam by Project Management Institute (PMI) is to ensure PMP credential holders have similar foundational knowledge.

1.1.2 PgMP Certification Process

The PgMP application occurs in two phases (or evaluations as PMI calls them):

- In Phase 1, the panel will review your completed application. Upon its completion, the applicant can proceed to Phase 2.
- Phase 2 is the PgMP examination in which you have one whole year to pass.

Note: PMI audits about 10–15% of the applications, and this occurs during Phase 1.

To start Phase 1, simply go to www.pmi.org to apply for the PgMP credential. Sign in to your account or create a new account. In the Certification Program page, click on "Apply for PgMP Credential." PMI also offers the following reference materials to aid in the credential process. These include:

1. PgMP Handbook
2. PgMP exam content outline (ECO)

Both of these publications can be found here: https://www.pmi.org/certifications/program-management-pgmp/exam-prep.

My suggestions for you are as follows:

1. Join PMI, if you are not a member already. The cost of the PgMP credential can be expensive ($800 for members and $1,000 USD for non-members at the time of writing). Therefore, the discount of $200 more than offsets the cost of PMI membership. Furthermore, included in the annual membership fee, you have access to the three important standards: Project, Program, and Portfolio. The Standard for Program Management – Fourth Edition costs about $40 at retail.

2. Download the Standard for Program Management – Fourth Edition and read it carefully. Make sure you gain a working knowledge of the five performance domains, by reading the Standard and reviewing Chapters 3–8 of this book. This knowledge will help you complete the application.

3. Complete the application process. In addition to developing a working knowledge of the five performance domains, make sure you start to document your program management experiences and key contacts who can serve as professional references.

4. After submitting the application, be prepared to be audited. (I had the "pleasure" of being audited on the PgMP and Portfolio Management Professional (PfMP) application process. It was not too painful.)

5. As stated in the handbook, the process time is 10 business days for online application and 20 days for paper applications. Early experience has shown the turnaround time to be much quicker.

6. Once PMI approves your application, then you have one year to pass the PgMP exam. Within this one-year period, you are allowed to take the exam up to three times. Each of the subsequent exams cost $600 for members and $800 for non-members. Given this expense, it is highly recommended to effectively prepare and pass the exam on the first or second attempt. If you fail the PgMP exam three times, you must wait for another year before you may reapply and resubmit your credentials all over again.

7. The exam policies and procedures are extensive. For those who have completed other PMI certifications, the exam policies and procedures are similar. Please re-read the PgMP Handbook to get reacquainted.

8. When scheduling for the exam, my recommendation is to schedule it for late morning, assuming the testing site is within an hour of where you live. The late morning, say 10 or 10:30 AM, gives you the ability to sleep late, eat a larger than usual but healthy meal, avoid morning rush traffic, drive leisurely to the exam site, and finish by a reasonable time in which you can avoid the rush hour drive home.

My company, PMO Advisory, has written extensively on this topic and presented in webinars. For more information, review this blog article: https://www.pmoadvisory.

com/blog/preparing-and-completing-pmi-certification-applications-pmp-pgmp-pfmp-acp-rmp/.

1.1.3 Some Quick Words on Maintaining PgMP Credential

Maintaining the PgMP certification is relatively straightforward, especially for those who have the PMP credential. This is because PgMP and PMP share the same professional development units (PDUs) and professionals can "double dip" on the PDUs. Remember, to maintain the PgMP Active status, professionals need to earn 60 PDUs every three years. The minimum education requirement is 35 PDUs, and the maximum Giving Back PDUs is 25.

Also, similar to PMP, PgMP can transfer up to 20 PDUs to the next continuing certification requirement (CCR) cycle. Only PDUs earned in the 12 months preceding the renewal qualifies can be applied to the next cycle.

For more information on maintaining credential status, please refer to the CCCR handbook: http://www.pmi.org/-/media/pmi/documents/public/pdf/certifications/ccr-certification-requirements-handbook.pdf.

1.1.4 PgMP Exam

The PgMP examination is similar in format with most of the PMI exams. It is composed of 170 questions of which 20 are pre-test questions and therefore do not affect the test score. These questions are placed randomly throughout the exam to test the validity of future exam questions. But since you do not know which questions are pre-test versus real exam questions, this distinction is largely useful only for PMI. For you as the test taker, your job is to complete 170 questions within the four hours for computer-based testing (CBT). In the next section, this book will present a test-taking strategy. It is important to adopt a strategy even before you study. This way, you will develop a helpful routine that should maximize your effectiveness during the actual exam.

Note: Since CBT is the standard method for administering the exam, this book covers only the CBT. PMI does offer a paper-based testing on an exception basis. Please refer to the PgMP Handbook's section on Examination Administration for more details.

1.2 Taking and Preparing for the PgMP Exam

Based on fairly substantial experience with PMI examinations, this book recommends that you plan the major steps backward from the end. While none of us can foresee the future with great accuracy, by envisioning the future state and slowly shifting backwards helps you plan better. Thus, this section covers three major steps, backwards:

i. Taking the exam
ii. Count down to the exam, five days prior to the exam time
iii. You passed Phase 1, Phase 2 starts, and the one-year countdown begins

1.2.1 Test-Taking Strategy

Other than the clothing your wear, two perhaps three pencils, blank papers for you to scribble notes, and possibly a pair of earplugs to block out noise, you enter the exam room with nothing else. Depending on the room setup, it may actually feel claustrophobic. So take a deep breath and get ready. Take time to make yourself comfortable like adjusting your seat, placing the keyboard and mouse in the optimal position, and adjusting the monitor if necessary. This is where you will spend the next four hours taking the test.

The exam is preceded by a tutorial on the computer-based training. If you finish the tutorial early, use the remaining minutes to relax your mind and calm your body. Once you exit the tutorial, the four-hour countdown begins. Table 1.1 shows my recommended test-taking strategy on how to spend these four hours. Figure 1.2 shows how to create a scoring sheet to help you track your progress and estimate your exam performance.

Table 1.1 Recommendation on Exam Time Utilization

#	Key Objective	Action	Est. Time
1	"Download" everything you can remember by recreating the exam aid Reduce anxiety.	Quickly recreate the exam aid (see the next section for a fuller discussion on exam aids). Writing them down will free your mind from the stress of memorization, which reduces anxiety. It will enable you to concentrate on the exam problems.	5–10 minutes
2	Create a simple scoring sheet so you can track your estimated performance. This will help you at the end as you gauge how well you are doing.	See Figure 1.2. Creating a scoring sheet will allow you to track your progress and estimate your exam performance.	10 minutes

(continued)

Table 1.1 (Continued)   Recommendation on Exam Time Utilization

#	Key Objective	Action	Est. Time
		Notes: 1. This step is not necessary for everyone. If you know the materials very well (or very poorly), this step is not going to add value. But for most of us mortals, it is highly desirable to have some guidance. 2. Depending on the number of pieces of paper you are given, you can easily adjust this procedure to fit your preference. 3. Also, for the CBT, there is an option to mark the question. This way, you can find the marked questions quickly.	
3	Sprint 1. Start taking the exam and track your performance. Note: See below for a sample score sheet.	Keep your test-taking routine simple. Go through the exam questions sequentially. Do not skip and always select an answer, even if it is a pure guess. On average, spend 1 minute per question. For answers that 1. You are certain, put a check mark in the 90% column. This assumes you are very sure with the near certainty of being correct. 2. You are able to eliminate two answers but unsure of the remaining two, put a check mark in the 75% column. 3. You are able to eliminate one answer and unsure of the remaining three answers, put a check mark in the 50% column. 4. You are not able to eliminate any answers. Put a check mark in the 25% column.	90 minutes

(continued)

Table 1.1 (Continued) Recommendation on Exam Time Utilization

#	Key Objective	Action	Est. Time
		When you complete the first 85 questions, check the time. Ideally, the countdown clock should be at around 2:00 hours. If you need to, take a 10-minute break (which counts toward the countdown). Use this time to stretch, relax, and clear your head.	
4	Sprint 2. Getting to the finish line.	Repeat the steps in #2 for the remaining questions.	80 minutes
5	Estimate your score. The target should be a minimum of 136 (or 80%).	Quickly count the numbers of 25%, 50%, 75%, and 90% in each of the sections. Multiply the count by the probability and add them together to get an estimated total score. For example, let's say you have achieved the following: • 25% -> 5 • 50% -> 10 • 75% -> 110 • 90% -> 45 The estimated score is 129, slightly below the target. Assuming you are objective and realistic about the %, then all you need do is to review a handful of 25% and 50% and convert them to 75% to pass the test.	10 minutes
6	Review and refine 25% and 50% questions.	Spend the remaining time on reviewing and rethinking the exam questions in which you marked 25% and 50%. Even though you may be guessing on the first pass, by going through all the questions in the exam, they may offer new insights to	30 minutes

(continued)

Table 1.1 (Continued) **Recommendation on Exam Time Utilization**

#	Key Objective	Action	Est. Time
		these tough questions. Plus, it is likely that another question can trigger thoughts and memories that can improve your odds on questions with 25% and 50%.	
7	Pass the exam and start gloating.	If you are taking the CBT, the exam results should be available almost immediately. Be prepared to gloat with your colleagues!	

Note: Creating and keeping a score sheet can be time intensive. If you are a slow test taker, you may wish to skip these steps and save about 15–20 minutes. But for many people, including myself, I believe keeping a score sheet is immensely helpful. It provides a degree of certainty (and sanity) as you progress through the questions. I was able to gauge my grades on multiple metrics: expected score, relative worst case, and relative best case. Also, remember to practice for test taking starting five days prior to the test.

#	25%	50%	75%	90%	#	25%	50%	75%	90%	#	25%	50%	75%	90%
1					31					61				
2					32					62				
3					33					63				
4					34					64				
5					35					65				
6					36					66				
7					37					67				
8					38					68				
9					39					69				
10					40					70				
11					41					71				
12					42					72				
13					43					73				
14					44					74				
15					45					75				
16					46					76				
17					47					77				
18					48					78				
19					49					79				
20					50					80				
21					51					81				
22					52					82				
23					53					83				
24					54					84				
25					55					85				
26					56					86				
27					57					87				
28					58					88				
29					59					...				
30					60					170				

Figure 1.2 **Sample scoring sheet.**

At this point, PMI does not publish the minimal passing score. It should be assumed to be in the range of other exams, such as PMP and PfMP. To be safe, our recommendation is to target for a minimum score of 80% or 136 questions correct – in both the practice and actual exam.

1.2.2 PgMP Exam Aid

For the purpose of preparing the exam, there are two types of exam aids:

a. Test *preparation* exam aids are designed to help students to prepare for the test. It contains important information, typically at a summary level, that can clarify confusions and help students to recall the relevant content.
b. Test-*taking* exam aids are more concise as students plan to recreate them during the exam. Since the PgMP exam is time limited, it is important to be concise.

My company has been providing the test preparation exam aid, as shown in Figure 1.3, to the PgMP training participants. The company has agreed to make it available here. If you are interested to receive a digital copy, please register this book at www.pmoadvisory.com/product-registration.

Readers can use the exam aid as is, but I highly recommend that you customize the exam aid for you. After all, you know your strengths and weaknesses and you should create one that is most suitable for you. Also, even if you adopt my firm's test *preparation* exam aid, I do not necessarily recommend you use this as the test-*taking* exam aid, mainly because recreating this can take considerable time. Remember, the PgMP exam is experience-based, and the standard is principle-based, therefore, there are few concepts, process orders, and inputs and outputs to remember.

1.2.3 Test Preparation Strategy – Count Down to the Exam (Five, Four, Three, Two, One, Zero, ...)

The final five days leading to the exam are especially important, and so use this time wisely. Ideally, you should spend an increasing amount of time to ensure retention of content and gain familiarity with any exam aids that you plan to use. Realistically, however, most of us have to work or have other responsibilities. But please make sure you spend at least a minimum of three to five hours on Days 5 and 4 and then increase it to six hours or more on Days 3 and 2. On the final day before the exam, it is perhaps more important for you to relax and get enough sleep rather than last minute cramming. It is more optimal to have a sharp mind than to remember a bunch of facts but be too tired to process.

Table 1.2 shows my recommendation on how to best maximize the five days leading to the exam.

PMO Advisory: PgMP Exam Aid

Standard for Program Management – 4th Edition

Term	Description
Program	Program activities conducted to authorize the program and develop the program roadmap required to achieve the expected results.
Program Definition Phase	Program activities performed to produce the intended results of each component in accordance with the program management plan.
Program Delivery Phase	
Program Closure Phase	Program activities necessary to transition program benefits to sustaining organization and formally close the program.
Benefits	The gains and assets realized by the organization and other stakeholders as the result of outcomes delivered by the program.
Component	A project, subsidiary programs, or other related activities conducted to support a program.

PgMP Standard Frameworks — Program Management Performance Domains

Program Life Cycle Management: Program Definition Phase · Program Delivery Phase · Program Closure Phase

Program Strategy Alignment · Program Stakeholder Engagement · Program Benefits Management · Program Governance

Benefits Identification · Benefits Analysis & Planning · Benefits Delivery · Benefits Transition · Benefits Sustainment

Earned Value Formulas

Term	Acronym	Formula	Example
Expected Monetary Value	EMV	Σ (prob. * impact)	$50,000
Budget at Completion, $	BAC, $		$50,000
Budget at Completion, Days	BAC, Days		100 Days
Planned Value	PV		$5,000
Earned Value	EV		$5,500
Actual Cost	AC		$4,500
Cost Variance	CV	EV - AC	$1,000
Schedule Variance	SV	EV - PV	$500
Cost Performance Index	CPI	EV / AC	1.22
Schedule Performance Index	SPI	EV / PV	1.10
Estimate at Completion	EAC	BAC / CPI or AC + ETC	$40,909
Estimate to Complete	ETC	EAC - AC	$36,409
Variance at Completion	VAC	BAC - EAC	$9,091
To-Complete Performance Index	TCPI	A (BAC-EV) / (BAC-AC) or B (BAC-EV) / (EAC-AC)	0.38
Time Estimate at Complete	TEAC	BAC Days / SPI	90.9
Time Variance at Complete	TVAC	BAC Days - TEAC	9.1

*** Example: Project X has a budget of $50,000 to be completed in 100 days. The planned burn rate is $500 per day on average. By Day 10, the project is clearly progressing faster, completing 10% more activities than planned and actually spent about 10% less budget than anticipated. At this point, the Earned Value calculations are shown in the Example column.

**** TCPI has two formulas. Use A when the project is under budget. Use B when the project is overbudget. In the example above, the project is under budget (since CPI is greater than 1).

Financial Formulas

Term	Acronym	Formula
Present Value	PV	Future Value / (1 + r)
Net Present Value	NPV	PV revenue – PV cost
Benefit-Cost Ratio	BCR	Cash flow / Project investment
Internal Rate of Return	IRR	% return on project investment
Payback Period	PP	Project cost / Annual cash flow

Other Important Formulas

Term	Formula
Float	LF – EF or LS - ES
PERT	(P + 4M + O) / 6
Standard Deviation	(P – O) / 6
Variance	((P – O) / 6)² or SD²
Communication Channels	N (N – 1) / 2
Planned Average Burn Rate	(BAC, $) / (BAC, Days)
Actual Average Burn Rate	EAC / (Actual Duration, Days)

Organizational Project Management — General Project, Program, Portfolio Lifecycle

Phase	Project Management (Traditional & Agile)	Program Management	Portfolio Management
Initiation	• Project vision • Business case • Scope statement* • Epics, product backlog, release planning** • Resource & constraint	In addition to Project Management: • Benefit management • Governance • Interdependencies • Stakeholder planning	• Mission, vision, culture, & people • Creation of executable strategy from business objectives
Plan	• Estimating schedule, cost, resources • Project management plan* • User stories** • Risk mitigation plan • Communication planning • Resources and team mobilizing • Procurement planning • Spring backlog**	In addition to Project Management: • Road-mapping • Capability gap analysis • Adoption management • Transition planning • Financial planning • Integration roadmap	• Portfolio management approach • Portfolio success metrics & criteria • Portfolio including categorization and prioritization • Approval of portfolio components
Execution	• Monitoring and controlling including audits • Prioritizing and Re-prioritizing Product Backlog** • Managing change	In addition to Project Management: • Executive dashboard • Benefit tracking • Rebalancing resources • Building steady state operational capability	• Portfolio governance • PMO to manage the execution of initiatives • Portfolio reporting and value
Closure	• Contract closure • Updating docs • Project post mortem • Validating Sprint** • Transition to operations*	In addition to Project Management: • Capability review • Adoption review • Benefit tracking • Operational review	• Benefit realization and alignment with strategic goals • Operational environment readiness

* Traditional Project Management Methodology ** Agile Project Management Methodology

To receive a digital version, register the book at www.pmoadvisory.com/product-registration

PMOAdvisory

Figure 1.3 Sample PgMP exam aid from PMO Advisory (used with permission).

Table 1.2 Exam Preparation – Five Days to Exam!

Day #	Key Objective	Description
5	Complete reading and reviewing of all content including study materials.	If you have not done so, please make sure you are familiar with the key concepts in the Standard and this book. You do not need to memorize everything yet, but there should not be any questions about what they are and how they are used. Assuming the above is done, spend at least two to three hours to review the key concepts, review your study sheets, and manually create the exam aids mentioned throughout this book using paper and pen. Practice makes perfect, and it will save considerable time during the exam. You should also decide on the exam aids that you plan to use. What I offer in this book are my suggestions; see Figure 1.3. You should customize them (or create new ones), so you are comfortable with them.
4	Recreate all the exam aids by heart.	Whether you use the exam aids from this book as-is or if you modify them, make sure you can recreate them manually by heart at this point. The exam aids offered in this book are designed to ease memorization, but feel free to modify them to suit your learning habits. You should also be able to complete most of the exam aids with the PgMP contents by heart. Mistakes at this stage are not ideal, but there are still three days left to remedy.
3	Recreate all of the exam aids and able to fill in the information by heart.	With only three days remaining, it is important to be able to create all the exam aids by heart and complete them without flaws. If there are minor errors, you still have Day 2 and Day 1 to work on them. Practice taking the sample exam. You should be able to pass the test with 136 correct answers (or 80%). For incorrect answers, it is important to understand why they are wrong and what the correct answers are.

(continued)

Table 1.2 (Continued)   Exam Preparation – Five Days to Exam!

Day #	Key Objective	Description
2	Recreate all of the exam aids and able to fill in the information by heart.	The goal is similar to Day 2, but in this case, there is no room for errors. You should be comfortable with the exam process, the recommended exam aids, and the ability to complete them flawlessly. If you have time, my suggestion is to complete the PgMP Exam Simulator again and make sure you can comfortably pass the test at 80%. While it is still not too late to cram new concepts at this point, it should be avoided. Our human brain works well on repetition. At this point, new concepts may actually cause confusion.
1	Relax, eat right, and sleep well.	At this point, unless you are desperate, it is a bit late to memorize new concepts or learn new ideas. Instead, spend your available time and review the content and recreate the exam aids and fill them in – all in a relaxed fashion. Most importantly, take time to relax, stretch, and even go for 50–75% of your routine exercise. Exercise is great for the brain. Sleep early at night and make sure you give yourself at least one extra hour of sleep than your routine.
0	Get ready for the exam.	In the morning of the exam, make sure you eat a healthy and nutritious meal (since it will be much harder to concentrate when you are hungry). Drink your favorite beverage but do not drink in excess (as bathroom breaks count against the four-hour limit). As stated earlier, my recommendation is for scheduling the exam for late morning (between 10 and 11 AM). This may not necessarily work for everyone, so please plan for the time which you know works best for you. Give yourself plenty of time to go to the exam site. You should plan to arrive at least 30 minutes before the start of the exam. Good luck.

1.2.4 You Passed Phase 1, Phase 2 Preparation Starts – A Sample Study Plan of 30 Days

Congratulations on completing Phase 1 of the PgMP credential process. Now the hard work starts. For the purpose of simplicity, let's assume you plan to start and complete Phase 2 in a one-month period with an average study time of four hours per day. This is aggressive but realistic. The duration and intensity can obviously be more or less, but not shorter than 2 weeks. Table 1.3 shows our recommended plan of action, but please customize with your preference.

Table 1.3 Sample 30 Days Study Plan

Day #	Key Objective	Description
30	Becoming familiar with the language and concepts in program management	Spend the first week carefully reading the Standard and this book. There may be an urge to skip; my recommendation is do not. Both books are organized for maximum effectiveness.
29		
28		
27		PMI also recommends an additional set of reference books (https://www.pmi.org/-/media/pmi/documents/public/pdf/certifications/program-management-reference-materials.pdf), and some of the questions are derived from these books. However, for the sake of the exam, reading these books is not an efficient use of your time. Thus, my recommendation is to skip them for exam preparation if you have limited time. These books excel at providing additional insights and tools for the practice of program management. But again, you should read them only if you have sufficient time.
26		
25		
24		
		Also procure or find a reputable set of PgMP practice questions. Preferably, the test bank is sufficiently large in which you can use multiple times without excessive duplications. This way, you can track your progress.

(continued)

Table 1.3 (Continued)   Sample 30 Days Study Plan

Day #	Key Objective	Description
23 22	Chapter 1: Introduction to Program Management Profession and Its Credential	Concentrate on Chapter 1 of both books. From the Standard, be prepared to explain the core concepts and an introduction to program management. From the book, understand the context of program management and the recommended test-taking approach. Feel free to customize the approach for your preference and learning style. But once determined, stick to the plan.
21 20	Chapter 2: Understanding Program Management Performance Domains	Concentrate on Chapter 2 of both books. From both the Standard and this book, be prepared to explain the five performance domains and the key principles.
19 18	Chapter 3: Understanding Program Strategic Alignment	Concentrate on Chapter 3 of both books which focuses on the program strategy alignment. This book extends the Standard by highlighting the three important questions to consider in this domain and incorporating key tasks from the ECO.
17 16 15	Chapter 4: Understanding Program Benefits Management	Concentrate on Chapter 4 of both books which focuses on the program benefits alignment. This book extends the Standard by highlighting the three important questions to consider in this domain and incorporating key tasks from the ECO.
14 13	Chapter 5: Understanding Program Stakeholder Engagement	Examine Chapter 5 of both books which focuses on the program stakeholder engagement. This book extends the Standard by highlighting the three important questions to consider in this domain and also incorporating key tasks from the ECO.

(continued)

Table 1.3 (Continued) Sample 30 Days Study Plan

Day #	Key Objective	Description
12	Chapter 6: Understand Program Governance	Concentrate on Chapter 6 of both books which focuses on the program governance. This book extends the Standard by highlighting the three important questions to consider in this domain and also incorporating key tasks from the ECO.
11		
10		
9	Chapter 7: Understanding Program Life Cycle Management	Concentrate on Chapter 7 of both books which focuses on the program life cycle management and the similarities and differences between the ECO and the Standard.
8		
7	Chapter 8: Understanding Program Activities	Concentrate on Chapter 8 of both books. From the Standard, be prepared to explain the core activities. From the book, spend time going through the practice questions.
6		

1.3 Program Management Overview

While this the primary purpose of the book is to prepare for the exam, it is valuable to understand some basic theories and concepts. Collectively, these will help you with the experience-based questions on the PgMP exam. Experience-based questions are difficult as organizations and situations are different. Yet, they are an integral part of the PgMP exam. Based on my experience as a certified PgMP, I believe understanding the context and learning to think like a program manager will be invaluable to tackle those prickly questions.

1.3.1 Context of Program Management

Today's organizations are complex and larger organizations have hundreds of business processes and thousands of activities. Depending on the type and function of the organization, they range from internal processes such as human resources to external or customer facing processes such as sales and marketing. Yet, amidst all these complications, all of these processes and activities can be simplified to just three pillars for *viable* organizations: planning, operating, and changing (Figure 1.4).

Planning addresses three essential questions: Who are we, what do we do, and where are we going? For smaller organizations, such as a mom-and-pop grocery store, this can be as simple as deciding what to sell, counting inventory of merchandise and deciding what to replenish, or setting a budget for store operations. For

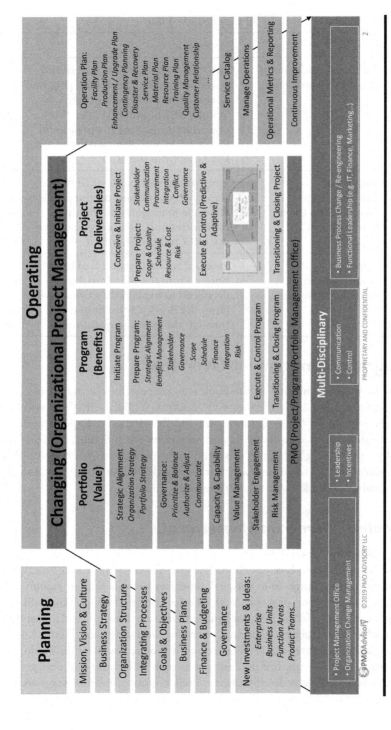

Figure 1.4 Strategic business execution framework (used with permission).[1]

larger organizations, this pillar can be vast ranging from formal strategic planning processes to budget, from visioning to communication, from market research to deciding what product to develop.

Operating has a simple purpose: How to keep the lights on by producing and selling its products and services? For a corner grocery shop, this is selling sufficient merchandise and making sufficient profit to keep on operating. For a manufacturing company, such as a cookie factory, operations include assembling the ingredients, forming the cookies, baking them, and then packaging the finished cookies with a minimal damage. For universities, it is preparing and teaching students and hopefully graduating and readying them for the next step of challenges, whether they are finding jobs or furthering their studies. While there are incremental enhancements or continuous improvements, the operating pillar largely focuses on maintaining the existing set of products and services.

If the external world remains static or if the organization itself remains static, then program management is largely irrelevant. But the world changes and organizations must adopt, evolve, and sometimes revolve to survive and thrive. In the past four decades, the pace of change is ever increasing. For organizations to remain *viable*, they must change. Hence, the ability to change successfully is often more important than planning and operating. For project professionals, change comes in the form of projects and programs that are designed to change the trajectory of the underlying products and services. Changing is often challenging, especially in larger organizations, and it requires a multi-disciplinary approach to ensure its success.

1.3.2 What Are Programs?

What are programs and how do they differentiate with projects and portfolios? Currently, there is a wealth of research and writing about project and project management. Even though project portfolio management also suffers from a dearth of publications, the conceptual relationship to financial portfolio management provides a solid underpinning of research. Plus, portfolio as a construct is more distinct than project and thus causes less misunderstanding. But programs somewhat caught between the realm of large projects and to a lesser extent project portfolios. Understanding program and hence program management is important for at least three reasons: (1) Undoubtedly programs are becoming more recognized as a distinct type of project work, the boundaries of this field need to be distinct. (2) As a discipline, program management gaining popularity as a mechanism of getting big and complex stuff done. A clear definition would encourage more studies and research, so the field can grow. (3) At a personal level, obtaining a program management certification such as Project Management Institute's Program Management Professional (PMI PgMP®) is seen as the next rational step in the growth of the project management career. For those who are preparing for the exam, it is important to develop the right mindset and perspective when thinking about program management and the associated exams.

According to PMI, a program is defined as a group of "related projects, subsidiary programs, and program activities managed in a coordinated manner to obtain

Figure 1.5 Spectrum of program centrality.[4]

benefits not available from managing them individually."[2] The problem with this definition is that the term "related" is not defined. Is this relatedness based on shared resources, shared sponsorship, and financial support, or something more such as dependencies of program objectives and benefits or projects within the program? The second part of the definition, "obtain benefits not available from managing them individually," is even more nebulous. After all, the entire field of management is about synergy and "doing more with less." Worse, this definition can be readily confused with large projects, which arguably have work that can be organized as smaller projects with the larger project. On the other extreme, a portfolio is also about a logical group of projects and other components too.

For this reason, in one of our latest publications, Brian Williamson and I defined a program as "a collection of highly related components, such as subprograms, projects, and other activities. When these highly related components are managed as a program, they can achieve great value and benefits not possible if they were managed separately."[3] We know, the definition is not perfect too. But since publishing that definition, I thought about it more and came up with the concept of "program centrality" to place greater emphasis on the uniformity or centrality of purpose. In short, we are advocating that programs should have a program centrality that are toward the right side of Figure 1.5. It is still a work in progress, but I believe to distinguish programs from large projects and portfolios, program centrality is important.

Program centrality is a measurement of the "tightness" of the components within a program, and it includes three important factors: relatedness, timeliness, and commonality of objectives.

1. Relatedness – Examines the interconnection of the program components which includes projects and other activities within a project, program, or portfolio.
2. Timeliness – Refers to the concerted effort and contiguous timeframe of implementation of these components.

3. Centrality of Objectives – Describes how tightly integrated are the component's objectives and their contribution toward the overall a program's objectives and benefits.

For a comparison of these factors, refer to Table 2.3. For PgMPs who are pursuing program management certifications, it is even more important to develop the right mindset and perspective in both the application and the examination.

Note: For a more detailed analysis of this topic, visit https://projectmanagement. co/blog/what-is-a-program/. This is an expanded article, also written by me, that contains more examples of programs and also finer category of distinctions between programs, portfolios, and projects.

1.3.3 What Is Program Management?

So what is program management? Program management is at the center of the changing pillar, and it is "the coordinated management of program activities by applying specific principles, knowledge, processes, tools, and skills to deliver results effectively." (Williamson and Wu, 2019). But it does not exist in isolation; for program management to be successful, a program must be aligned with planning and implemented in congruence with operating. As programs are generally much larger and much more encompassing than projects, programs often produce large and occasionally transformational change. Change at this scale is much more complex and involved, requiring an interdisciplinary approach.

Understanding of where program management exists in organizations and how it serves to advance organizational objectives are important to developing the right mindset. On the PgMP exam, it is paramount not only to memorize the core concepts and performance domains, but it is also just as important to think like one for experience-based questions. In real life, knowing how to think like a program manager is even more important. In the next section, I will present a simple framework on how to think like a program manager.

1.4 Nine Principles of Program Management

Even though the current Standard for Program Management is a principle-based standard, it does not provide a clear list of principles. Based on my experience as a practitioner, scholar, and research, here, I am proposing the following nine principles of program management:

1. Focus on strategic alignment
2. Direct on program performance and benefit achievement
3. Minimize surprises
4. Manage responsibly

5. Optimize approach
6. Empower teams
7. Communicate effectively
8. Manage up
9. Fact-based Management

Table 1.4 describes these nine principles.

Table 1.4 Nine Principles of Program Management

#	Name	Description
1	Focus on strategic alignment	Programs are complex and large endeavors with often long duration across its life cycle. Programs are tasked with achieving benefits for the sponsoring organizations. Therefore, it is vital for programs to be aligned with organization strategies at the onset and remained aligned throughout the program life cycle to ensure continual support.
2	Direct program performance and benefit achievement	Programs are engines of delivering significant benefits to the sponsoring organizations. Program managers should focus on program performance. Where possible, leverage lessons learned from past projects to enhance the likelihood of achieving results.
3	Minimize surprises	Program managers should look ahead and anticipate the road ahead at the next bent in the road. Irrespective of the program management approach, program manager's primary responsibility is to navigate the situation, establish and manage the processes, and drive toward results. Even positive surprises, or opportunities, can be perceived as poor program management if they occur unexpectedly as the program cannot take more advantage of the opportunity.
4	Mange responsibly	The challenge of management is to do more with less. For program managers who can potentially command a large amount of resources, it is important to be as effectively and efficiently as possible. Effective program management should deliver results at lower costs and with greater satisfaction. Program managers should also find the optimized method for implementing programs, such as selecting between the spectrum of approaches from the predictive to the adaptive for their program components.

(continued)

Table 1.4 (Continued)   Nine Principles of Program Management

#	Name	Description
5	Optimize approach	Assuming the resources given are feasible to achieve program benefits, in reality, program management is an optimization exercise – performing the art of possibility by dealing with competing priorities and needs with factors such as availability of time and resources. Effective program management strives to find the optimal balance between good planning without overthinking, developing the best paths and components to realize program benefits, make difficult trade-off decisions, risk taking, speedy execution with thoroughness, focusing on exceptions while maintaining solid control over execution progress, managing change versus adopting change, and trust but verify. Combined with Manage Responsibly, program managers need to adopt the optimal method that works best for the program AND the sponsoring organization.
6	Empower teams	This principle is especially important for programs as programs involving many teams and people. Program managers cannot simply "do it all," and thus, it becomes both vital and necessary for program managers to delegate responsibility appropriate to component leaders and their teams. Organizations should provide a nurturing environment in which teams and individuals can thrive and encourage their program managers to foster trust and independence in which teams can contribute.
7	Communicate effectively	Communication has always been an important contributor of success on programs. But in the era with a proliferation of technology tools such as social media, there may be a tendency toward too much information versus too little. With multiple components, long duration, and many people, program managers should develop clear program visions and establish expectations on communication and sharing of vital information.

(continued)

Table 1.4 (Continued)   Nine Principles of Program Management

#	Name	Description
8	Manage up	Most skilled program managers can manage both up and down one level effectively, but experienced program managers should strive to manage multiple levels up the organization chain. By developing the ability to think from the perspective of senior management, program managers can link their immediate program goals and benefits with the broader goals and key performance indicators of executives who are multiple levels above their current position. This is a sure way to ensure strategic alignment and continual support from the upper management.
9	Fact-based management	Complex program, especially those that are in a politically tense environment, can be intricate to manage. Program managers should always focus on the facts first and consider them first in their decision-making processes. Other sentiments can be important, and even if some ultimate decisions are political, program managers should be aware that their decisions are based on extrinsic factors beyond mere facts.

1.5 How to Think Like a Program Manager

Program managers are constantly challenged by three key questions:

1. What are the key business objectives of the program and how to stay continuously aligned?
2. How to define, deliver, and control program activities to achieve maximum effectiveness while mitigating risks?
3. What are the options and alternatives to accomplish more with less, such as better ways to define and integrate projects and other program activities, utilizing the precious resources to achieve more benefits, or leverage the economy of size and scale?

The answers to each of these questions vary greatly among organizations, their strategic outlook, internal capabilities, external environment, and their execution capabilities. For program managers to be truly effective, it is not enough that they understand quantitative or qualitative analysis. You need to think like a program manager. Here, based on my experience and knowledge, I highly recommend these four ways of thinking:

1. Think integration
2. Think stakeholder
3. Think execution
4. Think alignment

Naturally, this list is not exhaustive, but these four ways of thinking are foundational, and they go a long way in preparing for the PgMP exam.

1.5.1 Think Integration

Program managers by role are responsible for achieving program-wide strategic objectives, and the art of management is to find synergies that enable effective execution of programs. For program managers, program benefits are mainly derived in two major areas: (1) the strategic objectives that serve as the program outcome, and (2) the synergies and gains from managing the multiple components within the program during execution. Most of the "tightly integrated programs" have many interdependencies within the program. Furthermore, program managers can seek ways to improve the economy of scale and scope to more effectively utilize program resources. Remember the idea of synergy in which $1 + 1 > 2$.

The competing challenges of meeting immediate project outcomes and goals while remaining focused on the overall program objective require the ability of the program manager to manage across a wider range of responsibilities. To be an effective program manager, one must be able to think strategically, implement tactically, and by default, be a change champion for the program. Imagine an abstract scale of one to ten of business activities (see Table 1.5); program managers must be able to operate not only comfortably Levels 5 and 4, but also potentially at Level 6 and above.

1.5.2 Think Stakeholder

Programs are typically much larger and more complex requiring more time and resources than projects. One of the key differences between projects and programs is that many of the program attributes remain fuzzier and unclear for a much greater duration of time. Worse, the program benefits may not be uniformly shared by all the key stakeholders. Therefore, program managers need to engage stakeholders significantly more proactively than project management.

For example, let's examine an enterprise resource planning program. These programs are often less about the technology implementation than more about business process redesign in which the old way of working will undergo

Table 1.5 Organization Operating Level[5] – An Abstract Depiction

Level	Pillars		Name	Description
10	Planning		Corporate or enterprise strategy	This is the highest level of business strategy, and the focus is the entire enterprise. Questions at this level largely pertain to its identity, purpose, and direction.
9			Organization strategy	Following the corporate or enterprise strategy, organization addresses the question of how an organization needs to evolve over time to meet its business objectives. While mostly internally focused, it is built upon a realistic assessment of external and internal environment.
8			Business unit strategy	Depending on the organization, a business unit can be a product line, a geography, or other profit centers. Here, the strategy is less about coordination among the operating units and more about developing and sustaining advantages to advance its products and services.
7	Changing		Functional strategy	This is largely the realm of functional strategies including the specific business objectives for sales, marketing, operations, product management, information technology, etc.
6			Portfolio	Even though portfolios can exist at all levels of the organization, I am purposely putting it at Level 6 because this is where abstract planning starts to diminish and the hard work of getting things done starts. In addition, most portfolios exist cross-function and require the clear functional strategy.
5		Operating	Program	Programs can be seen as logical constructs of significant work components (other programs, projects, and operational initiatives) that require an organization to change. It is logical because of its relatedness and/or interdependencies. In PMI's definition, program focuses on delivering business benefits.

(continued)

Table 1.5 (Continued)   Organization Operating Level[5] – An Abstract Depiction

Level	Pillars		Name	Description
	Operating	Changing		
4		Changing	Project	Projects are typically more specific, concentrating on deliverables and outcomes. Portfolio, program, and projects are at the heart of the "changing" pillar.
3			Operational initiatives / quasi-projects	Operational initiatives are generally enhancement activities designed for the continuous improvement of operations. In some organizations, these are managed as quasi-projects, as they exhibit attributes of both project and operational endeavors. Occasionally, operational initiatives can be large and important to the overall business. In those cases, they are often managed as a part of programs.
2	Operating		Teams or tracks	Teams are specific work units with specific expertise that is the building block for operational initiatives, projects, or programs. For example, a track in software development can be development, quality assurance, deployment, or business analysis.
1			Tasks and activities	These are specific tasks and activities that operate the business and its routine processes. For example, for Sales, it can be making cold calls. For Developers, it is coding.

significant change. Prioritizing which business processes to tackle typically means that one area of the business will achieve greater benefits sooner than other areas. Worse, depending on nature of change, some areas may be negatively impacted. Therefore, assuming there is equal representation in the program leadership team of these key area executives, what are the chance that they agree upfront on these priorities and the ensuing benefits? These task conflicts are likely to be universal across all programs. Other complex programs such as merger and acquisition or creating new business capability all exhibit these task conflicts. These conflicts directly affect the ultimate program objectives and the perception of success. In other words, many measures of program success are in the eye of the beholders.

To manage these expectations and what ultimately constitute program success, program managers must engage stakeholders early, proactively, and continually throughout the program life cycle. During the Program Definition Phase, program managers should closely analyze the program stakeholders and prioritize them. Afterwards, program managers should develop specific plans to engage the stakeholders throughout the program life cycle. During the Program Delivery and Closure Phases, program managers should actively execute the plan, but also make changes depending on the effectiveness of the engagement plan. Just as important, as programs often have long durations in which strategic change can occur, program managers should be attentive to changes in stakeholders, especially when new ones suddenly appear.

One of the biggest challenges in program management is finding ways to transform active blockers to supporters. By proactive engaging stakeholders, program managers significantly improve their ability to successfully deliver the program and achieve program benefits.

1.5.3 Think Execution

One of the challenges confronting complex endeavors is getting started. Borrowing a concept from new product development, this is the problem of "fuzzy front end." The problem of fuzzy front end can occur on most ambiguous, complex, and high-stake activities, such as developing a new product or initiating a program. Especially at the beginning of the endeavor, chances are, there are many options such as varying voices and priorities or ways to tackle the program. Without a disciplined process of evaluating the options, prioritizing tasks, and quickly commit to actions, programs can become paralyzed by analysis. Worse, analysis paralysis can occur throughout the program life cycle. Program managers play a major role in this balancing act between thoughtful planning and execution. Without execution, even the best ideas in programs will remain as mere ideas. Therefore, it is vitally important for program managers to prioritize the program components and related activities and quickly enable the program team to work toward achieving program benefits.

To be a good program manager and also be able to pass the exam, it is important not only to know the key program management principles, but also have the discipline to distill the various options, prioritize program activities, determine a direction, and start to execute to achieve the program benefits as quickly as possible.

1.5.4 Think Alignment

As programs are resource intensive endeavors, organizations undertaking programs do so deliberately to achieve its strategic objectives. In addition, since programs can span across larger duration of time, situations can change from the inception to the completion of programs. Therefore, it is vitally important for program managers to maintain strategic alignment between their programs and organization strategies. Strategic alignment is "the process of linking and evaluating organizational strategy with program goals and objectives, taking into account the business environment and any implementation challenges." (Williamson and Wu, 2019).

Programs typically have business cases. Whether the program business cases are developed or inherited by the program manager, program managers should understand the details thoroughly during Program Definition Phase. Throughout the program life cycle, portfolio managers should proactively maintain alignment by performing these activities:

1. Maintain focus on the strategic perspective and the broad objectives of the program. This is especially important when making choices that may be convenient for the near term, but reduces or damages the strategic well-being of the program.
2. Develop close relationship with senior management, such as program sponsors, governance boards, and portfolio managers, to maintain the direct and strong linkage between the program and strategy.
3. Also, work closely with the component managers, such as the project and operation managers, to ensure coordination of component deliverables and their alignment with the program objectives.

Based on PMO Advisory's experience of helping hundreds, possibly thousands of aspiring program managers, developing the right thinking and adopting a program management mindset is likely the most important test preparation task. This is because a majority of the PgMP exam questions are experience-based questions, and I believe there is no better way to prepare for them than to learn how to think like a program manager.

1.6 Program Manager Skills

Program managers operate across a broad range of activities, from strategy alignment to tactical execution. Their primary skills can be simplified into one of these four sets of skills:

- ■ Coordinating
- ■ Facilitating
- ■ Managing
- ■ Leading

See Figure 1.6 for an illustration followed by a more detailed discussion.

The four primary skill sets of program managers are:

- ■ Coordinating – As coordinators, program managers primarily focus on running the program management processes as efficiently as possible. These include organizing activities related to business case development or validating, develop program roadmaps that include components and their execution plan, assembling the program charters, mobilizing program teams for implementation, scheduling program performance reports and meetings, and communicating to the necessary parties.
- ■ Facilitating – As facilitators, program managers concentrate on solving challenges and driving solutions. This includes engaging experts (e.g., financial experts on a program component's business case), promoting collaborative problem-solving, simplifying the complex problems, and managing conflicts and disagreements especially among program components.

Figure 1.6   Four primary skill sets for portfolio managers.

■ Managing – As managers, the focus is on ensuring the overall effectiveness of the program management processes and people. Specific activities include allocating resources, establishing process rules and guidelines, motivating teams, implementing program management processes, and managing stakeholders and their expectations.
■ Leading – Program managers can also be leaders. They set directions, maintain alignment with business objectives, ensure program benefits are achieved, determine risk management strategies, and make difficult decisions, especially with the allocation of resources and budget. Perhaps the most important role is making difficult decisions that often confront programs.

1.7 Important Information from the Standard

The Standard is written and organized as a reference manual. As such, it is neither an easy nor the most enjoyable read. Yet the descriptions and explanations are clear and vital to the profession. Personally, I enjoy all of PMI's standards because they help me organize my thoughts, knowledge, and experiences. Even when I disagree with PMI on some finer points, I relish the knowledge that PMI has done a superb job of advancing the profession.

As mentioned earlier, I will not repeat what PMI has so elegantly presented in the Standard. Therefore, I will focus on where I can add additional value, either by ways of clarification or expansion of the concepts in the Standard.

Since the standard is principle-based and the exam is mainly experience-based, the need to memorize for the PgMP exam is considerably less than some other PMI exams. Nonetheless, most people find that the PgMP exam is the most difficult of the PMI exams. For this reason, we continue to emphasize that aspiring program professionals should pay special attention to the following key tables and figures from the Standard.

1.7.1 Key Tables and Figures to Remember from the Standard

The Standard contains a number of figures and tables which I believe are essential to passing the exam. You should memorize the following items from the Standard:

■ Figure 1.1 on Page 5 shows the program life cycle. In the program life cycle, it is important to remember that all component delivery, such as projects, are managed in the "Program Delivery" Phase.
■ Figure 1.2 on Page 8 provides an example of program and where it lies in organizational activities. It's important to remember that projects, programs, and portfolios are distinct concepts and organizations choose to implement them in accordance with their needs. Thus, programs can be a part of

portfolio or not. But all programs have multiple components (e.g., projects and other program activities.)

■ Table 1.1 on Page 11. This table provides a high-level comparison of project, program, and portfolio management across a number of key characteristics.

■ Section 1.7.1 on Page 17 highlights the key program management skills. While questions on skills are typically indirect and often weaved into the context of the question, it is important to understand and appreciate all the skills listed.

■ Section 1.9 on Page 20 discusses program management office, which by definition is different from project management office, even though they share the same acronym "PMO" in most literature. In this book, we will make a distinction between project management office (PMO) and program management office (PgMO). PgMOs are established for the purpose of managing a specific program while PMOs tend to be a central office overseeing projects within the organization entity.

Based on my experience teaching program management bootcamps, it may also be important to review and apply the Earned Value Management (EVM) system. Calculation questions are infrequent, but inclusion and references of EVM concepts such as CPI (cost performance index) and EV (earned value) are still important.

1.8 Practice Questions

According to the PgMP Examination Outline, there are officially zero questions from this chapter. However, I believe there are core concepts in this chapter and hence critical to the successful preparation of the exam. Below are some sample questions for you to practice.

Question 1: What is the best definition of a program?

A.   Related projects, subsidiary programs, and program activities managed in a coordinated manner to obtain benefits not available from managing them individually

B.   Temporary endeavors undertaken to create a unique product, service, or result

C.   A collection of projects, programs, subsidiary portfolios, and operations managed as a group to achieve strategic objectives

D.   Related projects, subsidiary programs, and program activities managed individually to obtain benefits

Question 2: Ken Smith is working on a large-scale endeavor that is aligned with a number of strategic objectives of his organization. Currently, at the early phase of this endeavor, Ken is working to prioritize the various success factors by engaging key stakeholders. What kind of endeavor is this?

A. Ken is working on a project
B. Not enough information. The description is suitable for project, program, and portfolio
C. Ken is working on a program
D. Ken is working on a portfolio

Question 3: Organizations employ program management to:

A. Enable organizations to more effectively pursue their strategic goals through coordinated pursuit of projects, subsidiary programs, and other program-related activities
B. Ensure that an organization's programs, projects, and operations are aligned with an organization's strategy
C. Enable organizations to more efficiently and effectively generate outputs and outcomes
D. Enable organizations to more effectively pursue their strategic goals through coordinated pursuit of projects, subsidiary portfolios, and other program-related activities

Question 4: What are the five performance domains in program management?

A. Program Strategy Alignment, Program Benefits Management, Program Stakeholder Engagement, Program Governance, and Program Life Cycle Management
B. Program Strategy Alignment, Program Value Management, Program Stakeholder Engagement, Program Governance Leadership, and Program Life Cycle Management
C. Program Strategy Planning, Program Benefits Management, Program Stakeholder Engagement, Program Governance Leadership, and Program Life Cycle Management
D. Program Strategy Alignment, Program Benefits Management, Program Stakeholder Management, Program Governance Management, and Program Life Cycle Management

Question 5: A program manager should have the ability to do all except:

A.   Interact seamlessly and collaboratively with program steering committees and other executive stakeholders
B.   Facilitate understanding and agreement through the use of strong communication and negotiation skills
C.   Manage details while taking a complete, deliverable-focused view of the program
D.   Manage details while taking a holistic, benefits-focused view of the program

Question 6: Which of the following is not part of a program?

A.   Subsidiary programs managed in a coordinated manner to obtain benefits not available from managing them individually
B.   Program activities managed in a coordinated manner to obtain benefits not available from managing them individually
C.   Portfolio activities managed in a coordinated manner to obtain benefits not available from managing them individually
D.   Related projects managed in a coordinated manner to obtain benefits not available from managing them individually

Question 7: How do programs deliver their intended benefits?

A.   Through the correct application of all program management practices
B.   Through component projects and subsidiary programs that are presented to produce outputs and outcomes
C.   Through application of program management tools and techniques
D.   Through outputs and outcomes achieved from the execution of all projects and related programs within the organization

Question 8: The Standard for Program Management provides:

A.   Guidance on principles, practices, and activities of project management that are generally recognized to support good program management practices and that are applicable to most programs, most of the time
B.   Guidance on principles, practices, and activities of project management that are generally recognized to support good program management practices and that are applicable to all programs, all of the time
C.   Guidance on principles, practices, and activities of program management that are generally recognized to support good program management practices and that are applicable to most programs, most of the time
D.   Guidance on principles, practices, and activities of program management that are generally recognized to support good program management practices and that are applicable to all programs, all of the time

Question 9: Program managers focus on:

A. The generation of the specific outputs and outcomes required by an organization, as part of a project, a program, or a portfolio

B. Ensuring programs and projects are selected, prioritized, and staffed according to the organization's strategic plan for realizing desired organizational value

C. Delivering organizational benefits aligned with the organization's strategic plan through the coordinated management of program components

D. Delivering organizational outputs and outcomes aligned with the organization's strategic plan through the coordinated management of program components

Question 10: All of the following skills and competences are commonly required by program managers except:

A. Change management skills
B. Leadership skills
C. Analytical skills
D. Stakeholder management skills

1.8.1 Answer Key

1. A. Refer to Section 1.2 Program Definition of the Standard.
2. B. The question description is sufficiently vague that it can be any time of major endeavors such as a project, program, portfolio, or operational activity. Refer to Section 1.2 What is a Program and Glossary of the Standard.
3. A. Refer to Section 1.6 Business Value of the Standard.
4. A. Refer to Section 2.1 Program Management Performance Domain Definitions of the Standard.
5. C. Refer to Section 1.7 Role of the Program Manager of the Standard.
6. C. Portfolios are not part of a program. Programs are part of a portfolio. Refer to Section 1.2/Page 3 of the Standard.
7. B. Programs deliver their intended benefits through component projects and subsidiary programs that are presented to produce outputs and outcomes. Refer to Section 1.2/Page 3 of the Standard.
8. C. Refer to Section 1.1 Purpose of the Standard.
9. C. Refer to Section 1.4 The Relationship among Portfolio, Program, and Project Management of the Standard.
10. D. Refer to Section 1.7 Role of the Program Manager of the Standard. Program manager should *engage* stakeholders, not *manage* them.

Notes

1. Adopted from PMO Advisory training content library. Adapted with permission.
2. PMI Lexicon of Project Management Terms. Retrieved from https://www.pmi.org/pmbok-guide-standards/lexicon.
3. Williamson, B. and Wu, T. 2019. The Sensible Guide to Key Terminologies in Project Management, iExperi Press, Montclair, NJ. Glossary.
4. From PMO Advisory website. Reprint with permission.
5. Wu, T. 2016. The Sensible Guide to Passing the PfMP Exam, iExperi Press, Montclair. Table 11. Adapted with permission.

Chapter 2

Understanding Program Management Performance Domains

2.1 Overview

In the Standard, program management is organized by the five performance domains including:

1. Program Strategy Alignment (Chapter 3) – Identifies program outputs and outcomes to provide benefits aligned with the organization's goals and objectives
2. Program Benefits Management (Chapter 4) – Defines, creates, maximizes, and delivers the benefits provided by the program
3. Program Stakeholder Engagement (Chapter 5) – Identifies and analyzes stakeholder needs and manages expectations and communications to foster stakeholder support
4. Program Governance (Chapter 6) – Enables and performs program decision-making, establishes practices to support the program, and maintains program oversight
5. Program Life Cycle Management (Chapter 7) – Manages program activities required to facilitate effective program definition, program delivery, and program closure

Each of the respective chapters will discuss these performance domains in greater details. In this chapter, the goal is to provide an overview of these domains and how they interact and work together to successfully deliver programs.

2.2 Performance Domains and Their Interactions

Performance domains are logical cluster of knowledge and activities that focus on a specific set of outcomes, accomplishments, and values. The performance domains rarely work in isolation. Instead, they work collectively to create a synergistic environment for programs to achieve more value than what are possible if the components were managed individually. Furthermore, these domains run concurrently throughout the life cycle of the program, from Program Definition to Closure Phase.

During the Program Delivery Phase, the interactions of these domains become particularly intense. Partly this reflects the amount of effort and resources during the Delivery Phase and partly this is because components such as projects and other activities are also the most intense during the Delivery Phase. For example, in a typical merger and acquisition program in which two organizations are attempting to combine and unify their business processes and information technology systems, there may be hundreds of projects. During the Program Delivery Phase, many, if not most, of these projects are active at some level. To manage this program of hundreds of projects, all five of these domains are active helping to manage the overall endeavor.

2.3 Linkage between Organizational Strategy, Portfolio Management, and Program Management

Given the investment required to deliver program benefits, programs are generally based on organizational strategies. In advanced organizations with portfolio management, programs are one of the major components. In these cases, organizational and/or portfolio strategies are examined, evaluated, categorized, and prioritized. During program execution, constant alignment is required to enable programs to deliver the intended benefits. This dynamic is shown in Figure 2.1.

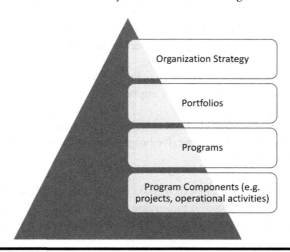

Figure 2.1   Linkage between organization strategy, portfolios, programs, and projects.

Table 2.1   Linking Organization Strategy, Portfolio Management, and Program Management

Organizational Strategy	Portfolio Management	Program Management
• Full spectrum of the organization's investments are evaluated, prioritized, and aligned • Portfolios and programs are evaluated as the business climate or organizational strategy changes	• Reinforce components of the portfolio that are in alignment and are achieving benefits and organizational objectives • Close initiatives that are not aligned with strategic objectives • New initiatives are proposed and analyzed during the portfolio review process • Programs are reviewed to assure they still meet strategic objectives • Business cases are reviewed to determine if new programs will be initiated	• When a program is approved, funding is provided, and a program manager is selected • During the Program Delivery Phase, program components are initiated, planned, executed, transitioned, and closed, while benefits are delivered, transitioned, and sustained • Programs are closed when benefits are achieved, or the program is no longer aligned with strategic objectives

The dynamic between organization strategy, portfolio management, and program management is explained in Table 2.1.

2.4 Comparison between Projects, Programs, and Portfolios

Conceptually, programs are somewhat caught between projects, especially large projects, on the one end and portfolios on the other end. Table 1.1 of the Standard attempts to clarify this confusion, and compare and contrast these dimensions: definition, scope, change, planning, management, monitoring, and success. To further clarify the similarities and differences, see Table 2.2, which is adopted from PMO Advisory training content, for a life cycle comparison between projects, programs, and portfolios.

Table 2.2   Comparison of Project, Program, and Portfolio Management

Phases	Project Management (Traditional and Agile)	Program Management	Portfolio Management
Initiation	• Project vision • Business case • Scope statement • Epics, product backlog, release planning • Resource and constraint	In addition to project management: • Benefit management • Governance • Interdependencies • Stakeholder planning	• Mission, vision, culture, and people • Creation of executable strategy from business objectives
Plan	• Estimating schedule, cost, resources • Project management plan • User stories • Risk mitigation plan • Communication planning • Resources and team mobilizing • Procurement planning • Spring backlog	In addition to project management: • Road-mapping • Capability gap analysis • Adoption management • Transition planning • Financial planning • Integration roadmap • Developing new (or expanding) project information systems	• Portfolio management approach • Portfolio success metrics and criteria • Portfolio including categorization and prioritization • Approval of portfolio components
Execution	• Monitoring and controlling including audits • Prioritizing and re-prioritizing product backlog • Managing change	In addition to project management: • Executive dashboard • Benefit tracking • Rebalancing resources • Building steady state operational capability	• Portfolio governance • Project management office (PMO) to manage the execution of initiatives • Portfolio reporting and value

(*continued*)

Table 2.2 (Continued)   Comparison of Project, Program, and Portfolio Management

Phases	Project Management (Traditional and Agile)	Program Management	Portfolio Management
Closure	• Contract closure • Updating docs • Project post mortem • Validating sprint • Transition to operations	In addition to project management: • Capability review • Adoption review • Benefit tracking • Operational review	• Benefit realization and alignment with strategic goals • Operational environment readiness

Since program, as a unit of work, is between projects and programs, there can be considerable confusion. Table 2.3 describes these three factors of relatedness, timeliness, and centrality of objectives for projects, programs, and portfolios.

See Section 1.3.2 for more description of programs.

2.5 Key Differences between Program and Project Management

Programs are often confused with large projects. Examining the differences between programs and projects, there are four key factors of distinction (See Table 2.4):

1. Uncertainty – This factor is related to risks and unknown throughout the life cycle.
2. Change – This factor describes the dynamism and fluctuations confronted by the underlying endeavor.
3. Methodology – This factor refers to the adoption of a particular approach and system of implementing projects and programs.
4. Complexity – This factor focuses on the intricacies of projects and programs involving ambiguity, unpredictable system and human behaviors.

Table 2.3 Comparison of Projects, Programs, and Portfolios on Relatedness, Timeliness, and Centrality of Objectives

Concept	Projects	Program	Portfolio
Relatedness	Project activities and tasks are specific, and they are working toward achieving the agreed deliverables or outcomes A good practice is developing a work-breakdown-structure (WBS) early on, identifying and determining all the work that is required	Program activities reside in components, and there can be considerable dependencies among these activities. A significant part of the program management effort is to ensure integrated management of the work as defined in program charter The component work should be very interrelated to achieve a specific benefit	The work included can be related in any way that the portfolio owner chooses. Typical portfolios include work that are grouped by same resource pool, delivered to the same client, conducted in the same accounting period, or fit in a similar strategic group The work may span a variety of diverse initiatives, and these initiatives are largely independent
Timeliness	Projects have a definite start and end dates, and even in adaptive methods, the work is performed continually until its completion	Like projects, programs are temporary. There is an existence on a clearly defined beginning, a future endpoint, and a set of defined benefits to be achieved Comparatively, as programs contain multiple components, programs tend to have much longer durations	Portfolios are reviewed regularly for decision-making purposes but are not expected to be constrained to end on a specific date. Portfolios have life cycles, but they can be very long duration sometimes spanning across decades. Portfolios can be altered, ended, or merged with other portfolios based on business environment changes

(continued)

Table 2.3 (Continued)   Comparison of Projects, Programs, and Portfolios on Relatedness, Timeliness, and Centrality of Objectives

Concept	Projects	Program	Portfolio
Centrality of Objective(s)	Project objectives are specific, often tangibly measurable	In a tightly managed program, program objectives tend to be broader and measured as substantial benefits. These benefits are decomposed and become the primary outcomes of projects and other components within the program. The failure of one program component jeopardizes the entire program objective	Portfolio objectives tend to be more loosely connected strategic objectives, often clustered in a common strategic group such as product families, business functional groups (e.g., IT portfolio), shared organizational objectives (e.g., revenue generation)

Table 2.4   Key Differences between Program and Project Management

Factor	Project	Program
Uncertainty	The expected outputs of projects are generally more certain than those of programs at the time of inception	Uncertainty is high at the beginning of a program, as the outcomes are not clear
Uncertainty	As a project proceeds, its ability to deliver on those outputs on time, on budget, and on scope becomes more certain as a result of progressive elaboration	Programs can change the direction on projects such as canceling projects, starting new projects, or modifying existing components – to adapt to changing circumstances
Uncertainty	Projects may produce outputs, products, or services as planned	In programs, the outcomes of projects may not contribute to the outcomes that were anticipated. Some outputs may have little value on its own
Change	Change within a project affects the defined deliverables at the tactical level	Changes within a program affect the delivery of benefits at the strategic level
Change	Employ change and change management to constraint or control the impact of variability on their baselines	Proactively use change management to keep the program components and intended benefits aligned with changes in organizational strategy and changes in the environment in which they are performed
Methodology	Projects largely utilizes one methodology or approach for implementation (e.g., traditional waterfall, Scrum, Lean, etc.)	Programs can utilize a variety of methodologies, depending on the optimal method of component execution and organizational culture. But having multiple methods of implementation incur an additional source of complexity on the program. Nonetheless, the gains offered by flexibility should offset additional management complexity

(continued)

Table 2.4 (Continued) Key Differences between Program and Project Management

Factor	Project	Program
Complexity	Complexity due to the uniqueness of projects. It can include the kind of thinking, action, and knowledge required to solve a problem or work on a complex task	Governance complexity results from the sponsor support for the program and the decision-making processes within the program
	Organizational complexity focuses on depth of the organization structure as well as the number of organizational units	Stakeholder complexity arises from the differences in needs and influence of stakeholders
	Dynamic complexity focuses on the project's behavior and how it changes over time	Definition complexity focuses on the agreement of a future state by stakeholders
		Benefits delivery complexity focuses on benefit management
		Interdependencies among components and not necessarily on issues within individual projects
		Resource complexity is another source of friction.
		Scope complexity arises from the difficulty of clearly defining the deliverables and the benefits of the programs and its components
		Change complexity arises from the impact change can potentially cause organizational issues
		Risk complexity arises from a high level of uncertainty due to the extended program life cycle

As readers prepare for the Program Management Professional (PgMP) exam, the concept of program must be defined better, not only to distinguish from project and portfolio, but also because the definition shapes how we view, understand, examine, learn, and analyze exam questions. Remember to adopt a mindset of defining programs as a "tightly integrated program."

2.6 Additional Features of Program Management

In addition to the distinctions between portfolio and project management, program management also exhibits a number of key features. Even though these features are relative and not absolute, practitioners should recognize these features as the plan of how to effectively manage programs.

2.6.1 Longer-Term Orientation and Strategic Goals

Program management aims for the accomplishment of goals synergized into program benefits. A program can have many combinations of projects and other activities to achieve its business objectives. Program managers can sometimes place projects in the different arrangement and define activities with distinct outcomes to achieve strategically important benefits. Program managers must state goals because not all the goals are associated with a single working area. This differs from projects in which project managers are more directly managing project deliverables. In addition, as programs are much larger collection of work requiring significant investments, organizations do not undertake programs lightly and often necessitate a close alignment of program and strategic goals of the sponsoring organization. Due to the much broader scope of work, strategic options of how to realize program benefits, programs can take much longer time to implement.

2.6.2 Resource Allocation

With the broader scope, program managers often allocate resources to various projects and other components within the program. This differs considerably with project managers whose primary job is to make the best use of the allocated resources. To make appropriate program resource decisions, program managers must understand the total resource needs of the program, determine the capability and capacity of the performing organizations, develop resource strategies to fill gaps, work with the component managers in the allocation of the resources, and occasionally adjust resources throughout the program life cycle to optimize the program performance by reallocating resources if needed. Hence, program managers are often negotiating resources among the components as compared with project management.

2.6.3 Measurement of Success

How to measure success? In a project, the primary focus is the tangible outcome or deliverables. Success metrics for project management are often processes oriented, including the ability to deliver agreed scope, on schedule and budget, and at the right quality. For programs, the success metrics are more strategic, such as the desired business benefits and the fitness of the outcome. Program management metrics are often beyond the common project management metrics and include the ability to make sound decisions, alignment with strategy, and engagement of key stakeholders. At the portfolio level, the success metrics are closely gained with business and organization metrics and key performance indicators.

On the flip side, the failure of projects, programs, and portfolios can be vastly different. Project failures can be painful, but they rarely threaten the existence of organization. Program failures can be catastrophic and even at a minimum, the resulting pain can be long lasting. At the portfolio level, failure of portfolios generally negatively impacts an entire area of the business if not the business itself.

2.7 Practice Questions

This section contains ten sample questions related to program management performance domains.

Question 1: Upon completing the initial preparation of program, a program may not have all of the following determined except:

A. Program manager
B. Scope
C. Budget
D. Timeline

Question 2: To assure that a program reflects the most suitable profile of the intended outcomes, all of the following are typically reviewed except:

A. Business case
B. Charter
C. Risk management plan
D. Benefits management plan

Question 3: The performance domain that identifies program outputs and outcomes to provide benefits aligned with the organization's goals and objectives is:

A. Program benefits management
B. Program governance
C. Program strategy alignment
D. Program life cycle management

Question 4: A big difference between portfolios and programs is that portfolios:

A. Are not expected to be constrained to end on a specific date
B. Contain projects
C. Do not get adjusted based on organizational strategic objectives
D. Are expected to be constrained to end on a specific date

Question 5: The performance domain that defines, creates, maximizes, and delivers the benefits provided by the program is:

A. Program life cycle management
B. Program benefits management
C. Program strategy alignment
D. Program stakeholder engagement

Question 6: All of the following is true about the five program management performance domains except:

A. They run consecutively throughout the duration of the program
B. Work within these domains is iterative in nature and is repeated frequently
C. They run concurrently throughout the duration of the program
D. Every program requires some activity in each of these performance domains during the entire course of the program

Question 7: Programs are characterized by the existence of all except:

A. An indefinite endpoint
B. Clearly defined beginning
C. A set of outcomes and planned benefits that are to be achieved during the conduct of the program
D. A future endpoint

Question 8: The performance domain that identifies and analyzes stakeholder needs and manages expectations and communications to foster stakeholder support is:

A. Program life cycle management
B. Program benefits management
C. Program stakeholder management
D. Program stakeholder engagement

Question 9: The performance domain that enables and performs program decision-making, establishes practices to support the program, and maintains program oversight is:

A. Program governance
B. Program benefits management
C. Program life cycle management
D. Program strategy alignment

Question 10: A critical difference between portfolios and programs is that in portfolios the work included is related in any way portfolio owners choose. However, in programs, in order to achieve the full intended benefits, work are likely be:

A. Interdependent
B. Separate and distinct
C. Conducted in series
D. Independent

2.7.1 Answer Key

1. A. Refer to Section 2.5 Program and Project Distinctions of the Standard.
2. C. Refer to Section 2.3 Organizational Strategy, Portfolio Management, and Program Management Linkage of the Standard.
3. C. Refer to Section 2.1 Program Management Performance Domain Definitions of the Standard.
4. A. Refer to Section 2.4 Portfolio and Program Distinctions of the Standard.
5. B. Refer to Section 2.1 Program Management Performance Domain Definitions of the Standard.
6. A. Refer to Section 2.1 Program Management Performance Domain Definitions of the Standard.
7. A. Refer to Section 2.4 Portfolio and Program Distinctions of the Standard.
8. D. Refer to Section 2.1 Program Management Performance Domain Definitions of the Standard.
9. A. Refer to Section 2.1 Program Management Performance Domain Definitions of the Standard.
10. A. Refer to Section 2.4 Portfolio and Program Distinctions of the Standard.

Chapter 3

Understanding Program Strategic Alignment

3.1 Introduction

The goal of the Program Strategic Alignment performance domain is to ensure the program management processes and activities are in support of the organization strategy, not just at the beginning of the program, but also sustained throughout the entire life cycle of a program.

This chapter is organized by the following sections:

1. Describe the purpose of Program Strategic Alignment and the high-level tasks and activities that program managers should tackle pertaining to this performance domain
2. Highlight the three most important questions that program managers should ask pertaining to this domain
3. Describe the key Program Strategic Alignment Skills
4. Provide ten sample questions for readers to practice

By the end of this chapter, readers should be able to perform the following:

- Describe strategic alignment and its importance
- Address the key questions that shape how program managers think about strategic alignment
- Articulate and potentially apply the important activities in this domain

3.2 About Program Strategic Alignment

Program managers achieve alignment through a series of tasks linking the strategic objectives and program benefits in a series of key program management artifacts including program business case, program charter, program roadmap, program environmental assessments, and program risk management. There are nine important tasks associated with this domain:

1. Perform initial program evaluation to ensure alignment with strategy
2. Create high-level roadmaps with milestones and preliminary estimates for initial approval
3. Refine high-level roadmap to establish a baseline for program execution
4. Create program mission statement
5. Evaluate organization's program and project management capability and capacity
6. Identify and determine program benefits, highlight direct and indirect benefits
7. Develop a high-level estimate to support the business case
8. Evaluate external implications of the program (e.g., regulatory, legal, social, cultural, political, ethical, security, and other considerations)
9. Obtain approval for the program initiation from organizational leadership
10. Assess opportunities for synergy, through integrated management of the program, environmental context, and the components within the program
11. Determine strategic opportunities aligned with the program objectives

Table 3.1 provides further description of the tasks, including the importance of this task and some general steps to perform this task.

3.2.1 Program Risk Management Strategy

An important part of Program Strategic Alignment is the development of the program risk management strategy since it serves as a vital input into subsequent program management artifacts such as program charter and program roadmap. As programs are significantly larger endeavor, uncertainties can arise from both internal program situations and external business environment. Successfully tackling risks are pivotal for the success of program delivery.

As program managers, it important to evaluate the program risk thresholds, which is the "the maximum amount or volume of uncertainty around an objective that a stakeholder or organization is willing to accept."[1] In addition, program managers perform a series of risk management activities, as shown in Figure 3.1, to tackle program risks:

1. Conduct an initial assessment of program risks
2. Evaluate their priorities, using factors such as impact and probability of occurrence

Table 3.1 Program Strategic Alignment Tasks

Task #	Task Description	Explanation of Importance	Steps to Perform This Task
1	Perform an initial program assessment by defining the program objectives, requirements, and risks in order to ensure program alignment with the organization's strategic plan, objectives, priorities, vision, and mission statement	Programs are expensive and large endeavors. To ensure continual support, alignment with strategy is essential	1. Review organization strategy and business objectives 2. Understand the business rationale and priority for the program 3. Understand if there are other options of fulfilling the business objectives 4. Review program objectives and evaluate the degree of alignments 5. Suggest alternatives or refinements, if appropriate
2	Establish a high-level road map with milestones and preliminary estimates in order to obtain initial validation and approval from the executive sponsor	Roadmaps, especially high-level roadmaps, are valuable tools for communication, expectation setting, and obtaining support	1. Identify the major components of the program 2. Define key milestones associated with the components and the program 3. Determine a preliminary approach to managing the program 4. Create an order-of-magnitude estimation of the scope, resources, and schedule of the program
3	Define the high-level road map/framework in order to set a baseline for program definition, planning, and execution	More detailed roadmaps can serve as blueprints for program definition, planning, and execution	1. Review and refine the earlier roadmap to create the next level of details suitable for planning 2. Solidify the program execution approach, especially focusing on the challenge of "fuzzy front-end" and strategic alignment

(continued)

Table 3.1 (Continued) Program Strategic Alignment Tasks

Task #	Task Description	Explanation of Importance	Steps to Perform This Task
4	Define the program mission statement by evaluating the stakeholders' concerns and expectations in order to establish program direction	Motivating program stakeholders around a common purpose	1. Confirm an approach to develop the mission statement (in general, there are three approaches: (a) top-down – ask executives, (b) middle – develop strawman and socialize, and (c) bottoms-up – socialize with team) 2. Engage selective stakeholders to develop program mission 3. Refine program mission, up or down the organization 4. Publish and share the program mission statement
5	Evaluate the organization's capability by consulting with organizational leaders in order to develop, validate, and assess the program objectives, priority, feasibility, readiness, and alignment to the organization's strategic plan	Creating an initial sense of feasibility and approach to execution	1. Work with leaders and managers to evaluate the organization's capability, capacity, change readiness, portfolio/program/project/Project Management Office (PMO) maturity, and alignment with strategy 2. Develop a gap analysis, clearly defining the current state, and outline the desired future state 3. Review and refine the analysis with key stakeholders, especially the core program team

(continued)

Table 3.1 (Continued) Program Strategic Alignment Tasks

Task #	Task Description	Explanation of Importance	Steps to Perform This Task
6	Identify organizational benefits for the potential program using research methods such as market analysis and high-level cost-benefit analysis in order to develop the preliminary program scope and define benefits realization plan	Reinforcing the business case for the program and then adopting the program management approach	1. Perform benefit analysis through identification of program features, outcomes, and potential benefits 2. Collect data to justify benefits
7	Estimate the high-level financial and nonfinancial benefits of the program in order to obtain/maintain funding authorization and drive prioritization of projects within the program	Determining the high-level cost to reinforce the business case	1. Analyze the updated information about the program including reviewing the business case and other supporting document 2. Work with the updated team, which may now include additional program team member, to critically examine the program scope, schedule, resources, and important deliverables, desired outcomes, and target benefits 3. Re-estimate the program based on the new information

(continued)

Table 3.1 (Continued)   Program Strategic Alignment Tasks

Task #	Task Description	Explanation of Importance	Steps to Perform This Task
8	Evaluate program objectives relative to regulatory and legal constraints, social impacts, sustainability, cultural considerations, political climate, and ethical concerns in order to ensure stakeholder alignment and program deliverability	Developing an initial understanding of the context and implications of program	1. Work with organizational specialists and subject matter experts to evaluate broader context of the program. These include, but not necessarily limited to, regulatory, legal, social, sustainability, cultural, political, ethical, security, supply chain, industry, competitor and other considerations 2. Document the analysis and determine implications for the program 3. Share the analysis and implications with key stakeholders
9	Obtain organizational leadership approval for the program by presenting the program charter with its high-level costs, milestone schedule, and benefits in order to receive authorization to initiate the program	Obtaining approval for the program initiation from organizational leadership	1. Review and confirm the appropriateness of the program charter, high-level estimates of costs, schedule, resources, and benefits 2. Work with organizational leaders to obtain approval 3. Ideally, also work with the organizational leaders to identify a program sponsor

(continued)

Table 3.1 (Continued) Program Strategic Alignment Tasks

Task #	Task Description	Explanation of Importance	Steps to Perform This Task
10	Identify and evaluate integration opportunities and needs (e.g., human capital and human resource requirements and skill sets, facilities, finance, assets, processes, and systems) within program activities and operational activities in order to align and integrate benefits within or across the organization	Achieving maximum effectiveness of program management through finding synergies and integration	1. Work with the important stakeholders (e.g., organizational leaders, other program managers, program component managers, operational executives, subject matter experts, functional managers, etc.) to evaluate program activities 2. Create an integration map that summarizes the activities across the program
11	Exploit strategic opportunities for change in order to maximize the realization of benefits for the organization	Maximize program benefits	1. Analyze the strategic opportunities in the organization and the environment as they are related to the program objectives 2. Identify ways to leverage the program work to maximize program benefits 3. Communicate with program stakeholders to gather their inputs and fresh perspectives 4. Define program and component activities in support of maximizing benefits 5. Obtain proper authorization for formal inclusion of these activities in the program

Figure 3.1 Risk management activities.

3. Develop program risk response strategy
4. Later in the program as appropriate, program managers and risk owners should execute the risk response strategy.

Even though this work should be performed early in the Program Definition Phase, program managers should monitor and conduct risk management activities throughout the life cycle of the program.

3.3 Key Questions for Program Strategic Alignment

As one prepares for the Program Management Professional (PgMP) exam, it is important think through two aspects of the current exam and Standard:

a. PgMP exam is mainly composed of experience-based, scenario driven questions. This places more emphasis on the task taker's experience than the pure knowledge that are a part of the Standard.
b. Furthermore, the current standard is a principle-based standard which means there are little in the way of memorization of processes and specific inputs and outputs. This means that the task taker's ability to assimilate their experience with the Standard's knowledge is more important than pure memorization.

Based on the knowledge gained from helping hundreds of professionals with passing the exam, it is far more important for the test taker to develop a proper mindset (as described in Section 1.5) and make them more specific for this performance domain. Here, this book achieves this by determining three of the most important questions for the Program Strategic Alignment performance domain:

1. How to ensure alignment between program objectives with organizational or portfolio strategies and stakeholder considerations to maximize program benefit?
2. What is the program roadmap that guides program component implementation?
3. How to achieve superior program implementation?

3.3.1 How to Ensure Alignment between Program Objectives with Organizational or Portfolio Strategies and Stakeholder Considerations to Maximize Program Benefit

Strategically, this is perhaps the most important of the program manager's tasks. Programs are generally derived from strategy and thus at the program inceptions, the alignment should be very strong. However, as program can take significant time for implementation, this alignment can shift and sometimes be weakened as situation changes. For program manages, making sure the strong alignment remains in place require constant monitoring, assessing, and adjusting.

This can be partially achieved by linking the program benefits through a series of program management artifacts including:

- Program business case – Often created either before the program's inception or during the Program Definition Phase, specifically during Program Formulation (see Figure I.3). The program business case is typically written from the perspective of the customer or sponsor, which may contain elements that are infeasible or too challenging to consider.
- Program charter – This is an important deliverable that formally authorizes the program for implementation. The charter is written from the perspective of the implementer, or the program management team. This shift in perspective is vital as the implementers tend to focus more practically on what is feasible.
- Program roadmap – This is a further distillation of the program scope and benefits as outlined in the charter. Since program often has many ways of implementation, the completion of the program roadmap signifies an agreement and commitment toward a specific path of implementation. Program roadmap also highlights the key components, which can be subprograms, projects, and other activities required to deliver program benefits.

In addition to aligning the goals, objectives, and benefits through this set of program management artifacts, program managers should also continually evaluate the broader environmental context for changes. These factors may include, but are not limited to, the business and organizational environment, market conditions, funding, resources, regulatory and legislative shifts, supply chain, technology, and other factors that can influence program implementation.

3.3.2 What Is the Program Roadmap That Guides Program Component Implementation?

Program roadmap is a conceptualized model that shows how the program is implemented through its components, which can include subprograms, projects, and other program activities. Like a typical roadmap, program roadmap highlights the direction of the program progression with milestones and dependencies. Further analysis of program roadmap can reveal important program considerations such as resources requirements, schedule of component approval and implementation, and accrual of benefits.

Depending on the program type, the component authorization can require significant time and attention. Assuming the components are projects, then project managers need to be assigned to lead the project, from initiation including developing the charter, to implementation, and eventually to project closure or transition.

3.3.3 How to Achieve Superior Program Implementation

This is a vital question for programs to achieve its objectives optimally, and there are a ton of research and books on this question alone. Here, for the purpose of exam preparation, it is important to remember that Project Management Institute (PMI) focuses on the following when taking the exam:

- Program management principles – This is described in Section 1.4.
- System and process thinking – This is important to achieve consistency of delivery and also enable continuous improvement

3.4 Program Strategic Alignment Skills

To perform Program Strategic Alignment effectively, program managers require developing the following skill sets:

- Business strategy
- Business/organization objectives
- Economic forecasting
- Feasibility analysis
- Financial measurement and management techniques
- Funding models
- Funding processes
- Intellectual property laws and guidelines
- Legal and regulatory requirements
- Marketing
- Portfolio management
- Program and constituent project charter development

- Program mission and vision
- Public relations
- Requirement analysis techniques
- Scenario analysis
- Strategic planning and analysis
- System implementation models and methodologies
- Trend analysis

For a description of these skills, refer to the skill glossary in Chapter 9 that highlights over 120 program management skills.

3.4.1 General Program Management Skills

In addition to the skills that are more specific to the Program Strategic Alignment performance domain, program managers should also consider the following business and management skills that are more general, but can be as vitally important as the specific skills:

- Active listening
- Analytical thinking
- Benefits measurement and analysis techniques
- Brainstorming techniques
- Budget processes and procedures
- Business environment
- Business ethics
- Business models, structure, and organization
- Capacity planning
- Change management
- Coaching and mentoring techniques
- Collaboration tools and techniques
- Communicating
- Communication tools and techniques
- Conflict resolution techniques
- Contingency planning
- Contract negotiation/administration
- Contract types
- Cost management
- Cost-benefit techniques
- Critical thinking
- Cultural diversity/distinctions
- Customer centricity/client focus
- Data analysis/data mining
- Decision-making techniques

- Distilling and synthesizing requirements
- Emotional intelligence
- Employee engagement
- Executive-level presentation
- Facilitation
- Human resource management
- Impact assessment techniques
- Industry and market knowledge
- Information privacy
- Innovative thinking
- Interpersonal interaction and relationship management
- Interviewing
- Knowledge management
- Leadership theories and techniques
- Leveraging opportunities
- Management techniques
- Managing expectations
- Managing virtual/multicultural/remote/global teams
- Maximizing resources/achieving synergies
- Motivational techniques
- Negotiating/persuading/influencing
- Negotiation strategies and techniques
- Organization strategic plan and vision
- Performance management techniques (e.g., cost and time, performance against objectives)
- Planning theory, techniques, and procedures
- PMI Code of Ethics and Professional Conduct
- Presentation tools and techniques
- Prioritizing
- Problem solving
- Problem-solving tools and techniques
- Project Management Information Systems (PMIS)
- Reporting tools and techniques
- Risk analysis techniques
- Risk management
- Risk mitigation and opportunities strategies
- Safety standards and procedures
- Social responsibility
- Stakeholder analysis and management
- Succession planning
- Sustainability and environmental issues
- Team development and dynamics
- Time management
- Vendor management

Similarly, refer to the skill glossary in Chapter 9 for a fuller description of these skills.

3.5 Practice Questions

This section contains ten sample questions pertaining to Program Strategic Alignment.

Question 1: A well-defined program risk strategy is critical for:

A.   Determination of the key performance indicators for the program
B.   The successful delivery of the program roadmap
C.   Development of the component risk reserve
D.   Determination of the quality assurance program

Question 2: In order to meet organizational strategic goals, program managers need to understand how the program will fulfill all of these except:

A.   Contract support necessary for project execution
B.   Portfolio and organization's strategy
C.   Goals and objectives
D.   Skills needed to align the program with goals

Question 3: The program charter formally expresses all of these except:

A.   Benefits achieved
B.   Organization's mission
C.   Organization's vision
D.   Benefits expected

Question 4: A chronological representation of the program which shows the linkage between business strategy and the program is:

A.   Program management plan
B.   Project charter
C.   Program roadmap
D.   Program charter

Question 5: The business case is required as:

A.   The document authorizing the execution of the program
B.   A deliverable before the program can be formally chartered and may be the secondary document to justify the business decision
C.   A deliverable after the program can be formally chartered and may be the primary document to justify the business decision
D.   A deliverable before the program can be formally chartered and may be the primary document to justify the business decision

Question 6: The business case may include all except:

A.   Alternative solutions
B.   Intrinsic and extrinsic benefits
C.   Quality assurance plan
D.   Social needs

Question 7: Environmental assessments need to be conducted to assess both:

A.   Internal influences and external influences to the program that may have an impact on program success
B.   The weather during the execution of the program to determine the type of clothing program participants should wear
C.   External influences to the program that may have an impact on program success
D.   Internal influences to the program that may have an impact on program success

Question 8: When environmental factors impact the overall strategic goals of the organization that misalign the program with the new organizational strategy, all of the following may be the resultant to a program except:

A.   Changed
B.   Put on hold
C.   Stay the same
D.   Canceled

Question 9: The initial program risk assessment identifies any risk to strategic alignment, and may include all of the following except:

A.   Program objectives not supportive of organizational objectives
B.   Program roadmap not aligned with organizational roadmap
C.   Component objectives not supportive of portfolio objectives
D.   Program objective not supportive of portfolio objectives

Question 10: Enterprise environmental factors refer to conditions that influence, constrain, or direct the program that are:

A.   Not under immediate control of the program team
B.   Directly related to the climate in the area the program is being executed
C.   Managed and directed by the steering committee
D.   Under immediate control of the program team

3.5.1 Answer Key

1. B. Refer to Section 3.5 Program Risk Management Strategy of the Standard.
2. A. Refer to Section 3.0 Program Strategy Alignment of the Standard.
3. A. Refer to Section 3.2 Program Charter of the Standard.
4. C. Refer to Section 3.3 Program Roadmap of the Standard.
5. D. Refer to Section 3.1 Program Business Case of the Standard.
6. C. Refer to Section 3.1 Program Business Case of the Standard.
7. A. Refer to Section 3.4 Environmental Assessments of the Standard.
8. C. Refer to Section 3.4.1 Enterprise Environmental Factors of the Standard.
9. C. Refer to Section 3.5.3 Initial Program Risk Assessment of the Standard.
10. A. Refer to Section 3.4.1 Enterprise Environmental Factors of the Standard.

Note

1. Williamson, B. and Wu, T. 2019. The Sensible Guide to Key Terminologies in Project Management, iExperi Press, Montclair, NJ. Glossary.

Chapter 4

Understanding Program Benefits Management

4.1 Introduction

The goal of the Program Benefits Management performance domain is to enable the program to deliver the agreed benefits and results. By focusing on the program benefits at the inception of the program, program managers can craft their program management plans and execution toward the fulfillment of these benefits.

This chapter is organized by the following sections:

1. Describe the purpose of Program Benefits Management and the high-level tasks and activities that program managers should tackle pertaining to this performance domain
2. Highlight the three most important questions that program managers should ask pertaining to this domain
3. Describe the key Program Benefits Management Skills
4. Provide ten sample questions for readers to practice

By the end of this chapter, readers should be able to perform the following:

- Describe benefits management and its importance
- Address the key questions that shape how program managers think about benefits management
- Articulate and potentially apply the important activities in this domain

4.2 About Program Benefits Management

To enable effective benefits management, program managers need to design and execute a series of processes that include benefits identification, analysis and planning, implementation and delivery, transition to ongoing management, and sustainment. There are eight important tasks associated with this domain:

1. Create the benefit realization plan
2. Determine program synergies
3. Create a program sustainment plan
4. Monitor program benefit realization throughout the program
5. Verify program benefits achieved are aligned with the program's strategic objectives
6. Maintain benefit register
7. Analyze program sustainment plan
8. Create a program transition plan

Table 4.1 provides further description of the tasks, including the importance of this task and some general steps to perform this task.

4.3 Key Questions for Program Benefits Management

Here are three of the most important questions for the Program Benefits Management performance domain:

1. What are the program benefits and how are they measured?
2. How are benefits created – through component execution, synergy amongst components, and cost savings?
3. How to monitor, control, and verify benefits achieved throughout the program life cycle while sustaining them in operations?

4.3.1 What Are the Program Benefits and How Are They Measured?

Programs can achieve many benefits for the sponsoring organization, and one of the key jobs of program managers is to direct the realization of these benefits. Benefits are typically initially identified in the business case. Leveraging that information, program managers should make an independent assessment of the benefits (unless the program manager also developed the business). Important steps in this assessment and identification include:

Table 4.1 Program Benefits Management Tasks

Task #	Task Description	Explanation of Importance	Steps to Perform This Task
1	Develop the benefits realization plan and its measurement criteria in order to set the baseline for the program and communicate to stakeholders, including sponsors	Identify how the program will realize the benefits	1. Analyze the program business case, charter, and other supporting document for program benefits 2. Develop how these benefits will be achieved across the program life cycle 3. Create the benefit realization plan and integrate with the program plans, such as the program milestone 4. Share the document with the key stakeholders
2	Identify and capture synergies and efficiencies identified throughout the program life cycle in order to update and communicate the benefits realization plan to stakeholders, including sponsors	Continuously improve program execution	1. Identify interdependent or related program activities in which there are potential areas of integrated management 2. Highlight areas of synergies throughout the program in which the value and benefits accelerate or enhanced using a program management approach 3. Analyze them to ensure feasibility 4. Capture the benefits through the integrated management 5. Share them with the program team and sponsor 6. Include them in the program planning

(continued)

Table 4.1 (Continued)   Program Benefits Management Tasks

Task #	Task Description	Explanation of Importance	Steps to Perform This Task
3	Develop a sustainment plan that identifies the processes, measures, metrics, and tools necessary for management of benefits beyond the completion of the program in order to ensure the continued realization of intended benefits	Ensure ongoing management to achieve benefit realization	1. Work with the operational managers, sponsors, and other executives to define how program results will be managed beyond the program implementation 2. Develop a program sustainment plan on the ongoing management of the program benefits and its realization 3. Make sure activities required for benefit sustainment and ongoing operations are considered in the program planning and implementation
4	Monitor the metrics (e.g., by forecasting, analyzing variances, developing "what if" scenarios and simulations, and utilizing causal analysis) in order to take corrective actions in the program and maintain and/or potentially improve benefits realization	Evaluate program success via the important metrics	1. Monitor and report on the benefit realization throughout the program (and working in conjunction with Task 7 in Strategy Alignment and Tasks 5 and 14 in Life Cycle Management) 2. Analyze results and determine additional areas of improvement

(continued)

Table 4.1 (Continued)   Program Benefits Management Tasks

Task #	Task Description	Explanation of Importance	Steps to Perform This Task
5	Verify that the close, transition, and integration of constituent projects and the program meet or exceed the benefit realization criteria in order to achieve a program's strategic objectives	Achieve program strategic objectives	1. Verify the achievement of program benefits throughout the program life cycle, especially at or near the program closure 2. Analyze results to make sure they are aligned with the program strategic objectives 3. Report deviations, positive or negative, to the program stakeholders 4. As necessary and feasible, develop action plans to improve program benefit realization
6	Maintain a benefit register and record program progress in order to report the benefit to stakeholders via the communications plan	Clearly understand the benefits that are being achieved throughout the program	1. Develop a program benefit register with the program benefits clearly identified, ideally with specific measures assigned 2. Monitor and update the register throughout the program life cycle 3. Report and communicate the program benefits

(continued)

Table 4.1 (Continued)   Program Benefits Management Tasks

Task #	Task Description	Explanation of Importance	Steps to Perform This Task
7	Analyze and update the benefits realization and sustainment plans for uncertainty, risk identification, risk mitigation, and risk opportunity in order to determine if corrective actions are necessary and communicate to stakeholders	Make sure sustainment risks are identified and managed from the onset	1. Review and analyze the program sustainment plan with the program core team and subject matter experts 2. Identify and analyze risks associated with the sustainment plan 3. Develop risk response and incorporate them in the program risk management plan 4. As necessary, assign risk owners to ensure proper management of risks in the benefits realization and sustainment plans
8	Develop a transition plan for operations in order to guarantee sustainment of products and benefits delivered by the program	Ensure smooth transition between program implementation and ongoing operations	1. Work with the operational managers, sponsors, and other executives to define how program results will be transitioned to the operational environment 2. Develop a program transition plan and highlight the tasks required during program to ensure smooth transition

- Thoroughly understand the program business case and program charter (if available) with an eye toward implementation feasibility
- Analyze the available information about organizational and business strategies
- Determine internal and external influences
- Examine program drivers to identify and qualify the benefits that program stakeholders expect to realize
- Work with program stakeholders and program governance to determine benefit metrics and measures

Program managers should also create a benefit register to capture all the findings. The register will henceforth serve as a valuable program management tool to monitor, evaluate, and make necessary adjustments throughout the life of the program. Common attributes to consider in the benefits register include:

- List of planned benefits
- Risk assessment and probability for achieving the benefit
- Establishment of processes for measuring progress against the benefits plan
- Mapping of the planned benefits to program components
- Person, group, or organization responsible for delivering each benefit
- Description of how each benefit will be measured
- Key performance indicators (KPIs) and thresholds for evaluation
- Status or progress indicator for each benefit
- Target dates and milestones for benefits achievement
- Tracking and communication processes to record program progress

4.3.2 How Benefits Are Created through Component Execution, Synergy Amongst Components, and Cost Savings

As a part of benefits identification, it is important for program managers to look beyond the business case. After all, by managing projects and components in a program, there are specific program management benefits from synergy and economy of scale and size. For example, instead of three projects separate contract consulting services from a company, the program is likely to achieve greater savings and vendor attention by procuring and managing these services centrally. See Table 4.2 for example of program benefits.

In addition to benefits identification, program managers should analyze and plan these benefits by:

- Establishing the benefits management plan
- Defining and prioritizing program components and their interdependencies
- Defining the KPIs and associated quantitative measures

Table 4.2   Sample Program Benefits

#	Source of Benefits	Description
1	Policy or legal requirement (mandatory)	Benefits that enable an organization to fulfill policy objectives or to satisfy legal requirements where the organization has no choice but to comply
2	Quality of service	Benefits to customers, such as quicker response to queries or providing information in a way the customer wants
3	Internal management	Benefits that are internal to the organization, such as improving decision-making or management processes
4	Process improvement (productivity or efficiency)	Benefits that allow an organization to do the same job with less resource, allowing a reduction in cost, or to do more
5	Personnel or HR management	The benefits of a better-motivated workforce may lead to a number of other benefits such as flexibility or increased productivity
6	Negative risk (or threats) reduction	Benefits that help enable an organization to be better prepared for the future by, for example, not closing off courses of action, or by providing new ones
7	Positive risk (or opportunities) exploitation	Benefits that help to enhance organization by sharing or expediting opportunities, for example, lobbying a particular policy to enhance the likelihood of success
8	Flexibility	Benefits that allow an organization to respond to change without incurring additional expenditure
9	Economy	Benefits that reduce costs while maintaining quality (often referred to as cost reduction)
10	Revenue enhancement or acceleration	Benefits that help enable increased revenue, or the same revenue level in a shorter timeframe, or both
11	Strategic fit	Benefits that contribute to or enable the desired benefits of other initiatives

■ Establishing the performance baseline for the program
■ Communicating program performance metrics to the key stakeholders

The benefits management plan is an important program management for managing benefits. Components of the benefit plan should include the following:

■ Define each benefit and associated assumptions and determine how each benefit will be achieved
■ Link component outputs to the planned program outcomes
■ Define the metrics (KPIs) and procedures to measure benefits
■ Define roles and responsibilities
■ Define how the resulting benefits and capabilities will be transitioned to achieve benefits
■ Define how the resulting capabilities will be transitioned to the individuals or group responsible for sustaining the benefits
■ Provide a process for managing the overall benefits management effort

Table 4.3 provides sample roles and responsibilities.

Table 4.3 Sample Program Benefits Management Roles and Responsibilities

#	Role	Responsibilities
1	Program manager (PgM)	The PgM is accountable for benefits realization at program level. He/she should help ensure that the Benefits Management Plan and Process are followed. The PgM owns the program's Benefits Profiles and Benefits Realization Plan
2	Project manager (PM)	Similar to the PgM, the person responsible for the setup, management, and delivery of the project
3	Organizational change manager (OCM)	The PgM (and PM) may appoint one or more OCMs to assist in the realization of benefits. The OCM typically comes from the business area most affected by the change and helps with the identification, and planning of benefits as well as the realization itself
4	Benefit owner	The individual responsible for realization of the benefit and who will "own" the Benefits Profile during the program and project implementation

4.3.3 How to Monitor, Control, and Verify Benefits Achieved throughout the Program Life Cycle While Sustaining Them in Operations

From a schedule perspective, most of the program life cycle time is spent in the Program Delivery Phase. Throughout this phase, program managers preform the following activities:

- Monitoring the organizational environment, program objectives, and benefits realization to ensure that the program remains aligned with the organization's strategic objectives
- Initiating, performing, transitioning, and closing components, and managing interdependencies among them (all component activities occur during benefits delivery!)
- Evaluating opportunities and threats affecting benefits and updating realized or obsolete risks affecting benefits
- Evaluating KPIs related to program financials, compliance, quality, safety, and stakeholder satisfaction in order to monitor the delivery of benefits
- Recording program progress in the benefits register
- Report to key stakeholders as directed in the program communications plan

As the program components are completed and the program start to wind down, program managers should start planning for the program benefits transition to operational areas. Successful transfer is crucial for the continual sustainment of benefits in subsequent phases. Specific transition activities include the following:

- Evaluate program performance against acceptance criteria and KPIs
- Review and evaluate acceptance criteria applicable to delivered components
- Review of operational and program process documentation
- Review of training and maintenance materials
- Review of applicable contractual agreements
- Assess to determine if resulting changes have been successfully integrated
- Spearhead of activities to improving acceptance of changes
- Transfer of risks affecting the benefits transitioned to the receiving organization
- Conduct of readiness assessment by the receiving person, group, or organization
- Dispose of all program-related resources

Finally, in Benefits Sustainment, the benefits achieved during the program delivery is now maintained and sustained, often by a separate team such as operations or portfolio management. To ensure the continued realization of the benefits delivered, a benefits sustainment plan should be developed prior to program closure to identify:

- Risk
- Processes
- Measures
- Metrics
- Tools

4.4 Program Benefits Management Skills

To perform Program Benefits Management effectively, program managers require developing the following skill sets:

- Benefit optimization
- Business value measurement
- Decision tree analysis
- Maintenance and sustainment of program benefits post delivery
- Performance and quality metrics
- Program transition strategies

For a description of these skills, refer to the skill glossary in Chapter 9 that highlights over 120 program management skills.

In addition to the skills that are more specific to the Program Benefits Management performance domain, program managers should also consider the more general business and management skills as described in Section 3.4.1.

4.5 Practice Questions

This section contains ten sample questions pertaining to Program Benefits Management.

Question 1: Program benefits delivery does what?

A. Monitors components, maintains benefits register, and reports benefits
B. Derives and prioritizes benefits and benefits metrics, establishes the benefits management plan, and maps benefits into the program management plan
C. Consolidates coordinated benefits and transfers ongoing responsibility
D. Monitors performance of benefits and ensures continued sustainment of benefits

Question 2: The program benefits management plan should:

A.   Provide a process for managing the overall deliverable management effort
B.   Define roles and responsibilities required to manage the deliverables
C.   Define how the resulting benefits and capabilities will be transitioned to operations to achieve benefits
D.   Link component outputs to the planned portfolio outcomes

Question 3: Benefits that cannot be easily measured such as improved employee moral or higher customer satisfaction are categorized as what?

A.   intangible benefits
B.   tangible deliverables
C.   intangible deliverables
D.   tangible benefits

Question 4: During program benefits delivery, strategic alignment focuses on:

A.   Ensuring that the program delivers the intended benefits
B.   Ensuring the linkage of enterprise and program plans, defining, maintaining, and validating the program value proposition, and aligning program and enterprise operations management
C.   Ensuring programs and projects are selected, prioritized, and staffed according to the organization's strategic plan for realizing desired organizational value.
D.   Ensuring the stakeholder engagement plan is synchronized with the program communication management plan

Question 5: A program may be terminated with no transition activities when:

A.   The program charter is fulfilled and operations are not necessary to continue realization of benefits
B.   The program charter is fulfilled and operations are necessary to continue realization of benefits
C.   The chartered program is still of value to the organization
D.   The program was completed ahead of schedule and the receiving organization was not prepared to accept the transition

Question 6: Program benefits analysis and planning does what?

A.   Consolidates coordinated benefits and transfers ongoing responsibility
B.   Identifies and quantifies benefits
C.   Derives and prioritizes benefits and benefits metrics, establishes the benefits management plan, and maps benefits into the program management plan
D.   Monitors performance of benefits and ensures continued realization of benefits

Question 7: The benefits register is developed during the benefits identification phase and is developed based on all of the following except?

A. Program business case
B. Organizational strategic plan
C. Other relevant program objectives
D. Other relevant project objectives

Question 8: Program benefits identification does what?

A. Identifies and quantifies benefits
B. Consolidates coordinated benefits and transfers ongoing responsibility
C. Monitors components, maintains benefits register, and reports benefits
D. Derives and prioritizes benefits and benefits metrics, establishes the benefits management plan, and maps benefits into the program management plan

Question 9: Benefits delivery activities include all of the following except:

A. Mapping the planned benefits to program components
B. Initiating, performing, transitioning, and closing components, and managing interdependencies
C. Evaluating KPIs to monitor the delivery of benefits
D. Recording program progress in the benefits register

Question 10: The purpose of program benefits management is to:

A. Focus stakeholders on the outcomes and benefits provided by various activities during the program life cycle
B. Focus the project management team on component schedules and milestones
C. Focus corporate leadership on benefits provided by the entire program at program completion
D. Focus stakeholders on the outcomes and deliverables provided by various activities during the program life cycle

4.5.1 Answer Key

1. A. Refer to Section 4.0 Program Benefits Management of the Standard.
2. C. Refer to Section 4.2.1 Benefits Management Plan of the Standard.
3. A. Refer to Section 4.0 Program Benefits Management of the Standard.
4. B. Refer to Section 4.3.2 Benefits and Program Governance of the Standard.
5. A. Refer to Section 4.4 Benefits Transition of the Standard.

6. C. Refer to Section 4.0 Program Benefits Management of the Standard.
7. D. Refer to Section 4.1.1 Benefits Register of the Standard.
8. A. Refer to Section 4.0 Program Benefits Management of the Standard.
9. A. Refer to Section 4.3 Benefits Delivery of the Standard.
10. A. Refer to Section 4.0 Program Benefits Management of the Standard.

Chapter 5

Understanding Program Stakeholder Engagement

5.1 Introduction

The goal of the Program Stakeholder Engagement performance domain is to effectively manage expectations of program stakeholders. Program managers generally do not have complete authority to make program-related decisions. They depend on stakeholders to react to the outcomes and benefits. Furthermore, program managers would require continual support from stakeholders throughout the program life cycle especially when dealing with certain risks and issues. Thus, it is important to keep stakeholders engaged in the decision-making process for the ultimate success of the program. Key steps and tools for stakeholder engagement are described below.

This chapter is organized by the following sections:

1. Describe the purpose of Program Stakeholder Engagement and the high-level tasks and activities that program managers should tackle pertaining to this performance domain
2. Highlight the three most important questions that program managers should ask pertaining to this domain
3. Describe the key Program Stakeholder Engagement Skills
4. Provide ten sample questions for readers to practice

By the end of this chapter, readers should be able to perform the following:

- Describe stakeholder engagement and its importance
- Address the key questions that shape how program managers think about stakeholder engagement
- Articulate and potentially apply the important activities in this domain

5.2 About Program Stakeholder Engagement

To effectively manage programs, program managers need successfully engage stakeholders and manage their expectations. There are seven important tasks associated with this domain:

1. Identify program stakeholders
2. Analyze program stakeholders
3. Negotiate with the program stakeholders
4. Maintain stakeholder management throughout the program life cycle
5. Manage important stakeholder through tailored communication
6. Engage stakeholders on risk management activities
7. Develop a positive relationship with program stakeholders

Table 5.1 provides further description of the tasks, including the importance of this task and some general steps to perform this task.

5.3 Key Questions for Program Stakeholder Engagement

Here are three of the most important questions for the Program Stakeholder Engagement performance domain:

1. Who are the stakeholders and what is their relative priority?
2. How are stakeholders engaged and how are detractors converted to supporters?
3. How to develop a positive working relationship with stakeholders that will enhance program success?

5.3.1 Who Are the Stakeholders and What Is Their Relative Priority?

A stakeholder is an individual, a group, or an organization that has the ability to influence or be influenced by decisions, actions, or results of a program. Accordingly, stakeholder engagement is the procedure through which a program manager interacts with its stakeholders to attain mutually agreed goals. Through stakeholder engagement, program managers get to know what their requirements and interests are, when they wish to achieve the program benefits, how engaged they are, and how the organizational strategies and actions will influence the overall results.

The first important step to stakeholder engagement is to identify stakeholders early in the program. The more a stakeholder will be influenced or impacted by the program, there will be more need to identify them early and keep them properly informed. This way, these stakeholders can take part in the program definition and delivery processes.

Table 5.1 Program Stakeholder Engagement Tasks

Task #	Task Description	Explanation of Importance	Steps to Perform This Task
1	Identify stakeholders, including sponsors, and create the stakeholder matrix in order to document their position relative to the program	Determine the program stakeholders, especially the most important ones	1. Work with the program sponsors and core team early in the program initiation to identify the key stakeholders 2. Develop a rudimentary understanding of the position and interest relative to the program
2	Perform stakeholder analysis through historical analysis, personal experience, interviews, knowledge base, review of formal agreements (e.g., request for proposal [RFP], request for information [RFI], contracts), and input from other sources in order to create the stakeholder management plan	Understand stakeholder positions and interests	1. Analyze and prioritize program stakeholders (based on the earlier task), especially evaluating their interests and influence 2. Create a stakeholder registry to capture the key information 3. Develop an engagement plan, especially with the important program stakeholders
3	Negotiate the support of stakeholders, including sponsors, for the program while setting clear expectations and acceptance criteria (e.g., key performance indicators [KPIs]) for the program benefits in order to achieve and maintain their alignment to the program objectives	Develop mutual interests to advance the program objectives	1. Negotiate with the program stakeholders to ensure the right level of support throughout the program life cycle 2. Update the stakeholder engagement plan as new information develops 3. Making sure the stakeholder engagement activities continuously align the stakeholder with the program objectives

(continued)

Table 5.1 (Continued) Program Stakeholder Engagement Tasks

Task #	Task Description	Explanation of Importance	Steps to Perform This Task
4	Generate and maintain visibility for the program and confirm stakeholder support in order to achieve the program's strategic objectives	Ensure sufficient support from the program stakeholders	1. Continually engage the program stakeholders throughout the program 2. Enable program visibility through communication and other engagement activities
5	Define and maintain communications adapted to different stakeholders, including sponsors, in order to ensure their support for the program	Ensure optimal communication, especially with the important stakeholders	1. Create special communication vehicles or reports that are suitable for the specific preference of the most important stakeholders 2. Monitor and adjust communication vehicles and engagement activities are necessary to ensure their continued support
6	Evaluate risks identified by stakeholders, including sponsors, and incorporate them in the program risk management plan, as necessary	Manage stakeholder expectations and develop closer relationship	1. Work with the key stakeholders and identify program risks from their perspective 2. Analyze the program risks including categorizing and prioritizing 3. Manage these risks using the program risk management plan

(continued)

Table 5.1 (Continued) Program Stakeholder Engagement Tasks

Task #	Task Description	Explanation of Importance	Steps to Perform This Task
7	Develop and foster relationships with stakeholders, including sponsors, in order to improve communication and enhance their support for the program	Ensure sufficient support from the program stakeholders	1. Analyze the stakeholders and determine the best member of the program team to engage with the stakeholder. Note: Even though the program manager is the de facto stakeholder manager, the program manager should involve the entire core program team, including the sponsor, in stakeholder management 2. Assign the best resource to manage the stakeholder 3. Engage the stakeholders to foster a positive relationship 4. Monitor and adjust course as necessary

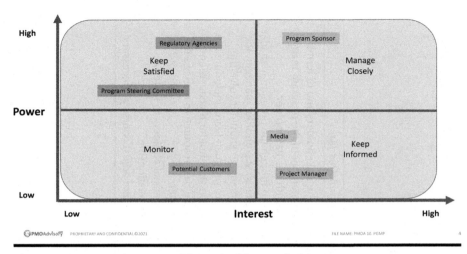

Figure 5.1 Power Interest Grid (used with permission).

Shortly after identifying the stakeholders, program managers should evaluate them for relative importance. Not all stakeholders are equal, in terms of their influence and impact. A common program management tool to evaluate stakeholder importance is the Power Interest Grid as shown in Figure 5.1.

5.3.2 How Are Stakeholders Engaged and How Are Detractors Converted to Supporters?

After identifying program stakeholders and arrange them by priority, the next step is to determine engagement, both the level of engagement and how to best engage them. Perhaps the single biggest challenge on some programs, especially those programs that are politically sensitive, is how to work with difficult stakeholders who are against the program and would actively block its progress and yet, their support is crucial for program success. Often caught in these difficult situations, program managers should develop a robust engagement plan, especially as they work with these difficult stakeholders (Table 5.2). Key steps to engage difficult stakeholders include:

1. Utilize strong communication
2. Negotiate where possible
3. Apply conflict management skills to reduce tension
4. Be as transparent and trustworthy as possible
5. Leverage the power of the masses and isolate the problematic stakeholders
6. Regularly monitor engagement results

Table 5.2   Steps to Engage Difficult Stakeholders

#	*Highlight*	*Description*
1	Utilize strong communication	Program managers should create a robust communication management plan, which includes an analysis of stakeholders' communication requirements. Furthermore, identify the optimal communication medium with each of the key stakeholders. These communication mediums may include the meeting conducts, the use of emails, and the intranet to keep them updated
2	Negotiate where possible	As there are likely disagreements with tasks and priorities, program managers should proactively negotiate with stakeholders to arrive at mutually acceptable positions. When regular negotiations are not possible, either because the stakeholder is being difficult or because the stakeholder has no interest in the program and yet you need their support, then work with others on the governance team enlarges the scope of the negotiation to include their interests
3	Apply conflict management skills to reduce tension	Whenever there are severe disagreements, conflicts may rise. Program managers should maintain a keen view toward deescalating tensions by applying conflict management skills. When combined with professional negotiation skills, program managers can seek to find common grounds while minimizing heated conflicts
4	Be as transparent and trustworthy as possible	On politically sensitive topics, program managers can be an objective meditator among conflicting parties. By being transparent with knowledge information (and where information cannot be shared, state that early) and treat all sides with open and honest communication, program managers can build trust with the key stakeholders
5	Leverage the power of the masses and isolate the problematic stakeholders	In certain situations, where there is little direct leverage with particularly difficult stakeholders, it may be important to gather as much support as possible. Achieving an overwhelming majority directly applies peer pressure to the isolated difficult stakeholders

(*continued*)

Table 5.2 (Continued)   Steps to Engage Difficult Stakeholders

#	Highlight	Description
6	Delegate where feasible	Even though program managers are often the "de facto" owner of stakeholder engagement, it is important for program managers to leverage all the people on the program team, and this includes the program governance members. This may be especially important when working with difficult executives
7	Regularly monitor engagement results	Throughout the program life cycle, program managers should closely monitor the progress of stakeholder engagement, especially on the delegated engagement activities. Furthermore, due to the longer duration of programs, situations and people can change. Therefore, program managers should also closely track changes on programs

5.3.3 How to Develop a Positive Working Relationship with Stakeholders That Will Enhance Program Success

Aside from applying professional skills including abiding to code of ethics of Project Management Institute (PMI), program managers should proactively engage stakeholders early in the program to develop a trust-based relationship. Here are some important planning considerations for developing a positive working relationship with stakeholders:

- Develop a deep understanding of the performing organization's culture and acceptance of change
- Evaluate the attitudes about the program and its sponsors
- Understand the expectation of program benefits delivery
- Assess the degree of support or opposition to the program benefits
- Measure the stakeholder's ability to influence the outcome of the program

Armed with this knowledge, program managers can now develop a mutually beneficial engagement plan that would enable the development of positive working relationships.

5.4 Program Stakeholder Engagement Skills

To perform Program Stakeholder Engagement effectively, program managers require developing the following skill sets:

- Customer relationship management
- Customer satisfaction measurement

- Expectation management
- Public relations
- Training methodologies

For a description of these skills, refer to the skill glossary in Chapter 9 that highlights over 120 program management skills.

In addition to the skills that are more specific to the Program Stakeholder Engagement performance domain, program managers should also consider the more general business and management skills as described in Section 3.4.1.

5.5 Practice Questions

This section contains ten sample questions pertaining to Program Stakeholder Engagement.

Question 1: Which of the following statements about program stakeholders is not accurate?

A.   Stakeholders can be internal or external to the program
B.   Stakeholders may have a positive or negative impact on the outcome of the program
C.   In many cases, stakeholders have more influence than the program manager
D.   Stakeholder communication is always considered direct communication

Question 2: William is a program manager. He is currently working on managing the groups that are interested in the program. Specifically, he is identifying highly influential parties and mapped their relationship to the program. These parties include customers and non-customers. What area of expertise should William be familiar with as it relates to this activity?

A.   Customer relationship management
B.   Program risk management plan
C.   Program stakeholder engagement plan
D.   Program stakeholder engagement plan

Question 3: When communicating with stakeholders, specific communication requirements should include which one?

A. A copy of the stakeholder register, the contact information for each stakeholder, and place of work
B. Details on the program team demographics, program performance information, and specific reporting format
C. What information should be communicated, language, format, content, and level of detail
D. The date and time of each stakeholder engagement meeting, the firm communication schedule, and reporting frequency

Question 4: In order to effectively share stakeholder questions and answers, a program manger should do what?

A. Only answer questions from each stakeholder and do not share information
B. Publish the questions and answers on a public site to allow all stakeholders access to the information
C. Capture and publish risks in a way that allows multiple stakeholders to benefit from the exchange
D. Capture and publish program questions in a way that allows multiple stakeholders to benefit from the exchange

Question 5: The program manager is who?

A. The person assigned by the performing organization to lead the team that is responsible for achieving project objectives
B. The person assigned by the performing organization to establish, balance, monitor, and control portfolio components to achieve strategic business objectives
C. The person who provides resources and support for the program and is accountable for enabling success
D. The individual authorized by the performing organization to lead the team responsible for achieving program objectives

Question 6: Because the list of stakeholders and their attitudes and opinions change as the program progresses and delivers benefits, stakeholder engagement is conducted when?

A. During benefits delivery
B. During project execution
C. Continuously throughout the program life cycle
D. During program closure

Question 7: In order to effectively conduct stakeholder engagement, all of the following aspects for each stakeholder are taken into consideration except which one?

A.   Organizational culture and acceptance to change
B.   Attitudes about the program and its sponsors
C.   The length of time the stakeholder has resided in their current position within the company
D.   Relevant phases applicable to stakeholder specific engagement

Question 8: Which of the following is often expressed as direct and indirect communication between the stakeholder person or group, and the program's leaders and team?

A.   Stakeholder interaction
B.   Stakeholder engagement
C.   Stakeholder communication
D.   Stakeholder management

Question 9: Program stakeholder engagement is the performance domain that does what?

A.   Identifies and analyzes stakeholder needs and manages expectations and communications to foster stakeholder support
B.   Defines, creates, maximizes, and delivers the benefits provided by the program
C.   Identifies program outputs and outcomes to provide benefits aligned with the organization's strategic goals
D.   Enables and performs program decision-making, establishes practices to support the program, and maintains program oversight

Question 10: The program steering committee is who?

A.   The individuals performing program activities
B.   The individuals performing constituent component activities
C.   A group of participants representing various program-related interests with the purpose of supporting the program under its authority by providing governance practices
D.   Groups representing consumer, environmental, or other interests

5.5.1 Answer Key

1. D. Refer to Section 5.5 of the Standard.
2. C. Refer to Section 5.3 of the Standard.
3. C. Refer to Section 5.5 Program Stakeholder Communications of the Standard.

4. D. Refer to Section 5.5 Program Stakeholder Communications of the Standard.
5. D. Refer to Section 5.1 Program Stakeholder Identification of the Standard.
6. C. Refer to Section 5.4 Program Stakeholder Engagement of the Standard.
7. C. Refer to Section 5.3 Program Stakeholder Engagement Planning of the Standard.
8. B. Refer to Section 5.4 of the Standard.
9. A. Refer to Section 5.0 Program Stakeholder Engagement of the Standard.
10. C. Refer to Section 5.1 Program Stakeholder Identification of the Standard.

Chapter 6

Understanding Program Governance

6.1 Introduction

The goal of the Program Governance performance domain is to provide oversight and make key program decisions. Specific activities include establishing and approving program vision, securing funding and resources, addressing escalated program issues and risks, championing program interests and activities, and supporting the program manager and the program management team. By establishing and implementing robust program governance, program managers improve the overall likelihood of delivering program benefits by fortifying executive support.

This chapter is organized by the following sections:

1. Describe the purpose of Program Governance and the high-level tasks and activities that program managers should tackle pertaining to this performance domain
2. Highlight the three most important questions that program managers should ask pertaining to this domain
3. Describe the key Program Governance Skills
4. Provide ten sample questions for readers to practice

By the end of this chapter, readers should be able to perform the following:

- Describe governance and its importance
- Address the key questions that shape how program managers think about benefits management
- Articulate and potentially apply the important activities in this domain

6.2 About Program Governance

Program Governance involves processes, skills, and techniques in which programs determine, approve, direct, and support key program decisions. The program manager plays a vital role in the design, establishment, and management of the program governance processes. Successful program governance provides a proper structure to handle escalated problems, risks, and challenges. Good governance also helps to tackle risks and ultimately achieve the agreed benefits. Furthermore, with the appropriate governance framework, programs can more easily stay aligned with the organizational strategy. There are 11 important tasks associated with this domain:

1. Develop program and project management methods for the program
2. Determine an optimal program governance model
3. Obtain approval for program progression
4. Evaluate key performance indicators (KPIs)
5. Establish the Program Management Information System (PMIS)
6. Manage program risks
7. Escalating issues and risks
8. Utilize the PMIS throughout the program life cycle
9. Apply lessons learned
10. Monitor the environmental context of the program
11. Develop program integration management plan to enable proper integration management throughout the program life cycle

Table 6.1 provides further description of the tasks, including the importance of this task and some general steps to perform this task.

6.3 Key Questions for Program Governance

Here are three of the most important questions for the Program Governance Engagement performance domain:

1. How to design the optimal governance structure for program?
2. What are program governance roles?
3. What are important governance decisions?

6.3.1 How to Design the Optimal Governance Structure for Program

Early in the program and during the Program Definition Phase, program managers should work with the program sponsor to design and establish good governance structure and processes. One of the key program management artifacts

Table 6.1 Program Benefits Management Tasks

Task #	Task Description	Explanation of Importance	Steps to Perform This Task
1	Develop program and project management standards and structure (governance, tools, finance, and reporting) using industry best practices and organizational standards in order to drive efficiency and consistency among projects and deliver program objectives	Enable program implementation excellence	1. Evaluate and review the various program and project methodologies that exist within the organization and/or industry 2. Work with the component managers to agree on the best approach to implement the components and the overall program 3. Tailor the program and project management standards and structure as appropriate. If required, obtain support from the PMO and other organizational units 4. Communicate the methodology and if needed conduct training 5. Update the methodology as appropriate, especially if there are significant changes in the program
2	Select a governance model structure including policies, procedures, and standards that conform program practices with the organization's governance structure in order to deliver program objectives consistent with organizational governance requirements	Establish how important decisions on the program will be made	1. Evaluate and review the various program and project governance models and structures that exist within the organization (e.g., PMOs) and/or industry 2. Select the program governance model that maximizes the effectiveness while minimizing inefficiencies and/or side effects 3. Refine the governance model as required, especially consider the component project governance model and activities 4. Communicate the governance model and if needed conduct training 5. Continually refine the governance model as required, especially if there are significant changes in the program

(continued)

Table 6.1 (Continued)   Program Benefits Management Tasks

Task #	Task Description	Explanation of Importance	Steps to Perform This Task
3	Obtain authorization(s) and approval(s) through stage gate reviews by presenting the program status to governance authorities in order to proceed to the next phase of the program	Determine major program review cycles	1. Define the major stages of the program 2. Agree on the entrance and exit criteria for these stages 3. Agree on the mechanism to review, approve, and authorize the progression of program stages 4. Document the agreement and the processes 5. Implement the processes to obtain authorizations and approvals in program execution
4	Evaluate KPIs (e.g., risks, financials, compliance, quality, safety, stakeholder satisfaction) in order to monitor program benefits throughout the program life cycle	Monitor program progress	1. Work with the program governance and component managers to agree on the KPIs (including leveraging the work accomplished in Life Cycle Management Task 14) 2. Monitor the KPIs including the benefits attained
5	Develop and/or utilize the PMIS, and integrate different processes as needed, in order to manage program information and communicate status to stakeholders	Effective management of knowledge and information	1. Develop and implement an effective PMIS for the program (including leveraging the work accomplished in Life Cycle Management Task 11) 2. Refine the PMIS utilization by integrating different components and processes as required throughout the program life cycle 3. Communicate and share the knowledge in PMIS with the program stakeholders

(continued)

Table 6.1 (Continued)   Program Benefits Management Tasks

Task #	Task Description	Explanation of Importance	Steps to Perform This Task
6	Regularly evaluate new and existing risks that impact strategic objectives in order to present an updated risk management plan to the governance board for approval	Effectively manage program risks	1. Conduct regular review of program risks, especially the high priority risks with the program governance 2. Focus on the risk implications and responses. For innovative and exploratory programs, there may need to be an emphasis on managing the "unknown unknown"
7	Establish escalation policies and procedures in order to ensure risks are handled at the appropriate level	Manage the program execution effectively	1. Clearly define escalation methods for various project situations including issues, risks, and changes with the goal of timely intervention at the appropriate level 2. Communicate and conduct training, if necessary, with the entire program team
8	Develop and/or contribute to an information repository containing program-related lessons learned, processes, and documentation contributions in order to support organizational best practices	Effective management of knowledge and information	1. Develop processes to make sure important knowledge and program-related artifacts are captured in the PMIS 2. Encourage teams to utilize the PMIS including creating enforcement activities 3. Create instructions and/or conduct trainings to enable the entire program team with the knowledge on how to best use the PMIS
9	Identify and apply lessons learned in order to support and influence existing and future program or organizational improvement	Continuously improve program execution	1. Obtain and review lessons learned from previous programs, with the goal of improving current program execution 2. Share and review component-level lessons learned throughout the life cycle of the program as components are closed

(continued)

Table 6.1 (Continued)   Program Benefits Management Tasks

Task #	Task Description	Explanation of Importance	Steps to Perform This Task
10	Monitor the business environment, program functionality requirements, and benefits realization in order to ensure the program remains aligned with strategic objectives	Minimize external surprises on the program	1. Monitor the external environment of the program regularly to minimize surprises. These can include industry trends, competitive movements, macroeconomic situations, regulatory changes, and legal environment 2. Analyze these observations and determine if actions and changes are required. It is especially important to evaluate the impact to the program assumptions, which are risks if the assumptions may be changing 3. Manage these changes as issues, risks, and/or program changes are required
11	Develop and support the program integration management plan in order to ensure operational alignment with program strategic objectives	Effectively manage program integration activities	1. Develop the program integration management plan by leveraging the previous work in Strategy Alignment Task 10 2. Share the program integration plan with the program team and ensure proper understanding 3. Regularly monitor and control program integration activities to achieve synergy

is the creation of the Program Governance Plan, which lays out the systems and methods to be used to monitor, manage, and support the program. A good governance plan when properly executed can handle most if not all the program governance activities. Specifically, the purpose of the governance plan is as follows:

- Facilitate the design and implementation of effective governance
- Provide guidelines for the establishment of governance frameworks, functions, and processes
- Determine and describe the systems and methods to be used to monitor, manage, and support the program

Key components of a robust governance plan include the following:

- Program vision and goals
- Governance roles and responsibilities
- Governance practices
- Level of authorization, including component authorization
- Program dependencies, assumptions, and constraints
- Governance meetings, especially special meetings to address urgent issues and risks
- Agreement on program success criteria, program benefits, performance metrics, and constraints
- Process of conducting periodic health checks

By establishing good governance processes and systems, program managers can address program challenges often before they occur. See Figure 6.1 for good governance practices.

Figure 6.1   Good governance practices.

6.3.2 *What Are Program Governance Roles?*

Depending on program and organization, there can be many roles in program governance teams. Common roles include:

- Program Steering Committee – A group of participants with the purpose of supporting the program under its authority providing guidance and oversight
- Program Sponsor – An individual or a group that provides resources and support for the program and is accountable for enabling success
- Program Management Office – A management structure that standardizes the program-related governance processes and resource sharing
- Program Manager – The individual in the organization that maintains responsibility for leadership, conduct, and performance of the program
- Project and Component Manager – The person assigned by the performing organization to lead the team that is responsible for achieving project objectives
- Other Stakeholders – Include the manager of the portfolio and operational managers receiving the capabilities delivered by the program

Since the role of program steering committee is especially important for program success, here are some key responsibilities of the steering committee:

1. Provide governance support for the program to include oversight, control, integration, and decision-making functions
2. Provide capable governance resources to oversee and monitor program uncertainty and complexity related to achieving benefits delivery
3. Ensure program goals and planned benefits align with organizational strategic and operational goals
4. Conduct planning sessions to confirm, prioritize, and fund the program
5. Endorse or approve program recommendations and changes
6. Resolve and remediate escalated program issues and risks
7. Provide oversight and monitoring so program benefits are planned, measured, and achieved
8. Provide leadership in making, enforcing, carrying out, and communicating decisions
9. Define key messages that are to be communicated to stakeholders and ensure they are consistent and transparent
10. Review expected benefits and benefits delivery
11. Approve program closure or termination

6.3.3 What Are Important Governance Decisions?

Program governance, specifically the program steering committee, is responsible for making key decisions on programs that are typically beyond the authorization of the program manager and program sponsor. Selective decisions include:

1. Approval of important program management artifacts such as the program business case, program charter, program management plans, benefits realization, and program closure
2. Major change to programs, especially those changes that impact program direction
3. Escalated issues and risks
4. Approval of program components such as subprograms, projects, and other program activities

Program business case is the first major artifact for approval as this document serves as a formal projection of the benefits that the program is expected to deliver and a justification for the resources that will be expended to deliver it. Program charter is the next major artifact as the approval of this document authorizes the program management team to use organizational resources to pursue the program and links the program to its business case and the organization's strategic priorities. Program management plan or its components (such as the governance management plan) are also important as they provide guidance for program implementation. Toward the end of the program life cycle, governance team should provide the final approval to closeout or transition the program.

On programs, managing change and escalated issues and risks are an integral part of governance. Depending on the size and complexity of programs, there can be multiple levels of steering committees. In these multi-level governance situations, program managers should clearly delineate roles and authority level. For example, on a large SAP implementation, the program steering structure contained three levels of governance. The tactical layer is composed of business level directors, and their authority was to make changes up to $50k. The next layer is composed of area vice presidents, and changes at this level typically impact business unit operations. Their authority is to approve changes up to $250k. The final level is the most senior level, and the team is made of some C-level executives and other senior or executive vice presidents. Their budgetary authority has no pre-determined limit.

One of the key decisions for program steering committee is the approval of program components by reviewing and evaluating component business cases. Approval of the initiation of a new program component generally includes the following:

■ Reconfirming the component business case and in some cases the program business case too
■ Ensuring the availability of resources to perform the component

- Defining or reconfirming individual accountabilities for management and pursuit of the components
- Ensuring the communication of critical component-related information to key stakeholders
- Ensuring the establishment of component-specific, program-level quality control plans
- Authorizing the governance structure to track the component's progress against its goals

As a program nears completion, program steering committee either approves closure or recommends to the senior management the program for closure. Program closure can occur two distinct reasons:

- Happy path – the program has met the stated objectives and achieved the agreed benefits
- Unhappy path – the program is terminated underperformance or a change in the environment that diminishes program benefits or needs

At program closure, transition occurs from program governance to operational governance to maintain and sustain the benefits realized by the program.

6.4 Program Governance Skills

To perform Program Governance effectively, program managers require developing the following skill sets:

- Archiving tools and techniques
- Business/organization objectives
- Closeout plans, procedures, techniques and policies
- Composition and responsibilities of the PMO
- Financial closure processes
- Go/no-go decision criteria
- Governance models
- Governance processes and procedures
- Metrics definition and measurement techniques
- Performance analysis and reporting techniques (e.g., earned value analysis [EVA])
- Phase gate reviews
- Program and project change requests
- Statistical analysis

For a description of these skills, refer to the skill glossary in Chapter 9 that highlights over 120 program management skills.

In addition to the skills that are more specific to the Program Governance performance domain, program managers should also consider the more general business and management skills as described in Section 3.4.1.

6.5 Practice Questions

This section contains ten sample questions pertaining to Program Governance.

Question 1: How does the program charter provide governance to the program?

A. Serving as a formal projection of the benefits that the program is expected to deliver and a justification for the resources that will be expended to deliver it

B. Authorizes the program management team to use organizational resources to pursue the program and links the program organizational strategic priorities

C. Assess a program's ongoing performance and progress toward the realization and sustainment of benefits

D. Establishes the minimum acceptable criteria for a successful program and the methods by which those criteria will be measured, communicated, and endorsed

Question 2: Program governance is the performance domain that does what?

A. Defines, creates, maximizes, and delivers the benefits provided by the program

B. Identifies program outputs and outcomes to provide benefits aligned with the organization's strategic goals

C. Identifies and analyzes stakeholder needs and manages expectations and communications to foster stakeholder support

D. Enables and performs program decision-making, establishes practices to support the program, and maintains program oversight

Question 3: The program business case provides governance to the program by what means?

A. Authorizes the program management team to use organizational resources to pursue the program and links the program organizational strategic priorities

B. Assesses a program's ongoing performance and progress toward the realization and sustainment of benefits

C. Establishes the minimum acceptable criteria for a successful program and the methods by which those criteria will be measured, communicated, and endorsed

D. Serves as a formal projection of the benefits that the program is expected to deliver and a justification for the resources that will be expended to deliver it

Question 4: The two governance documents that provide program approval, endorsement, and definition are what?

A. Program business case and program charter
B. Program benefits management plan and program charter
C. Program business case and program benefits management plan
D. Program stakeholder engagement plan and program benefits management plan

Question 5: Program success criteria:

A. Establishes the minimum acceptable criteria for a successful program and the methods by which those criteria will be measured, communicated, and endorsed
B. Serving as a formal projection of the benefits that the program is expected to deliver and a justification for the resources that will be expended to deliver it
C. Authorizes the program management team to use organizational resources to pursue the program and links the program organizational strategic priorities
D. Assess a program's ongoing performance and progress toward the realization and sustainment of benefits

Question 6: Program escalation that involves individuals outside of the program includes all of the following except:

A. Program steering committee
B. Other stakeholders
C. Component teams
D. Program management team

Question 7: Program decision-point reviews may include all of the following except which one?

A. Program resource needs and organizational commitments in addition to capabilities for fulfilling them
B. Program confirmation of support for business or organizational strategy
C. Information critical to strategic prioritization or operational investments of the organization as part of its portfolio management activities
D. Potential need for changes to elements of the program, in order to further improve the program's performance and likelihood of success

Question 8: Program reporting and controlling documents may include all except:

A. Project information management
B. Operational status and progress of programs, components, and related activities
C. Expected or incurred program resource requirements
D. Issues and issue response plans

Question 9: Common factors optimizing program governance include all of the following except:

A. Project manager selection
B. Alignment with portfolio and organizational governance
C. Program funding structure
D. Decision-making hierarchy

Question 10: In order to ensure the program is conforming to established governance expectations and agreements, the program governance plan is referenced when?

A. At the beginning of each phase of the program life cycle
B. At the end of each program life cycle
C. During the program benefits delivery phase
D. Throughout the program duration

6.5.1 Answer Key

1. B. Refer to Section 6.1.3 Program Approval, Endorsement, and Definition of the Standard.
2. D. Refer to Section 6.0 Program Governance of the Standard.
3. D. Refer to Section 6.1.3 Program Approval, Endorsement, and Definition of the Standard.
4. A. Refer to Section 6.1.3 Program Approval, Endorsement, and Definition of the Standard.
5. A. Refer to Section 6.1.4 Program Success Criteria of the Standard.
6. C. Refer to Section 6.1.6 Program Risk and Issue Governance of the Standard.
7. B. Refer to Section 6.1.9 Program Governance Reviews of the Standard.
8. A. Refer to Section 6.1.5 Program Monitoring, Reporting, and Controlling of the Standard.
9. A. Refer to Section 6.3 Program Governance Design and Implementation of the Standard.
10. D. Refer to Section 6.1.1 Program Governance Plan of the Standard.

Chapter 7

Understanding Program Life Cycle Management

7.1 Introduction

The goal of the Program Life Cycle Management performance domain is to manage the program from start to finish. The program life cycle is similar with the project life cycle, and the only real differences is that the program involves multiple components and each of the components have a life cycle within the larger program structure. As such, programs are more complex than projects to manage these additional interactions and linkages.

This chapter is organized by the following sections:

1. Describe the purpose of Program Life Cycle Management and the high-level tasks and activities that program managers should tackle pertaining to this performance domain
2. Highlight the three most important questions that program managers should ask pertaining to this domain
3. Describe the key Program Life Cycle Management Skills
4. Provide ten sample questions for readers to practice

By the end of this chapter, readers should be able to perform the following:

- Describe program life cycle management and its importance
- Address the key questions that shape how program managers think about benefits management
- Articulate and potentially apply the important activities in this domain

7.2 About Program Life Cycle Management

The program life cycle can be defined as the series of different stages involved throughout the life of a program from its inception to completion. The program life cycle is quite similar to the project life cycle. The key difference between the two is that the objective of program management is to provide long-term benefits to the organization and programs by definition contains multiple components, which can be subprograms, projects, and other activities.

As readers prepare for the Program Management Professional (PgMP) exam, the two important publications, the PgMP Examination Content Outline (ECO) and Standard for Program Management – 4th Edition (Standard), have different program life cycle phases. This is partly because these publications are published in different years. This difference can cause some confusion. See Figure 7.1 for mapping of the phases across the two models.

Since the PgMP exam is technically based on the ECO, this book will first describe the ECO's five-phase schema for program management life cycle and the associated tasks in the next section.

7.2.1 ECO's Program Life Cycle – Initiating

In Program Initiation Phase, there are six important tasks:

1. Develop program charter
2. Create high-level scope, based on the strategic objectives of the program
3. Create high-level milestones based on the available information
4. Create a Responsibility Assignment Matrix (e.g., RACI) to clearly identify the roles
5. Determine the program management success metrics and measures
6. Organize and facilitate program kick-off meeting(s) with important stakeholders

Table 7.1 provides further description of the tasks, including the importance of this task and some general steps to perform this task.

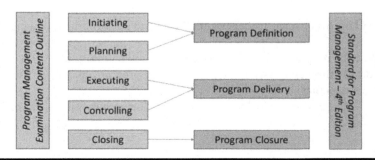

Figure 7.1 Aligning two models of program life cycle.

Table 7.1 Program Life Cycle Management – Initiating Tasks

Task #	Task Description	Explanation of Importance	Steps to Perform This Task
1	Develop program charter using input from all stakeholders, including sponsors, in order to initiate and design program and benefits	Program charter is one of the most useful program artifacts, not only serve as an initial contract but also can be used as an important communication vehicle	1. Work with the organizational leaders, especially program sponsors and the core program team to create the overall program scope, constraints, business cases, preliminary resources requirements, milestones, budgets, risks, and challenges 2. Develop the program charter and make sure core team members review and agree with it
2	Translate strategic objectives into high-level program scope statements by negotiating with stakeholders, including sponsors, in order to create a program scope description	Preliminary scope statement help an organization to understand "what" they are doing	1. Work with the organizational leaders to understand the strategic objectives of the program, including the desired outputs and benefits 2. Review the organizational strategies to ensure alignment 3. Develop the high-level scope for the program
3	Develop a high-level milestone plan using the goals and objectives of the program, applicable historical information, and other available resources (e.g., work-breakdown-structure [WBS], scope statements, benefits realization plan) in order to align the program with the expectations of stakeholders, including sponsors	Preliminary schedule; can also be served as an executive-level program schedule	1. Collect the source of program information 2. Determine what are the attributes of program milestones 3. Determine the program milestones with a focus on selectivity (as there can be many program milestones) 4. Share the milestones with the program management team and important stakeholders

(continued)

Table 7.1 (Continued)   Program Life Cycle Management – Initiating Tasks

Task #	Task Description	Explanation of Importance	Steps to Perform This Task
4	Develop an accountability matrix by identifying and assigning program roles and responsibilities in order to build the core team and to differentiate between the program and project resources	Clearly define the roles and responsibilities, especially across projects and programs and sometimes with projects	1. Work with sponsors and executives to identify the program structure 2. Work with the component managers to clearly define the roles of program, projects, and other component team members 3. Create the Responsibility Assignment Matrix (RAM). Note: RACI is a popular form of RAM 4. Share it with the broader program team to achieve understanding, buy-ins, and agreements
5	Define standard measurement criteria for success for all constituent projects by analyzing stakeholder expectations and requirements across the constituent projects in order to monitor and control the program	Define the success criteria	1. Develop a strawman of program metrics and specific measures for managing the program 2. Review the metrics with the executives to understand their perspective 3. Work with the program and component teams to agree on the how to best collect the data objectively 4. Publish the success metrics and share it with the entire program team

(continued)

Table 7.1 (Continued)   Program Life Cycle Management – Initiating Tasks

Task #	Task Description	Explanation of Importance	Steps to Perform This Task
6	Conduct program kick-off with key stakeholders by holding meetings in order to familiarize the organization with the program and obtain stakeholder buy-in	Making sure the program team are on the same page	1. Plan the kick-off meetings required for the program, as there can be multiple kick-off meetings 2. Work with the sponsors and component managers to determine the important topics for the program kick-off meeting. Clearly define the objectives and the desired outcomes 3. Collect the required information and assemble the materials 4. Organize the kick-off meetings by inviting the relevant stakeholders. Tailor for virtual and international team members 5. Conduct the kick-off meetings 6. Monitor and measure the outcome and adjust and refine as required in the future program meetings

7.2.2 ECO's Program Life Cycle – Planning

In Program Planning Phase, there are nine important tasks:

7. Develop a detailed program scope statement
8. Develop the program WBS with assignments
9. Develop the program management plan
10. Refine the program management plan
11. Establish the project management information system (PMIS) for the program, which is an environment for collecting and sharing of program information
12. Identify and determine methods to resolve issues
13. Plan for program closure by focusing on transitioning to operations, achieving synergy among project components in the program and program closure
14. Determine the key performance indicators (KPIs) for the program (and leverage the earlier work on metrics and KPIs)
15. Monitor program resources, especially people, to enable clearly performance targets are being achieved

Table 7.2 provides further description of the tasks, including the importance of this task and some general steps to perform this task.

7.2.3 ECO's Program Life Cycle – Executing

In Program Executing Phase, there are nine important tasks:

16. Authorize the implementation of components (e.g., projects)
17. Implement and manage the agreed program management processes
18. Develop mechanisms for communication and knowledge sharing
19. Manage people and talents through the program
20. Direct project managers
21. Implement the various plans in the program management plan
22. Develop the program performance report
23. Manage the program progress through performance reports
24. Approve closure of program components

Table 7.3 provides further description of the tasks, including the importance of this task and some general steps to perform this task.

Table 7.2 Program Life Cycle Management – Planning Tasks

Task #	Task Description	Explanation of Importance	Steps to Perform This Task
7	Develop a detailed program scope statement by incorporating program vision and all internal and external objectives, goals, influences, and variables in order to facilitate overall planning	Refine the program scope from the Initiating phase	1. Review the high-level scope statement from the Initiating phase 2. Work with the program sponsors and teams to refine the scope statement 3. Develop greater details and specificities of the program scope, including better definition of vision, objectives, goals, and requirements 4. Create the detailed program scope statement 5. Share it with the broader program team
8	Develop program WBS in order to determine, plan, and assign the program tasks and deliverables	Drive greater clarity on the program activities	1. Work with the program team, including the component team managers to clearly define program vs. project and other component level activities 2. Develop the program WBS based on the agreed program activities 3. Assign resources to the program activities 4. Communicate and share the program WBS with the program core team

(continued)

Table 7.2 (Continued)   Program Life Cycle Management – Planning Tasks

Task #	Task Description	Explanation of Importance	Steps to Perform This Task
9	Establish the program management plan and schedule by integrating plans for constituent projects and creating plans for supporting program functions (e.g., quality, risk, communication, resources) in order to effectively forecast, monitor, and identify variances during program execution	Create the "operating" document for the program to ensure common understanding	1. Work with the program team, including the component team managers to clearly define program processes and management of exception. It is also important to work with the component managers to define and agree on the approaches and methodologies for program implementation (e.g., waterfall, agile, etc. for the various components) 2. Create the subsidiary components of the program management plan (e.g., scope, schedule, cost, risk, quality, etc.) 3. Review with the component managers to ensure both integration and distinction from the component (e.g., project) management plans 4. Inform and receive approval from program sponsors and program steering committees of the important activities in the program management plan 5. Share the program management plan with the broader team

(continued)

Table 7.2 (Continued)   Program Life Cycle Management – Planning Tasks

Task #	Task Description	Explanation of Importance	Steps to Perform This Task
10	Optimize the program management plan by identifying, reviewing, and leveling resource requirements (e.g., human resources, materials, equipment, facilities, finance) in order to gain efficiencies and maximize productivity/synergies among constituent projects	Make sure this document is kept current and relevant through continuous refinement	1. Over the course of the program life cycle, regularly review and update the program management plan with the latest developments 2. Refine the program management plan to ensure currency and relevancy. Continuously improve the document especially on important program-level activities such as resource allocations, procurement activities, re-optimization of budgets, etc. 3. Track changes to the program management plan 4. Re-publish the document as appropriate 5. If there are significant changes, conduct review sessions with the broader program teams
11	Define PMIS by selecting tools and processes to share knowledge, intellectual property, and documentation across constituent projects in order to maximize synergies and savings in accordance with the governance model	Enable effective management of information and knowledge	1. Work closely with the sponsors and project managers to agree on the important functions for the PMIS 2. Develop, set up, and establish the PMIS and the associated processes including standards such as file naming, storage locations, and keyword tags for the program 3. Develop instructional materials, including training programs, to educate the program and component team members

(continued)

Table 7.2 (Continued)   Program Life Cycle Management – Planning Tasks

Task #	Task Description	Explanation of Importance	Steps to Perform This Task
12	Identify and manage unresolved project-level issues by establishing a monitoring and escalation mechanism and selecting a course of action consistent with program constraints and objectives in order to achieve program benefits	Enable proper and timely management of issues	1. Review with the program/project managers and sponsors on unresolved issues across the program, including component-level challenges 2. Develop a mechanism for properly channeling and escalating these issues to the appropriate level on a timely basis. Integrate this with the program governance 3. Make sure the agreed mechanism(s) is captured properly in the program management plan
13	Develop the transition/ integration/closure plan by defining exit criteria in order to ensure all administrative, commercial, and contractual obligations are met upon program completion	Plan for the "day after" to ensure benefit sustainment	1. Work with the various operational teams within the organization to clearly define the program exit criteria 2. Sometimes, as programs are significant undertaking, it is a part of the program's responsibility to develop the sustaining organization for continuous operation. Make sure these projects are properly incorporated in the overall program 3. Work with the sponsors and executives to achieve agreement of the exit criteria and the approach for ongoing management

(continued)

Table 7.2 (Continued)   Program Life Cycle Management – Planning Tasks

Task #	Task Description	Explanation of Importance	Steps to Perform This Task
14	Develop KPIs by using decomposition/mapping/ balanced scorecard (BSC) in order to implement scope and quality management system within a program	Improve focus and executive communication	1. Based on the earlier work on performance and success metrics, identify the KPIs which should be used to guide the major decisions and progress of the program 2. Review with the executives to achieve agreement. Often there will be refinement as to integrate the KPIs with the business metrics beyond the program 3. Work with the program and project teams to determine how to best incorporate the KPIs in program performance reports 4. Continually monitor, communicate, and refine the KPIs throughout the program
15	Monitor key human resources for program and project roles, including subcontractors, and identify opportunities to improve team motivation (e.g., develop compensation, incentive, and career alignment plans) and negotiate contracts in order to meet and/or exceed benefits realization objectives	Monitor productivity, encourage people, and intervene as necessary	1. Work closely with the sponsors and project managers to monitor the performance of the important, often expensive, and sometimes scarce resources, especially people 2. Adjust and improve as required to continually optimize the resource allocations and utilizations throughout the program. Examples of activities include renegotiating contracts, substituting resources for something or someone better, reallocating fund from one resources to another, etc.

Table 7.3 Program Life Cycle Management – Executing Tasks

Task #	Task Description	Explanation of Importance	Steps to Perform This Task
16	Charter and initiate constituent projects by assigning project managers and allocating appropriate resources in order to achieve program objectives.	Enable effective project execution with common understanding and proper resourcing	1. Work with the sponsors and program steering committee on the prioritization and approval of components for implementation 2. Work with the component managers on the agreeing and refining the component scope, schedule, etc. to ensure tight integration with the program and the other components in the program 3. Potentially conduct additional program kick-off meetings to ensure proper communication
17	Establish consistency by deploying uniform standards, resources, infrastructure, tools, and processes in order to enable informed program decision-making	Enable effective project execution by using agreed implementation method(s)	1. Deploy the program management processes, standards, tools, etc. in the executing phase 2. As required, conduct training sessions with the broader program and project teams to ensure common application of the agreed methods
18	Establish a communication feedback process in order to capture lessons learned and the team's experiences throughout the program	Continuous improvement on the program execution	1. Make sure there are processes for sharing knowledge, communicating important learning, and collaborating throughout the program life cycle 2. Leverage the PMIS and be an advocate for the proper use 3. As required, create special communication forums, such as Wikis or lunch-and-learn to enable team collaboration

(continued)

Table 7.3 (Continued) Program Life Cycle Management – Executing Tasks

Task #	Task Description	Explanation of Importance	Steps to Perform This Task
19	Lead human resource functions by training, coaching, mentoring, and recognizing the team in order to improve team engagement and achieve commitment to the program's goals	Focus on people development	1. As programs are large endeavors, they are often excellent activities for professional development. Identify the important resources on the project and work with the human resources to define development plans for selective individuals 2. Work with the individuals (or assign senior people to work with the individuals) on the agreed development goals including coaching, mentoring, training, and other performance enhancement activities 3. Regularly check to make sure goals are being accomplished 4. Develop activities to motivate and encourage people
20	Review project managers' performance in executing the project in accordance with the project plan in order to maximize their contribution to achieving program goals	Focus on the program and project execution and developing the program leadership team	1. Similar to above, it is often the program manager's responsibility to work directly with the project managers and guide them through the program. Understand the important motivational factors why the project managers are working on the program. Address the question "what's in it for them" 2. Develop activities to work with the project managers (and in conjunction with the Human Resources) so the project managers can achieve their goals 3. Conduct regular performance review sessions as appropriate

(continued)

Table 7.3 (Continued) Program Life Cycle Management – Executing Tasks

Task #	Task Description	Explanation of Importance	Steps to Perform This Task
21	Execute the appropriate program management plans (e.g., quality, risk, communication, resourcing) using the tools identified in the planning phase and by auditing the results in order to ensure the program outcomes meet stakeholder expectations and standards	Ensure proper execution of the agreed program management processes	1. Implement the plans within the program management plan (as previously created in Life Cycle Management Task 9 and refined in Life Cycle Management Task 10) 2. Monitor the progress and performance of the implementation and make adjustments and refinements as necessary 3. As required, updated the program management plan with the latest changes 4. Communicate the changes with the program team
22	Consolidate project and program data using predefined program plan reporting tools and methods in order to monitor and control the program performance and communicate to stakeholders	Consolidating the program progress reporting to enable timely decision-making and intervention	1. Work with the project managers and other component managers to collect and review the component performance data. Leverage the work performed earlier, especially on the KPIs (Life Cycle Management Task 14) 2. Consolidate the performance data and transform them into the agreed KPIs 3. Regularly monitor these KPIs and update them on a timely basis 4. Share the consolidated program reports, especially the KPIs with the relevant stakeholders

(continued)

Table 7.3 (Continued) Program Life Cycle Management – Executing Tasks

Task #	Task Description	Explanation of Importance	Steps to Perform This Task
23	Evaluate the program's status in order to monitor and control the program while maintaining current program information	Close manage program performance through active intervention	1. Evaluate the program performance including the KPIs and apply expert judgment 2. As required, intervene to make sure the program and the components are performing properly 3. Report to the sponsors and other stakeholders on progress, especially when there are issues and risks
24	Approve closure of constituent projects upon completion of defined deliverables in order to ensure scope is compliant with the functional overview	Close constituent projects and transition benefits into the programs	1. Review constituent project progress to make sure the project scope and the desired outcome are completed. As programs can have many constituent components with different time horizons, program managers will need to approve and authorize closure of projects and to make sure the component outcomes and benefits are properly transitioned to the program 2. Work with the project managers to make sure the project or component outcomes are as planned and they are properly transitioned into the program environment 3. Work with the program sponsor and/or steering committee to authorize the closure of the project 4. Work with the project manager to close the project, including the demobilization of project resources with the potential of leveraging them elsewhere on the program

7.2.4 ECO's Program Life Cycle – Controlling

In Program Controlling Phase, there are six important tasks:

25. Analyze program data to derive business intelligence
26. Update the program management plans
27. Tackle program-level issues
28. Manage program-level change
29. Conduct impact analysis on program changes and make recommendations
30. Manage program-level risks

Table 7.4 provides further description of the tasks, including the importance of this task and some general steps to perform this task.

7.2.5 ECO's Program Life Cycle – Closing

In Program Closing Phase, there are five important tasks:

31. Develop a program performance analysis report for program closure
32. Work with the stakeholders to close the program
33. Complete program by closing out all program activities including transitioning them to other teams
34. Conduct post program review
35. Capture the lessons learned and good practices to enable knowledge management

Table 7.5 provides further description of the tasks, including the importance of this task and some general steps to perform this task.

7.3 Standard's Program Life Cycle Management

According to the Standard for Program Management – 4th Edition (Standard), there are three major phases of program life cycle as shown in Figure 3. The three phases are Program Definition, Program Delivery, and Program Closure. This section will provide further details on these phases.

7.3.1 Program Definition Phase

Program Definition is the earliest phase of the program life cycle. Here, the purposes and content of the program are defined, and the program management plan is to be made. Ultimately, the goal is to seek approval of the program and prepare the program for implementation. This phase is further sub-categorized into two somewhat overlapping parts: Program Formulation and Program Planning.

Table 7.4 Program Life Cycle Management – Controlling Tasks

Task #	Task Description	Explanation of Importance	Steps to Perform This Task
25	Analyze variances and trends in costs, schedule, quality, and risks by comparing actual and forecast to planned values in order to identify corrective actions or opportunities	Continuously monitor and improve program execution through data analysis	1. Review and analyze the program performance data collected across the program and the components 2. Work with the component managers to fully understand the meaning of the data 3. Develop insights and business intelligence from the data, to identify corrective actions or improvement opportunities 4. Share the insights with the key program stakeholders
26	Update program plans by incorporating corrective actions to ensure program resources are employed effectively in order to meet program objectives	Continuously monitor and improve program execution through consistent planning and adaptation	1. Update the components of the program management plan as changes, either from addressing problems or finding new opportunities, come up. This should be viewed as continuous improvement to refine the program management. Substantial changes may require the re-approval from the program sponsor and the steering committee 2. Communicate and share the updates with the program teams

(continued)

Table 7.4 (Continued) Program Life Cycle Management – Controlling Tasks

Task #	Task Description	Explanation of Importance	Steps to Perform This Task
27	Manage program-level issues (e.g., human resource management, financial, technology, scheduling) by identifying and selecting a course of action consistent with program scope, constraints, and objectives in order to achieve program benefits	Continuously monitor and improve program execution through proactive issue management	1. Work with the program sponsor and steering committee to tackle the program-level issues and obstacles 2. Determine the course of action. Often this requires a close working relationship with the component managers to implement these actions 3. Monitor and refine the actions as necessary in order to achieve the program benefits
28	Manage changes in accordance with the change management plan in order to control scope, quality, schedule, cost, contracts, risks, and rewards	Continuously monitor and improve program execution through effectively managing program changes	1. Work with the program sponsor and change control board to manage the program-level changes 2. Work with the component managers to fully analyze and determine the implications across the program including the components. For larger changes, conduct full impact analysis (see next activity, Life Cycle Management Task 29) 3. Make recommendations with the program change control board 4. Receive approval (or not) to implement the change 5. Document the change in the PMIS and communicate with the relevant stakeholders

(continued)

Table 7.4 (Continued) Program Life Cycle Management – Controlling Tasks

Task #	Task Description	Explanation of Importance	Steps to Perform This Task
29	Conduct impact assessments for program changes and recommend decisions in order to obtain approval in accordance with the governance model	Continuously monitor and improve program execution through diligent analysis and approval of program changes	1. Work with the change submitter and the impacted components and teams to fully understand the implications of change 2. Develop a detailed impact assessment. Remember to include "business-as-usual" scenario too 3. Share the analysis with the impacted stakeholders to ensure agreement 4. Submit and report the impact analysis with the program governance and/or the program change control board
30	Manage risk in accordance with the risk management plan in order to ensure benefits realization	Continuously monitor and improve program execution through management of program risks	1. Work with the program sponsor and steering committee to identify, categorize, and prioritize of the program-level risks 2. Determine the best strategy to manage opportunities or threats 3. Develop risk responses and contingency plans as required, in conformance with the program risk management plan 4. Assign risk owners, as required, to ensure strong ownership of program risks

Table 7.5 Program Life Cycle Management – Closing Tasks

Task #	Task Description	Explanation of Importance	Steps to Perform This Task
31	Complete a program performance analysis report by comparing final values to planned values for scope, quality, cost, schedule, and resource data in order to determine program performance	Evaluating overall program performance	1. Analyze the consolidated program performance data from the program life cycle 2. Compare and contrast with the planned metrics across the program attributes such as scope, cost, schedule resources, procurement, governance, etc. 3. Apply expert judgement to determine program performance; rely on objective and quantitative data as much as possible 4. Summarize and develop the program analysis 5. Share with the program stakeholders
32	Obtain stakeholder approval for program closure in order to initiate close-out activities	Secure stakeholder approval to enable proper program closure	1. Work with the key program stakeholders to review their expectations and accomplishments 2. Obtain their approval to close the program 3. Initiate program closeout activities; for programs that have follow-up phases, start to transition the program with the new program team

(continued)

Table 7.5 (Continued)   Program Life Cycle Management – Closing Tasks

Task #	Task Description	Explanation of Importance	Steps to Perform This Task
33	Execute the transition and/or close-out of all program and constituent project plans (e.g., perform administrative and PMIS program closure, archive program documents and lessons learned, and transfer ongoing activities to functional organization) in order to meet program objectives and/or ongoing operational sustainability	Enable smooth program closure and benefit realization	1. Close out the program activities, which can include transitioning to operations, to other programs or portfolios, to various business units and teams responsible for maintaining program deliverables 2. Agree with the management on the closure or successful transition 3. Ensure all important documentation and tasks are updated in the PMIS
34	Conduct the post-review meeting by presenting the program performance report in order to obtain feedback and capture lessons learned	Identify areas of strengths and improvements, to enable continuous improvement of program management	1. Organize a program post-review to capture lessons learned. Make sure to include the program and the important component stakeholders 2. Conduct and facilitate the meeting(s) and focus on what worked well, what can be improved, what should be avoided, and other important lessons learned 3. Consider organizing a wider program-level knowledge sharing with all the team members
35	Report lessons learned and best practices observed and archive to the knowledge repository in order to support future programs and organizational improvement	Enable continuous improvement of programs through knowledge sharing	1. Capture the lessons learned, good and best practices, and other important knowledge from the program 2. Store them properly in the PMIS for future use

- The purpose of Program Formulation is to pin down the desired outcomes and to establish the strategic goals of the program.
- In Program Planning, the goal is to prepare the program by creating a detailed plan which entails how the defined outcomes and objectives are to be achieved.

The Program Formulation involves the development of the program business case which states the overall expected benefits. At this point, program sponsors are usually assigned, and they have the key responsibilities of:

- Securing financing
- Selecting the program manager

The sponsor, program manager, and sponsoring organization work together to:

- Initiate studies and estimates of scope, resources, and cost
- Develop an initial risk assessment
- Develop a program charter and roadmap

At the same time, program managers perform the initial risk assessment to analyze threats and opportunities confronting the program. Once completed and approved, the program charter formally authorizes the commencement of the program, gives the program manager authority to execute the program, and connects the program to the organization's ongoing work and strategic priorities. Occasionally, program may be terminated here. Even if the program is not authorized, the information should still be recorded in the lessons learned repository for future use.

In the Program Planning part, the primary goals are to establish the program governance, define the program structure, and assemble the program team to develop the program management plan. The program management plan is a master operating plan for the program, and it can contain many specific plans including:

- Benefits Management Plan
- Stakeholder Engagement Plan
- Governance Plan
- Change Management Plan
- Communications Management Plan
- Financial Management Plan
- Information Management Plan
- Procurement Management Plan
- Quality Management Plan
- Resource Management Plan
- Risk Management Plan

- Schedule Management Plan
- Scope Management Plan
- Program Roadmap

Typically, the approval of the program management plan signifies the program is ready to enter the next phase – Program Delivery. Before exiting Program Definition, program managers should have identified the following:

- Program vision, objectives, and success criteria
- Stakeholder needs and expectations
- Strategy associated with the program and the resulting changes
- Program interdependencies with other programs and portfolios
- Program component interdependencies and ideally the sequencing leading to a program roadmap
- Program resources, including funding, people, and other scarce resources
- Benefits realization plan
- Program governance and reporting structure
- Important roles and responsibilities across the program

7.3.2 *Program Delivery Phase*

The Program Delivery Phase starts when the program governance board evaluates and approves the program management plan. In this phase, the all program components are initiated, implemented, and closed during Program Delivery. Each program component progress through three parts:

- Component authorization and planning
- Component oversight and integration
- Component transition and closure

Component management plans are developed at the component level and integrated at the program level to deliver the program benefits, and include:

- Cost management
- Scope management
- Schedule management
- Risk management
- Resource management

It is important to remember that ALL component implementation occur during the Program Delivery Phase. Closure of the Program Delivery Phase depends on the attainment of planned benefits through component implementation. Program managers, working with the component mangers, should create regular program performance reports informing program steering committee of progress and benefits attained. The report of achieved goals helps the management to decide on whether the program will continue to work or be terminated. Before exiting Program Delivery, program managers should have completed (or largely completed) the following:

- Delivery of program components, satisfactorily
- Completed the transition and sustainment planning
- Making sure program integration at all levels are being achieved
- These levels include, but not limited to strategic, inter-program/inter-portfolio, program components, functional integration, and other supporting program activities
- Updated benefit realization plan
- Signals from customers and sponsors that program delivery is completed

7.3.3 *Program Closure Phase*

The Program Closure Phase includes program activities necessary to transition program benefits to the sustaining organization and formally close the program in a controlled manner. Upon the completion of major work, program steering committee is consulted to determine if either:

- A program has met all desired benefits and that all transition work has been completed within the component transition, or
- There is another program or sustaining activity that will oversee the ongoing benefits

There are often additional required to transition the resources, responsibilities, knowledge, and lessons learned to another sustaining entity. The program manager will receive approval from the sponsoring organization to close the program once all transitioning activities are completed. As described earlier, there are generally two paths at completion.

The "happy path" is when the program goals and objectives are achieved, sponsor and customers are happy with the outcome, the intended business benefits are achieved, and even if there are specific challenges, the important stakeholders largely agree with the completion of the program

Unfortunately, there are many "unhappy paths," such as the program is terminated by the sponsor, with or without cause; program closed by default as funding or other resource ran out; or program closed for cause, such as poor implementation to date. While programs can occur over multiple years, all programs should come to an end.

Before completing the program, program managers should have finished the following:

- Obtain formal approval from the sponsor on program closure
- Capture the knowledge and lessons learned
- Demobilize the program team
- In some organizations, it is the responsibility of the program managers to work with human resources to reassign program team members
- Create the program closure report
- Provide timely and accurate performance reports, especially on valuable contributors
- Making sure vital resources and knowledge are properly transitioned
- Celebrate the successful completion of the program!

7.4 Program Life Cycle Management Skills

To perform Program Life Cycle Engagement effectively, program managers require developing the following skill sets:

- Benchmarking
- Closeout plans, procedures, techniques, and policies
- Decomposition techniques (e.g., WBS)
- Financial closure processes
- Logistics management
- Performance and quality metrics
- Phase gate reviews
- Procurement management
- Product/service development phases
- Program and constituent project charter development
- Program and project change requests
- Program initiation plan
- Program management plans
- Quality control and management tools and techniques
- Resource estimation (human and material)
- Resource leveling techniques
- Root cause analysis
- Schedule management, techniques, and tools
- Scope management
- Service level agreements
- Statistical analysis
- Strategic planning and analysis
- SWOT analysis

- Talent evaluation
- Team competency assessment techniques
- Training methodologies

For a description of these skills, refer to the skill glossary in Chapter 9 that highlights over 120 program management skills.

In addition to the skills that are more specific to the Program Life Cycle Management performance domain, program managers should also consider the more general business and management skills as described in Section 3.4.1.

7.5 Practice Questions

This section contains ten sample questions pertaining to Program Life Cycle Management.

Question 1: The program closure phase is what?

A.   Consists of program activities conducted to authorize the program and develop the program roadmap required to achieve the expected results

B.   Comprises the program activities performed to produce the intended results of each component in accordance with the program management plan

C.   Includes the program activities necessary to transition the program benefits to the sustaining organization and formally close the program in a controlled manner

D.   Involves the development of the program business case which states the overall expected benefits to be addressed by the program in support of the strategic initiatives

Question 2: In the program life cycle, program scope management includes all of the following except:

A.   Program scope closure
B.   Program scope assessment
C.   Program scope management planning
D.   Program scope monitoring and controlling

Question 3: Program performance monitoring and controlling is performed during delivery management by?

A.   Program-level components
B.   Both program-level and project-level components
C.   Project-level components
D.   Program steering committee

Question 4: The program charter contains all of the following questions and associated answers except which one?

A. Risks and Issues: What are the initial risks and issues identified during the preparation of the program roadmap?
B. Timeline: What is the total length of the program, including all key milestone dates?
C. Program Closeout: What was the reason that the program was closed out?
D. Benefit Strategy: What is the approach to ensure the realization of the planned benefits?

Question 5: All components should be what before the program can be closed?

A. Completed, ongoing, and all contracts formally closed
B. Initiated, canceled, and all contracts formally closed
C. Completed, canceled, and all contracts opened
D. Completed, canceled, and all contracts formally closed

Question 6: An effective program management information system incorporates all of the following except:

A. Portfolio management tools
B. Software tools
C. Documents, data, and knowledge repositories
D. Configuration management tools

Question 7: The program delivery phase is what?

A. Consists of program activities conducted to authorize the program and develop the program roadmap required to achieve the expected results
B. Includes the program activities necessary to transition the program benefits to the sustaining organization and formally close the program in a controlled manner
C. Comprises the program activities performed to produce the intended results of each component in accordance with the program management plan
D. Involves the development of the program business case which states the overall expected benefits to be addressed by the program in support of the strategic initiatives

Question 8: Components may produce benefits in all cases except which one of the following?

A. As individual components
B. Integrated with other components before the associated benefits may be realized
C. Once all components are complete
D. During the program formulation subphase

Question 9: Program delivery activities include which one of the following?

A. Define the expected program outcomes and benefits and seek approval for the program

B. Initiate studies and estimates of scope, resources, and cost and develop an initial risk assessment

C. Formalizing the scope of the work to be accomplished by the component and identifying the deliverables that will satisfy the program's goals and benefits

D. Formalizing the scope of the work to be accomplished by the program and identifying the deliverables that will satisfy the program's goals and benefits

Question 10: Program management refers to the _____ of various components to achieve the planned program goals.

A. Sequential planning
B. Parallel planning
C. Alignment
D. Misalignment

7.5.1 Answer Key

1. C. Refer to Section 7.1.1 Program Life Cycle Phases Overview of the Standard.
2. A. Refer to Section 7.2.3 Mapping of the Program Life Cycle to Program Activities of the Standard.
3. B. Refer to Section 7.2.2 Program Integration Management of the Standard.
4. C. Refer to Section 7.1.2 Program Definition Phase of the Standard.
5. D. Refer to Section 7.2.2 Program Integration Management of the Standard.
6. A. Refer to Section 7.2.2 Program Integration Management of the Standard.
7. C. Refer to Section 7.1.1 Program Life Cycle Phases Overview of the Standard.
8. D. Refer to Section 7.1.3 Program Delivery Phase of the Standard.
9. C. Refer to Section 7.1.3.1 Program Delivery Phase of the Standard.
10. C. Refer to Section 7.2 of the Standard.

Chapter 8

Understanding Program Activities

8.1 Introduction

In addition to the performance domains, there are many supporting program-level activities throughout program life cycle. For those who are familiar with the *PMBOK®* *Guide*, these activities are closely associated with the project management knowledge areas, except they are now at a program level. In Chapter 8 of the Standard, these activities are organized by the three program management phases of Program Definition, Program Delivery, and Program Closure. These activities include:

- Program Change Management
- Program Communications Management
- Program Financial Management
- Program Information Management
- Program Procurement Management
- Program Quality Management
- Program Resource Management
- Program Risk Management
- Program Schedule Management
- Program Scope Management

8.2 Program Definition Activities

The main purpose of the Program Definition Phase is to confirm that the program is appropriate for full implementation. This is achieved by reviewing and approving the program business case and start to plan for the program implementation. Key deliverables in this phase include program charter and program roadmap. Furthermore, this phase can be divided into two parts: program formulation and program planning.

8.2.1 Program Formulation Activities

At the very beginning of the program, the program itself is still being shaped as program managers start to understand the purpose of the program, its scope, constraints, and planned benefits. Program managers are likely seeking various alternatives that can achieve the program goals. Therefore, much of the work in this early part of the project are **evaluative** and **explorative**. In some cases, program managers and sponsors may decide that the business cases are just too weak, and programs can terminate at this point. Specific assessment activities include the activities in Table 8.1.

Table 8.1   Program Formulation Activities

Activity	Description	Input To (Program)
Change	**Evaluate and/or explore** potential change management considerations, including the sources, the sensitivity, and the magnitude of change and impact	• Business case • Charter • Change management planning
Communication	**Evaluate and/or explore** the complexity of the communication and the various program stakeholders	• Stakeholder engagement plan • Communication management planning
Cost	**Evaluate and/or explore** cost by reviewing the business case and developing an initial, rough order of magnitude estimate for the program. If there are significant deviations from the business case, then these differences should be examined before moving forward with the implementation	• Business case • Charter • Cost estimation
Information	**Evaluate and/or explore** optimal ways of managing information and knowledge. A program will generate a large amount of documents during its life cycle, and therefore, it is important for the program manager to develop ways to collect, share, and maintain information. These may have an impact on program team efficiency and stakeholder perception of the program	• Business case • Charter • Information management planning

(continued)

Table 8.1 (Continued)   Program Formulation Activities

Activity	Description	Input To (Program)
Procurement	**Evaluate and/or explore** the need for external resources and at the same time, develop a good understanding of the procurement policies and practices. This way, program managers can determine any supply chain challenges	• Business case • Charter • Procurement management planning
Quality	**Evaluate and/or explore** the various components of quality including organization's quality standards, quality constraints, expectations, risks, and controls	• Business case • Charter • Quality management planning
Resource	**Evaluate and/or explore** program resources for program implementation. Estimate resources that are required for the program. Program resources include people, office space, laboratories, data centers, equipment, software, vehicles, and office supplies	• Business case • Charter • Resource management planning
Risk	**Evaluate and/or explore** important uncertainties on the program and identify their impact. At the same time, program managers should assess the organization's risk appetite. This can determine the level of monitoring	• Business case • Charter • Cost estimate • Roadmap • Risk management planning
Schedule	**Evaluate and/or explore** program duration by developing an initial estimate of schedule required to implement the program	• Business case • Charter • Roadmap • Schedule management planning
Scope	**Evaluate and/or explore** the program scope that help to define the program-level benefits. Understanding scope is required for the development of the program charter	• Charter

8.2.2 *Program Planning Activities*

In the second part of Program Definition Phase, program managers shift the attention to more concretely prepare the program for implementation. Here, a program organization is first defined, and the program manager leads the core program team to develop the program management plan. The program management plan is a vital part of the program planning, and it is developed based on the following inputs:

- Organization's strategic plan
- Business case
- Program charter
- Outputs from the assessments completed during Program Formulation

The program management plan contains many parts, but one of the most important part is the program roadmap. When finalized, the program roadmap shows the arrangement and order in which the program components will be implemented. The roadmap will be invaluable during the Program Delivery Phase to help monitor and control program delivery.

With the evaluative and explorative activities performed during Program Formulation, now in Program Planning, attention turns to "**Plan**" (see Table 8.2).

Table 8.2 Program Planning Activities

Activity	Description	Key Program Output(s)
Change	**Plan** on how to evaluate the impact of change to program outcomes. Program managers should develop program change management principles and procedures	• Change management plan • Change threshold
Communication	**Plan** information and communication needs of program stakeholders. Program communication management includes activities for generation, collection, distribution, storage, retrieval, and disposition of program information. Communications management plan must take into account: • Culture and language differences • Time zones • Other factors associated with globalization	• Communications management plan • Communication requirements, serving as inputs to the stakeholder register

(continued)

Table 8.2 (Continued) Program Planning Activities

Activity	Description	Key Program Output(s)

Financial Model	**Plan** funding model and timing. Program financing objective is to obtain funds to bridge the gap between paying money for development and obtaining program benefits. Due to the high cost of programs, the funding organization has significant inputs to program management and decision-making by key stakeholder	• Financial Framework
		• Updates to
		  • Business case
		  • Communications management plan
		  • Stakeholder engagement

Financial	**Plan** financial management of the program by: • Identifying the program's financial sources and resources • Integrating the budgets of the program components • Developing the overall budget for the program • Controlling the costs during the program Financial planning also serves as input to program risk management	• Financial metrics • Financial management plan • Program budget (still preliminary) • Funding schedules • Component payment schedules • Operation costs
Information	**Plan** how the program's information assets will be prepared, collected, organized, and secured. This is composed of information management policies, distribution lists, appropriate tools, templates, and reporting formats	• Information management plan • Information management tools and templates
Procurement	**Plan** to acquire external resources to meet the needs of the program Program manager should understand the resources required for the delivery of program benefits and can use techniques such as make-or-buy	• Procurement standards • Procurement management plan • Budget/financial updates

(continued)

Table 8.2 (Continued)   Program Planning Activities

Activity	Description	Key Program Output(s)
	decisions and the program work-breakdown-structure (PWBS) charts	
Quality	**Plan** program quality policies, objectives, and responsibilities. Program management is responsible for planning quality assurance criteria throughout the life cycle of the program	• Quality management plan that includes quality metrics, policy, standards, cost of quality, and checklists
Resource	**Plan** all required resources for the program, including those that are made available to component managers to enable program benefits delivery	• Resource requirements • Resource management plan
Risk	**Plan** how to approach and conduct risk management activities. While this activity is conducted early in the Program Definition Phase, this activity should continue throughout the program life cycle	• Risk management plan • Risk register

Schedule	**Plan** the order and timing of components, estimates the amount of time to accomplish each one, identifies program milestones, and documents the outcomes	• Schedule management plan
		• Master schedule
		• Inputs to
		  • Risk register
		  • Roadmap

Scope	**Plan** all activities required to deliver program benefits, including management activities such as strategic alignment. Program scope encompasses all program benefits, which are reflected in the PWBS. The PWBS includes program management artifacts such as plans, procedures, standards, processes, program management deliverables, and project management office (PMO) support deliverables	• Scope statement • Scope management plan • PWBS

8.3 Program Delivery Activities

During the Program Delivery Phase, program managers' attentions are turned toward the execution of the plans created in the Program Definition Phase. Shifting from evaluating, exploring, and planning, the key actions in Program Delivery are managing, engaging, **monitoring, and controlling** the work of the component managers (see Table 8.3).

Table 8.3 Program Delivery Activities

Activity	Description	Key Program Output(s)
Change	**Monitor and control** program changes and assure all approved change requests: • Recorded in the program change log • Communicated to appropriate stakeholders • Reflected in updates to component plans	• Approved change requests • Updates to program change log
Communication	**Monitor and control** the timely and appropriate generation, collection, distribution, storage, retrieval, and disposition of program information. One piece of vital information is program reports, which provide consolidated performance information to key stakeholders	• Various communication needs such as program health and status information, change request notifications, financial reports, updates about program progress, etc.
Financial	**Monitor and control** program funds and manage according, including raise funding concerns with program steering committee or raise change requests pertaining to financial changes as required. An important part of the control is the program budgets, which should include costs for both program components and resources to manage the program	• Updates to program financial plan and related items such as contracts, components, and program cost forecasts • Revised cost estimates

(continued)

Table 8.3 (Continued)   Program Delivery Activities

Activity	Description	Key Program Output(s)
Information	**Monitor and control** exchange of information among program management, component management, portfolio management, program stakeholders, and program governance. An important information is lessons learned, which can be frequent as program components are completed throughout the program. Program managers should compile these insights in a Lesson Learned database	• Updates to program information repository • Inputs to how program information is distributed and reported • Lessons learned reports and inputs to program management plan
Procurement	**Monitor and control** program procurement activities including contracts. A good practice is to direct all procurement activity to be conducted at the program level rather than at the component level	• Updates to procurement processes and deliverables such as Request for Information (RFI), Request for Quote (RFQ), and Request for Proposal (RFP) • Procurement reports, such as vendor performance reports, earned value reports
Quality	**Monitor and control** related to quality evaluation to assure the program will comply with quality policies and standards. This should include quality audit (proactive to prevent quality issues) and quality control (reactive to address defects)	• Quality assurance audit findings • Quality change requests • Quality control checklists, inspection reports, or test/measurement reports
Resource	**Monitor and control** program resource utilization. As required, program managers may re-prioritize scarce resources and optimize their	• Resource prioritization • Updates to resource management plan

(*continued*)

Table 8.3 (Continued)   Program Delivery Activities

Activity	Description	Key Program Output(s)
	use as well as examine resource interdependencies to avoid bottlenecks	

Risk	**Monitor and control** program risk responses. But at the same time, continue to identify and analyze new and emerging risks that can occur through the program life cycle	• Updates to
		  • Risk management plan
		  • Risk register
		 • Risk responses (new and updates)
		 • Risk reports showing trends
		 • Potential change request

Schedule	**Monitor and control** of program schedule to ensure timely delivery of program benefits and capabilities. This should include tracking and monitoring the start and finish of each component activity and milestone against the master schedule	• Updates to
		  • Master schedule
		  • Risk register
		  • Roadmap

Scope	**Monitor and control** program scope with particular attention toward scope changes, which may originate from stakeholders, components within the program, previously unidentified requirement issues, or external sources	• Updates to
		  • Scope statement
		  • Program management plan
		  • PWBS
		  • Program roadmap

8.4 Program Closure Activities

Program closure can be triggered for happy or unhappy reasons. For the unhappy path, the steering committee may decide to stop the program. There can be a number of reasons. For example, if the sponsoring organization is experiencing strategic changes and deprioritized the program or if the program is not meeting its goals. For the happy path, this is when the program components have delivered their results and the program benefits have been achieved. Regardless of the happy or unhappy paths, all programs must come to an end.

During the Program Closure Phase, the primary goal is to enable a smooth winding down of the program, including releasing resources, completing contracts, transitioning benefits to operations, updating knowledge artifacts to reflect the work performed, capture lessons learned, and complete program closeout report (see Table 8.4).

Table 8.4   Program Closure Activities

Activity	Description	Results
Financial	**Close** program finances. There may be residual activities to oversee ongoing benefits, which may be structured as an individual project or program, as new work in a separate program or portfolio, or in new or existing operations. Program financial transition is completed once sustainment budgets are developed, benefits are delivered, and sustainment has begun	• Close program budgets • Input to financial reports and plans
Information	**Archive** information and knowledge from program and component management. This may be used by other elements of the organization. Program manager should include the transfer of program knowledge to sustainment supporting organization(s) which includes training, documentation, and materials. The final lessons learned from the program team should be shared with the organization and archived	• Input to organization knowledge repository • Lessons report
Procurement	**Close** program contracts after making sure all deliverables have been satisfactorily agreed, payments are made, and there are no outstanding contractual issues. For early termination of programs, the program managers should negotiate with vendors and avoid unnecessary costs	• Closed contracts • Contract closeout reports • Updates to lessons learned
Resource	**Transition and/or close** program resource. Reassign resources to other programs, components, or organizational units	• Release resources
Risk	**Transfer and/or close** program risk. For risks that may continue to undermine benefit realization, program manager should transfer these risks and the supporting analysis to that organization and/or the PMO	• Input to other risk register

Upon satisfactorily completing the above activities, program managers should work with the program steering committee to obtain the final sign-off to close the program.

8.5 Practice Questions

This section contains ten sample questions pertaining to Program Activities.

Question 1: The program management plan is what?

A. Is iterative and can change as the program matures
B. Is fixed at the completion of the program definition phase
C. Is fixed at the completion of the program delivery phase
D. Is finalized by the program steering committee at the end of program formulation

Question 2: Outputs of the program financial closure do not include which one?

A. Inputs to the program final report
B. Updates to the program financial management plan
C. Revised estimate at completion
D. Inputs to the knowledge repository

Question 3: Supporting program closing activities include all of the following except?

A. Program procurement management
B. Program resource transition
C. Program risk management transition
D. Program financial closure

Question 4: Residual activities to oversee ongoing benefits may be structured as all of the following except:

A. An individual project or program
B. New work in a separate program or portfolio
C. An extension of the current program until all benefits have been sustained
D. In new or existing operations

Question 5: During program formulation, the outputs of the program resource requirements estimate are inputs to all of the following except:

A. Program business case
B. Program charter
C. Program resource management planning
D. Program quality management planning

Question 6: During which subphase is the program organization defined and an initial team deployed to develop the program management plan?

A. Program planning subphase
B. Program delivery subphase
C. Program formulation subphase
D. Program transition subphase

Question 7: Program definition activities do what?

A. Establishes and confirms the business case for the program, and develops the detailed plan for delivery
B. Identifies sources of change, the sensitivity of the programs proposed business case to changes in organizational strategy, and the possible frequency and magnitude that stem from components during program delivery
C. Are estimates of the overall program cost and level of confidence in the estimate is critical to the business case
D. Are identifiers of the key risks that may occur and the likelihood and impact should be developed

Question 8: During program formulation, the outputs of the program information management assessment are inputs to all of the following except:

A. Program change management planning
B. Program business case
C. Program charter
D. Program information management planning

Question 9: What is developed based on the organization's strategic plan, business case, program charter, and outputs from the assessments completed during program definition?

A. Project management plan
B. Program plan
C. Program management plan
D. Component management plan

Question 10: The program manager can direct the risk register to be updated for many reasons. Which of the following is the least likely reason for updating the risk register?

A. Fallback plans for use as a response to a risk that has occurred and the primary response proves to be inadequate

B. Risks originally identified in the risk register are realized and the appropriate risk mitigation plan implemented

C. Residual risks that are expected to remain after planned responses have been taken, as well as those that have been deliberately accepted

D. Secondary risks that arise as a direct outcome of implementing the risk response

8.5.1 Answer Key

1. A. Refer to Section 8.1.2 Program Planning Phase Activities of the Standard.
2. C. Refer to Section 8.3.1. Program Financial Closure of the Standard.
3. A. Refer to Section 8.3. Program Closure Phase Activities of the Standard.
4. C. Refer to Section 8.3.1. Program Financial Closure of the Standard.
5. D. Refer to Section 8.1.1 Program Formulation Activities of the Standard.
6. A. Refer to Section 8.1.1 Program Formulation Activities of the Standard.
7. A. Refer to Section 8.1 Program Definition Activities of the Standard.
8. A. Refer to Section 8.1.1 Program Formulation Activities of the Standard.
9. C. Refer to Section 8.1.2 Program Planning Phase Activities of the Standard.
10. B. Refer to Section 8.2.8 Program Risk Monitoring and Control of the Standard.

Chapter 9

Program Management Skills

The Program Management Professional (PgMP) Examination Content Outline lists 126 important program management skills. Some of these skills pertain to one or two performance domains while others are more generally applicable to all or nearly all performance domains. In Chapters 3–7, this book has provided a list of these skills. This chapter provides a broad description of these skills as they apply to program management.

Note: The description of these skills is licensed and adopted from PMO Advisory's Program Management Training Contents (See Table 9.1).

Table 9.1   Program Management Skills

#	Skills	Description
1	Active listening	*Analytical* listening entails the skill and the ability of a program manager to appropriately interpret any given information. *Active* listening extends beyond the comprehension of information that is being communicated by examining the intention of the speaker. It involves the ability to break complicated messages into pieces, especially getting to the crux of the communication. Active listening appears deceptively simple, as it requires the listener to separate the core meaning from extraneous information. In addition, good listening skills can also aid analytical listening. The ability to rapidly deduce logical connections and likely inconsistencies in the information is the hallmark of active listening.

(continued)

Table 9.1 (Continued)   Program Management Skills

#	Skills	Description
2	Analytical thinking	Analytical thinking refers to the capacity of examining information, either in a qualitative or quantitative form, to identify trends or deeper meaning within the information. Analytical thinking often entails engaging deductive thinking without deep professional knowledge, like understanding the fundamental arrangement of a sequence of interactions; rationally determining identical statements; and deducing from the presented details what might be accurate or must be accurate. As a program manager, analytical thinking strengthens one's comprehension of various aspects of a project. In essence, it decomposes tasks or projects into component parts.
3	Archiving tools and techniques	In program management, an archive focuses on methodical storage of program and component artifacts (such as project plan, designs, and documents) at the completion of a project. For administrative closure, storing program articles and documents is essential. Additionally, historical project records can serve as a support for current or prospective projects. Stored project articles also help in providing answers to questions on the project. Note: Depending on organization policies, not ALL information and artifacts should be archived. Certain sensitive information may need to be permanently destroyed.

(*continued*)

Table 9.1 (Continued) Program Management Skills

#	Skills	Description
4	Benchmarking	Benchmarking is a method that constantly compares the program management strategies of one's company with that of a leading organization or a group of companies in the same industry to gain insights to enhance performance. Insights gained can be adopted to develop strategies and procedures for implementation and give one's company a competitive edge. Benchmarking is a sustained activity of study and assessment. It is necessary to be decisive on the areas to benchmark because it is not feasible to analyze all the areas of program management. It is imperative to focus only on critical success areas that will be beneficial to the company.
5	Benefit optimization	Benefit optimization is the approach used by program professionals to objectively analyze the project and program benefits intending to enhance the overall value for the program.
6	Benefits measurement and analysis techniques	Benefit measurement is an approach used for project and component selection and is centered on the key metrics, such as the current financial worth of the projected cash inflow and outflow. For decision-making, cost benefits are analyzed and juxtaposed with other projects. The different types of analysis used in benefit measurement are benefit/cash ratio, economic model, scoring model, payback period, net present value, discounted cash flow, interest rate of return, opportunity cost, constrained optimization methods, and non-financial considerations. Since project and component selection can be done in a variety of ways, it is essential for an organization to pursue various approaches and evaluate a wide variety of variables before selecting a project to ensure that the most suitable decision has been chosen for the organization.

(*continued*)

Table 9.1 (Continued) Program Management Skills

#	Skills	Description
7	Brainstorming techniques	Brainstorming describes a circumstance in which several people come together to address a particular area of interest intending to draw up an action plan. During this process, those that are involved in the task are motivated to come up with ideas that can be deliberated upon as a group. Every idea is expected to be documented, but occasionally only ideas that are appealing to the group are documented. Brainstorming is a vital technique in addressing challenges and it helps with team building by ensuring that each member of the group is given the free idea without fare or favor.
8	Budget processes and procedures	Budget processes are tasks of calculating the cost estimates of a program to establish the total cost estimate that enables a formal cost baseline. Thus, the budget is developed based on the baseline. The budget represents the funds approved for the execution of the project and other related activities. The process aims to approve and allocate the funds necessary for the completion of the project and hand it over as scheduled. The process is usually carried out at the beginning of project planning in conjunction with the project scheduling process. This process facilitates the preparation of a budget that considers major cost factors relevant to program task timelines.

(continued)

Table 9.1 (Continued)   Program Management Skills

#	*Skills*	*Description*
9	Business environment	The business environment are the external factors that *may* influence the program. Business environment includes all individuals, organizational and other forces external to the program manager's control. The economic, cultural, governmental, technical, and other distinct forces that exist outside an organization are also components of its environment which are composed of individual users, the management, client associations, rivals, press, courts, and other institutions operating outside the performing organization.
10	Business ethics	Business ethics focuses on applying ethical principles to business conduct (e.g., accountability, fairness, morality, honesty, integrity, etc.). Ethics is concerned with making the most suitable decision for individuals, resources (monetary and non-monetary), and the community. Ethical decisions minimize risk, increase morale, assess lasting successes, and maintain a good public image. Business ethics encompasses everything from management strategies, sales methods, and accounting procedures, to relationships with stakeholders and product responsibility concerns. Business ethics refers to the discretionary actions made in everyday circumstances by organizations and employees. Business ethics is vital for the successful implementation and delivery of projects, programs, and portfolios.

(*continued*)

Table 9.1 (Continued)   Program Management Skills

#	Skills	Description
11	Business models, structure, and organization	A business model refers to how an organization functions. For profit-oriented businesses, a business model refers to how an organization maintains financial viability and serves as the backbone for the operations of companies, including the development and distribution of products and services. A business model is developed by the leadership of an organization and can convey the management's judgment and perception of client needs, and how to effectively incorporate strategies and procedures for profitable benefit. Business structure refers to the composition of the organization: single ownership, partnership, and corporation. Selecting a corporate structure requires legal and tax concerns. Business models and structures of organizations can shape how the sponsoring and performing organizations tackle major endeavors such as projects, programs, and portfolios in terms of financing and funding, cash flow management, tax implication, and other considerations.
12	Business strategy	Business strategy is a long-term plan that describes how an organization creates value, sustains its business, abides by its core beliefs and philosophy, and remains viable. Based on an organization's mission and vision, business strategies can be distilled into specific goals and objectives, products and services, and plans for customers, innovation, and other considerations that further its vision.

(*continued*)

Table 9.1 (Continued) Program Management Skills

#	*Skills*	*Description*
13	Business value measurement	The standardized measurement of "worth" for business organizations. Value should encompass both financial and non-financial benefits and the added value of a given endeavor. The idea of business value is relative and is based on the objectives of the program. Factors involved in the measurement of business value are revenue, profitability, market share, brand recognition, customer loyalty, customer retention, share of wallet, cross-selling ratio, and customer satisfaction. Note: Even though projects and programs can naturally have value, the term value is more abstract than the outcome (e.g., project) and benefit (e.g., program), and thus value is more often applied toward portfolios.
14	Business/ organization objectives	This refers to the general objectives and aims of an organization that have been set by its management and conveyed to its employees. The organizational goals should be consistent with an organization's mission and usually reflect an organization's long-term operational intentions and its general management strategy, which can offer valuable direction for personnel trying to satisfy their purposes. The objectives of the organization will assume a significant part in the formulation of organizational strategies and the distribution of organizational resources. The accomplishment of objectives enables an organization to fulfill its general strategic goals. There can be several factors in setting objectives. An organization can have one objective or several objectives; however, there must be a timeline for achieving the objectives. Decision-makers in the organization should be dedicated to the attainment of the objectives.
15	Capacity planning	Capacity planning is the system of deciding the program capacity required to tackle the planned endeavor. In program management, it is referred to as high-level evaluation and estimation of the key resources required. Capacity planning is also the mechanism of deciding the way to secure resources.

(continued)

Table 9.1 (Continued)   Program Management Skills

#	Skills	Description
16	Change management	In program management, changes occur frequently and can affect planned activities, procedures, systems, and work operations. Change management refers to the techniques and strategies that are used to address change and its impact on the implementation team in an integrated manner. Change management handles change with the aim that anticipated behaviors and operations would be geared toward achieving organizational goals.
17	Closeout plans, procedures, techniques, and policies	The aim of the closeout plans, procedures, techniques, and policies is to ensure the proper closure of projects, programs, and portfolios. The primary goal is to review the completed work, secure completion sign-off, extract experience gained, update key documentations, and gain insights for future endeavors. These activities involve the sponsor, client, and stakeholder to validate the work completed and attain sign-offs. Furthermore, the program manager should check that all deliverables, benefits, and value have been achieved, supplied, and/or acknowledged. The closeout process is a system to complete or settle all contractual requirements for a tangibly complete contract. Closeout is accomplished when all managerial activities have been finalized, differences settled, and final payment completed. Project closeout procedure includes termination notices, close expense accounts, and a complete closeout checklist.

(*continued*)

Table 9.1 (Continued)   Program Management Skills

#	Skills	Description
18	Coaching and mentoring techniques	Coaching and mentoring are mainly concerned with enhancing efficiency and effectiveness in a particular field of expertise. The targets are normally set with or at the recommendation of the coach. The learner is primarily responsible for achieving the target, and the coach primarily handles the process. The coach gives the learner feedback (extrinsic observation). Mentoring is a relationship where a more experienced person offers to guide a less skilled individual. This can be an enduring relationship where targets are established and modified. The less experienced individual gives the coach feedback (intrinsic observation). Selective techniques include goal setting, addressing roadblocks, developing self-knowledge, and motivating creative thinking.
19	Collaboration tools and techniques	A collaboration tool enables individuals to collaborate. The tool intends to assist a team of two or more persons to achieve a shared goal. These tools consist of items like paper, flip charts, whiteboards, and software. In program management, collaborative tools are often applied to solve problems using tools such as Asana, Trello, Microsoft Project Central, or Oracle Primavera that promote teamwork by enhancing communication, file sharing, and exchange of ideas.

(*continued*)

Table 9.1 (Continued)   Program Management Skills

#	Skills	Description
20	Communicating	Communication is essential to program management. Effective communication with all stakeholders is important for effective execution. Projects, programs, and portfolios can collapse owing to ineffective communication. Communication is described as the sharing of knowledge and the transmission of opinions, thoughts, and emotions using facial expressions, body language, words, and written documents. In program management, this implies the sharing of information, expertise, and experience. There are the three primary communication domains for program management: • Internal sharing of information (decision-making process, meetings, regular scrums, task assignments, etc.) • Knowledge management (important project information is conveyed to all involved parties, project changes are also conveyed, training, operating procedures, etc.) • Project marketing (project presentation and show to staff, clients, sponsors, etc.)
21	Communication tools and techniques	Communication is a vital aspect of program management. Communication tools and techniques refer to activities, templates, processes, and other devices employed by program managers to aid communication. Selective tools and techniques include communication analysis, communication plan, technology-based tools to aid with communication, team list, structured agenda, and clear outline of agreements at the end of meetings. Collectively, these tools and techniques help to enhance the overall dissemination of information and knowledge required for high-performing teams.

(continued)

Table 9.1 (Continued)   Program Management Skills

#	Skills	Description
22	Composition and responsibilities of the program management office (PgMO)	The PgMO is described as an organizational framework that can be applied to optimize the portfolio, project-associated governance processes, program, and promote the distribution of resources, strategies, equipment, and techniques. PgMOs also efficiently monitor and distribute resources throughout all projects by determining priorities based on schedules, budgets, resource levels, and what-if analysis details and supplying the necessary resources appropriately. On any specific project, PgMO also describes the roles and responsibilities required.
23	Conflict resolution techniques	There are five common conflict resolution techniques: 1. **Withdraw/avoid:** Pulling back from a real or probable situation of conflict; deferring the situation to be adequately prepared or be handled by others. 2. **Smooth/accommodate:** Highlight areas of consensus rather than discrepancy; grant one's role to other people's needs for peace and relations. 3. **Compromise/reconcile:** The quest for solutions that satisfy all parties to fix the conflict momentarily or partly. Often this strategy leads to a lose-lose scenario. 4. **Force/direct:** Forcing one's standpoint without considering others and presenting win-lose options only. This is generally applied via a power stand to address an urgent situation. This tactic often leads to a win-lose circumstance. 5. **Collaborate/problem-solve:** Integrating various viewpoints and ideas from different perspectives; needs a mutual mindset and an open discussion that tends to lead to an unanimous agreement and commitment. This strategy will lead to a win-win circumstance.

(continued)

Table 9.1 (Continued)   Program Management Skills

#	Skills	Description
24	Contingency planning	A contingency plan is an alternative or backup plan. In essence, a contingency plan for program management is a specified, substantive plan that can be implemented if the perceived risk arises. In program management, contingency plans are a part of risk management and must be included in the risk management strategy. It is also called a fallback plan.
25	Contract negotiation/ administration	Negotiation is a procedure between two or more individuals with opposing roles and desires. The goal is to seek a mutually agreeable outcome. Depending on the degree of differences and conflicts, the outcome can be win-win, win-lose, lose-win, or lose-lose. Successful negotiations can sometimes be lose-lose, but ultimately all parties overcome the impasses and achieve more strategic success. Common negotiations include procurement and contract negotiations. Procurement managers usually lead negotiations, but both the purchaser and the vendor program managers are also engaged in contract negotiations. It is the responsibility of program managers to facilitate the discussion to resolve the technical problems. Contract administration is a means to ensure that the vendor honored the contracts in the agreement. To certify that the vendor meets its commitments, the program manager and the contract administrator of all parties work closely together.

(*continued*)

Table 9.1 (Continued)   Program Management Skills

#	Skills	Description
26	Contract types	Contract type refers to the contract structure of an agreement. There are three common contract types:
		1. **Fixed price contracts:** This type of contract includes a fixed price for a specified product or service. These types of contracts are proposed when the context of operation is fully specified and concluded. The different types of fixed price contracts are firm fixed price, fixed price incentive fee, and fixed price and economic price adjustments.
		2. **Cost reimbursable contracts:** This type of contract includes the reimbursement of costs (payments to the work performed) for the costs incurred during the contracted work execution. It is accompanied by a pre-defined fee indicating the profit of the vendor. This is advised if it is anticipated that the mode of operation could change during the contract term. The types of cost reimbursable contracts are cost plus fixed fee, cost plus incentive fee, and cost plus award fee.
		3. **Time & material contracts (T&M):** This is a blended form of contract that incorporates both fixed and cost-reimbursable contract characteristics. This is sometimes used where there is no identified/agreed contractual condition (scope). This sort of contract is also effective for the acquisition or recruitment of professionals, project staff needed for a specific period.
27	Cost management	Cost management is the method of calculating, allocating, and regulating the costs of a project. To lessen the possibilities of exceeding the budget, it enables a company to forecast future expenses. At the planning stage of a project, estimated costs are calculated and must be authorized prior to initiating the project. As the project schedule is implemented, expenses are recorded and monitored to stay within the cost management plan. Predicted costs versus. real costs are analyzed after the project is finished, establishing benchmarks for prospective cost management plans and project budgets.

(*continued*)

Table 9.1 (Continued)   Program Management Skills

#	Skills	Description
28	Cost-benefit techniques	Cost-benefit analysis (CBA) is a basic technique used for generating non-critical financial decisions. It entails adding the benefits of a specific action and then giving a comparison of the related costs. The outcomes of the analysis are presented as a payback period, which is the amount of time required for the benefits to pay back the costs. In program management, CBA is an essential tool, and it is effective in cases such as assessing a new project, reviewing any strategic change, and ascertaining the viability of diverse purchases. Before estimating the return on investment (ROI), net representative value (NPV), and internal rate of return (IRR), an effective CBA lists project costs as well as significant benefits.
29	Critical thinking	Critical thinking involves the constructive questioning of procedures, projects, and essential business principles that are generally accepted. Critical thinking is used to strengthen analysis for the whole team's advantage. Selective critical thinking strategies that boost productivity and team cohesion include: (1) refrain from making rash assumptions; (2) recognize possible issues (and their implications) from the outset; (3) utilize the "Five Whys" to discover root causes.
30	Cultural diversity/ distinctions	Cultural diversity is a pattern of beliefs and behaviors that acknowledge and respect the existence of all different groups in a society or workplace and promotes their continuous participation in an inclusive cultural sense that empowers everyone. Program managers working in cross-cultural or global environment should concentrate their effort toward cultural diversity to achieve greater innovation and overcome challenges and poor communication. Cultural literacy and experience are vital keys for handling diversity.

(*continued*)

Table 9.1 (Continued)   Program Management Skills

#	*Skills*	*Description*
31	Customer centricity/client focus	Customer-centered (also called client-centered) is an entrepreneurial approach that puts customers first. This is often at the heart of the sponsoring organization to generate meaningful interactions and long-lasting relationships. By placing customers at the center of attention, program managers can better understand customer viewpoints rather than on preconceived notions and faulty assumptions.
32	Customer relationship management	Customer relationship management (CRM) is the management process of focusing on the customer and managing their needs and expectations. By applying active listening, stakeholder engagement, communication planning, and other techniques and tools to enhance customer interactions, program managers can more effectively identify requirements, understand root issues or pain points, apply solutions, and manage customer expectations.
33	Customer satisfaction measurement	Customer satisfaction is about recognizing, identifying, assessing, and managing customer needs in such a way that their desires are met. As such, these measurements are designed to evaluate customer approval quantitatively or qualitatively. In program management, customer satisfaction is an essential component of scope and quality management. It assures that the policies, goals, and obligations are fulfilled by the program. Customer satisfaction measurement tools include interviews, surveys, questionnaires, and other feedback mechanism that enable the managers to evaluate, monitor, and improve the customer experience.

(*continued*)

Table 9.1 (Continued)   Program Management Skills

#	Skills	Description
34	Data analysis/data mining	Data analysis is a method of examining, cleaning, manipulating, and modeling data to find valuable knowledge, informing insights, and promoting decision-making. Data mining is the process of finding trends in broad sets of data that include techniques at the interface of machine learning, statistics, and database processes. In program management, the data-driven analytical approach allows teams to evaluate specified data to understand trends. Program managers will use this research to assess project and personnel progress and what strategic decisions they will take to enhance efficiency.
35	Decision tree analysis	The decision tree is a type of diagram that specifically addresses the possible outcomes of a set of similar choices. In program management, a decision tree analysis approach would enable project leaders to quickly compare various courses of action and determine the costs, the probability of success, and the possible benefits linked to each other. It is necessary to remember that the ideal decision tree has four components: decision nodes, chance nodes, end nodes, and branches.
36	Decision-making techniques	Decision-making is the procedure by which the program manager and project team decide on the plan, strategies, and appropriate actions of the project. Techniques are methods or systems of making decisions such as building consensus through meetings, obtaining buy-in from key stakeholders, using surveys to gather viewpoints, and collaborating in decision analysis. Decision techniques include the use of specific analysis such as SWOT (strengths, weaknesses, opportunities, and threats) analysis, Maslow's pyramid, Pareto principle, Monte Carlo simulation, and decision tree analysis. Decision-making is used for all areas of program management, e.g., approval of a business case, assessment of potential proposals, choice of vendor or services to carry out the project, risk reduction, and authorization of proposed changes. Decisions that are taken have a wide-ranging impact on the project and can lead to a distinction between successes or failures.

(*continued*)

Table 9.1 (Continued) Program Management Skills

#	Skills	Description
37	Decomposition techniques (e.g., work-breakdown-structure, WBS)	Decomposition is described as a tool and technique for dividing and subdividing complex activities into smaller work packages until the component is understandable and feasible. Decomposition techniques can be applied to project activities, risks, resources, and other complex activities. For example, a WBS is often created to decompose project scope into specific activities. The lowest level of decomposition is called a work package, and this is the basis of the estimation of time, resources, and costs for the given activity. The volume of the job package after decomposition depends on the size and the complexity of the activity.
38	Distilling and synthesizing requirements	This is the process of progressively refining business requirements through intelligently and logically combing through requirements for overlaps, inter-connectivities, and dependencies. At the same time, lower priority or outlandish requirements are deprioritized and potentially removed. Where possible, feasibility and "how-to" analysis are conducted to determine implementation resources, challenges, and risks. The outcome is a refined set of requirements that serve as the basis for future decisions and implementation.
39	Economic forecasting	Economic forecasting is an aim to predict the prospective condition of the economy using a set of significant and highly supported indicators. Economic forecasting requires the development of statistical models with contributions from a variety of major factors or metrics, usually to reach a specific outcome. Key economic metrics for projects, programs, and portfolios comprise funding and cash flow, inflation, cost of capital (or interest rates), team and vendor productivity, consumer assurance, level of stakeholder engagement, and currency exchange rate (for international projects).

(*continued*)

Table 9.1 (Continued)   Program Management Skills

#	Skills	Description
40	Emotional intelligence	Emotional intelligence (EI) is the capacity to feel, comprehend, regulate, and utilize the information and power of emotions as an important source of vitality, motivation, and interaction with team members. There are five main parameters that are employed to assess EI: social skills, motivation, empathy, self-regulation, and self-awareness. The success of projects is influenced by the level of EI that the program manager and the project team have. It is essential for managers to understand the emotions of the team members and how to effectively communicate with different stakeholders of the project. Program managers also need to be conscious of their behaviors and understand how to motivate their team for success.
41	Employee engagement	Employee engagement is the degree to which workers are excited about their jobs and are committed to the program. This emotional engagement means that committed workers are passionate about their job and the underlying endeavor. An employee is assumed to be actively engaged if he or she is completely immersed in his or her work or motivated to do his or her work above what is usually required in his or her job position.
42	Executive-level presentation	The executive-level presentation is a concise report or a proposal that program managers present to the executives of the company. It could be an update on a recently concluded project or a plan for a prospective one. It can be referred to as an executive brief.
43	Expectation management	Expectation management is among the most effective strategies for managing stakeholders by setting and managing a set of anticipations and beliefs. In program management, staying ahead of expectations should be an intentional task that requires diligent planning and careful execution with regular reviews.

(*continued*)

Table 9.1 (Continued)   Program Management Skills

#	Skills	Description
44	Facilitation	Facilitation is an important skill that is employed in meetings to draw out the best and address the worst in a team, in the interest of achieving certain objectives. Typically applied during a meeting, good facilitation skills steer the team toward the desired objectives by focusing on common ground and balancing the multi-dimensional needs of the various stakeholders, resources, and constraints.
45	Feasibility analysis	A feasibility study is an examination that takes into consideration all the related variables of a program, namely economic, technological, legal, and timing, to assess the probability of effectively executing the endeavor. Before spending substantial time and resources on the endeavor, program managers use feasibility reports to evaluate the advantages and disadvantages of executing a project. Feasibility studies may also provide critical data to the management of an organization which may discourage the organization from blindly joining risky investments.
46	Financial closure processes	Financial closure processes are activities by which all project-related financial operations are completed, financial accounts are finalized and closed, assets are disposed of, and the job site or project environment is released. It is a criterion for program closure and post-implementation analysis. Until all financial dealings are concluded, a program should not be closed, or else there would not be the approval of funds to offset pending fees and invoices. As a key element of the post-implementation analysis, financial closure sets final costs for comparison to budgeted costs. Lastly, financial closure guarantees that certain properties and resources are properly disposed of or transitioned.

(continued)

Table 9.1 (Continued)   Program Management Skills

#	Skills	Description
47	Financial measurement and management techniques	There are several financial measurement techniques available to help professionals to comprehend the operations' strengths and weaknesses. Some techniques include: 1. Estimating, calculating, and analyzing common project metrics such as Benefit-Cost Ratio, Payback Period, Net Present Value, IRR, and Cost Performance Index. 2. In financial accounting, perform *Horizontal Analysis* which includes calculating the change in percentage of the classifications of financial statements over a period of time OR *Vertical Analysis*, which is the method of reporting every item on a collection of financial statements as a proportion of a bigger item. Advanced skills may involve the anticipation of currency exchange rate fluctuations, time value of money analysis, and complex investment funding requirements.
48	Funding models	A funding model is an analytical and institutionalized technique used to create a stable base of funds that will sustain the program. Traditional project funding models are rooted in periodic (annual, semi-annual, or quarterly) portfolio re-planning practices that incorporate updated estimates for active investments and demands for financing new ones. The funding model for an investment could be a one-time payment, phase-gate, or periodic disbursement as the project progresses.
49	Funding processes	This is a process of providing financial resources for a program. This term is primarily employed when a business uses its internal resources to fulfill its need for capital or funds.
50	Go/no-go decision criteria	Go/no-go decision criteria are the important factors for making key decisions to either progress or stop the progress of a program. These criteria can be based on a variety of key factors such as financial, product, competitive, organizational, strategic, or performance of the program.

(continued)

Table 9.1 (Continued)   Program Management Skills

#	Skills	Description
51	Governance models	The governance model tends to identify the roles and duties of a decision-making body overseeing the program. Program governance models are typically inherited from the organization's governance model and are refined for the specific situation. Governance models typically include overseeing strategic, compliance, risk, financial, and audit activities. When defining a suitable governance model that supports the organization, the program manager should assess the level of rigor that they want to integrate. Overbearing governance models can slow down progress, but a lack of good governance may result in loss of stakeholder involvement and poor performance.
52	Governance processes and procedures	Governance is a regulatory and accountability system that determines and monitors the outputs, results, and benefits of projects, programs, and portfolios. It is also the method by which the sponsoring company maintains financial and technological influence over the development of the program. Governance involves people, program operations, and policies that help determine the company's decisive actions and strategic practices. Governance practices should address these core considerations: leadership issues, change management, resource management, strategic communications, knowledge management, meeting management, risk management, product and service validation, procurement of strategic resources, and performance of the program.

(continued)

Table 9.1 (Continued)   Program Management Skills

#	Skills	Description
53	Human resource management	Human resource management (HRM or HR) is a systematic approach to the successful management of personnel in projects, programs, and/or portfolios to help them achieve a competitive edge in their industry. It is structured to optimize employee efficiency for the goals of the endeavor. Human resource management is mainly associated with handling personnel within organizations, focusing on strategies and processes. The ultimate objective of human resources (HR) is to make sure that the organization can achieve its objectives via employees working in a team environment. The team is generally made up of individuals with exceptional skills and duties.
54	Impact assessment techniques	Impact assessment is an appraisal whose intent is to assign results and impacts to program. There are multiple techniques involved. A common technique is to perform the impact assessment by setting up a counterfactual event, which would have existed if the project was absent. The counterfactual event distinguishes the impact assessment from all other types of project evaluation. It is important to eliminate conflicting interpretations for the findings reported and therefore "ascribe" the findings reported to the program. Other methods include scope analysis, qualitative analysis, quantitative analysis, aggregation, and comparison of choices (e.g., cost-benefit analysis), support for participation and involvement (e.g., internet consultation), presentation and involvement of data, and monitoring and evaluation of events.

(*continued*)

Table 9.1 (Continued)   Program Management Skills

#	Skills	Description
55	Industry and market knowledge	Industry knowledge is the awareness of business patterns in a given industry. It improves the ability to make strategic decisions and to offer excellent advice to other businesses about surpassing competitors in the industry. Market knowledge is about comprehending the market setting where a company operates. Market knowledge also includes the prospective customer's behavior that is explicitly and implicitly relevant to the goods and services that can be provided.
56	Information privacy	Information protection is the connection between the gathering, storage, and distribution of data, innovation, the public right to privacy, and the legitimate and legislative concerns pertaining to them. It is sometimes referred to as data privacy or data security. Information privacy is a dimension of information technology (IT) that interacts with the right of an entity or person to decide which information in a computer system can be communicated with external parties.
57	Innovative thinking	Innovative thinking focuses on the opening of thoughts, promoting collaboration with a diverse team, and seeking ways to look beyond the obvious. Successful innovative thinking enhances an organization's ability to develop new products, new processes, and new models.
58	Intellectual property laws and guidelines	Intellectual property is a valuable resource and is typically protected by trademarks, licenses, patents, or copyrights. For organizations, it is important to develop policies that govern intellectual property usage to safeguard against economic theft or misuse by unlicensed entities or persons. Intellectual property laws ensure the rights of the proprietor or the permitted individual to claim the economic benefit, copyrights of the resource, and the liberty to restrict use.

(*continued*)

Table 9.1 (Continued)   Program Management Skills

#	Skills	Description
59	Interpersonal interaction and relationship management	Interpersonal interaction refers to a close affiliation between people working together in a relatively close environment (which can be both in physical proximity or intellectually on the same endeavor). Personnel who are working together need to develop an effective relationship to maximize performance. Individuals need to be truthful with one another to promote a healthy social dynamic and positive workplace.
60	Interviewing	An interview is an organized conversation where questions are posed by one party and responses are given by another party. The information obtained from the conversation can be used or made accessible to other people immediately or afterwards. Interviews can take place face to face and in both physical and virtual settings.
61	Knowledge management	Knowledge management is the diligent management of the intellectual knowledge created during projects, programs, and/or portfolios. This information can be of utmost importance, generating value, achieving tactical and strategic obligations, or sustain business operations. Knowledge management consists of processes, procedures, methods, and mechanisms that enable and improve the storage, evaluation, distribution, and refining of knowledge.
62	Leadership theories and techniques	Leadership theories are perspectives on how to develop and nurture leaders. Well-known theories include the "great man theory," the trait theory of leadership, the skills theory of leadership, the style theories of leadership, the situational leadership theory, the contingency theory, transactional leadership theory, transformational leadership theory, leader-member exchange theory, and servant leadership theory. Leadership technique is the art of providing guidance, executing strategies, and inspiring citizens. Selective leadership styles include autocratic, authoritative, pacesetting, democratic, and coaching.

(*continued*)

Table 9.1 (Continued)   Program Management Skills

#	Skills	Description
63	Legal and regulatory requirements	A regulatory requirement is a policy placed on an organization by a government agency, external regulatory agency, or professional body. Almost all organizations are regulated by certain legislations. Regulations control how companies handle their operations and people, communicate with customers and markets, and manage internal and external activities. Usually, regulations are put in place to safeguard somebody or something, including workers, customers, the public in general, or the dignity of trade or business operations.
64	Leveraging opportunities	Leverage is a technique used to maximize advantages through the use of other resources or situations. For example, a program sponsor had a difficult time advocating for a major program. However, by leveraging a recent legislative change that was favorable for the program, the sponsor was able to win sufficient support to advance the program.
65	Logistics management	Logistics management is a supply line management field that is designed to satisfy program needs through the preparation, monitoring, and execution of efficient transportation and storage of relevant information, products, and services from source to endpoint. Logistics management enables businesses to minimize costs and boost customer support. Logistics management promotes process strategy, preparation, and execution by adhering to business requirements and professional standards.

(*continued*)

Table 9.1 (Continued)   Program Management Skills

#	Skills	Description
66	Maintenance and sustainment of program benefits post delivery	Programs require a significant investment of time and resources, especially during the Delivery Phase. To extract benefits, program teams need to manage, maintain, and sustain the operation of the program results to attain intended value. The sustainment of program benefits is often conducted through the operation of the program results.
67	Management techniques	Management techniques are ways in which program managers apply their skills to carry out specific tasks and activities. There are many techniques for planning, organizing, executing, and controlling work, including specialized techniques to manage program challenges such as management of issues, risks, conflicts, assumptions, and changes.
68	Managing expectations	Managing expectations are a collection of statements that represent what is planned or predicted, not what currently exists. Steps to managing expectations include early planning, involvement of stakeholders, getting the commitment of all stakeholders, defining roles of all the parties, and ensuring good communication among stakeholders for projects, programs, and portfolios.

(*continued*)

Table 9.1 (Continued)   Program Management Skills

#	Skills	Description
69	Managing virtual/ multicultural/ remote/global teams	Cultural, language, and geographical heterogeneity are among the most common differences that can affect the job performance of a multinational virtual team. In diverse and remote teams, participants are geographically dispersed and do not meet face-to-face. Members of the team may have cultural differences, language differences, or can be based in diverse parts of the world. These types of discrepancies affect communication and cooperation among the team members, which may cause incomprehension or disagreement in the team. It is crucial to understand this dynamic in program management, especially when it comes to forecasting, managing, and monitoring potential problems and setbacks, collaborating on activities, and completing work. It is essential to be mindful of differences: consider the background of various team members and use that as an advantage toward the success of projects and programs. Ways of managing this global team include assigning roles among the team members, establishing an effective communication structure, selecting the most feasible communication channel, agreeing on a specific communication language, and clarifying the meanings of some words. Managers should also track key member's commitment and share leadership roles as appropriate to enable team engagement.
70	Marketing	Marketing is a business function of communicating and promoting products and services to the target groups of audiences. For large projects, programs, and/or portfolios, the marketing of key features and benefits can enhance the overall success of the underlying endeavor.

(*continued*)

Table 9.1 (Continued)   Program Management Skills

#	Skills	Description
71	Maximizing resources/ achieving synergies	Synergy is the idea that the worth and output of two activities combined would be better than the summation of the distinct individual parts. The achieving synergy gained through the effort can be credited to several factors: streamlining processes, achieving economy of size and scope, and reducing overlapping work and hence cost.
72	Metrics definition and measurement techniques	Metrics are quantitative or qualitative indicators widely used for the evaluation, comparison, and monitoring of results or output. Measurement techniques include recording of empirical observations, automatic collection through pre-programmed and automated systems, and pre-determined inputs from program stakeholders.
73	Motivational techniques	Program managers should develop approaches to increase and sustain team performance and apply motivational techniques such as setting feasible goals, communicating a well-defined vision, providing feedback to the team members regularly, emphasizing benefits, boosting relationships among the team members, assigning clear responsibilities to each member, and providing enough room for creativity and input among team members.
74	Negotiating/ persuading/ influencing	Negotiation is a procedure that includes activities required to settle conflicts by holding consultations between the stakeholders to achieve an agreement. In program management, the negotiation process can be divided into stages: preparation, discussion or debate, proposal, and analysis. Persuasion is described as a process of attempting to convince a person of something or a means of advising a person to undertake something. Influence can also be described as the capacity to control or manipulate based on reputation, resources, capability, or role.

(continued)

Table 9.1 (Continued)   Program Management Skills

#	Skills	Description
75	Negotiation strategies and techniques	Negotiation strategies and techniques are applied to achieve the maximum interest, preferably for all parties. Negotiation strategies can be broadly classified as interest-based negotiation and positional bargaining: • Interest-based negotiation is a strategy to problem-solving that concentrates on wants, wishes, interests, and fears of both parties instead of positions. An interest is the reason behind the position. Interest-based negotiation mostly results in win-win situations where each party meets their needs and expectations or addresses their concerns and doubts. • Positional bargaining is a negotiating technique that includes maintaining a fixed concept or position about what each party expects. For inexperienced negotiators, positional bargaining is often the first tactic they employ. This is also troublesome because as talks move forward, negotiators dig-in deeper and they become increasingly loyal to their positions by constantly reassuring and maintaining them. A deep determination to protect a position typically shows a lack of consideration to the fundamental concerns of both parties. Positional bargaining is more likely to result in a win-lose situation.
76	Organization strategic plan and vision	Strategic planning is a management exercise that aims to define goals, concentrate energy and assets, improve operations, ensure that all staff and other players work to achieve common objectives, define consensus on the desired results, and assess and adjust the course of the organization to meet the evolving business climate. Strategic vision is a simple, detailed picture of an organization in the near future. It gives clarity because it explains what the company wants to look like to thrive in that future.

(*continued*)

Table 9.1 (Continued)   Program Management Skills

#	Skills	Description
77	Performance analysis and reporting techniques (e.g., earned value analysis, EVA)	Performance analysis and reporting techniques examine the actual performance versus the planned. The primary aim of performance analysis is to present management with a comprehensive and detailed examination of the major performance metrics of program management. A common analysis of projects and programs is the EVA, which focuses on cost and schedule analysis. Based on the analysis, forecasts can be drawn to provide a logical prediction of the outcome. This comprehension is important for arriving at good decisions when assessing the project, exploring possibilities, reducing unwanted variances, and providing assurance of outcome.
78	Performance and quality metrics	Performance metrics are project-specific data employed to identify and evaluate the progress and conditions of projects, programs, and portfolios. There are many categories of metrics including skills and ability of managers and team members, scope and quality metrics about the product, and process rigor pertaining to the discipline of management. Popular performance indicators can include cost and schedule performance indicators, product sales, ROI, client satisfaction, sector and market feedback, and the image of an organization with its clients. Examples of quality metrics include defect frequency, cost control on-time performance, and failure rate.
79	Performance management techniques (e.g., cost and time, performance against objectives)	Performance management is a critical process for projects, programs, and portfolios. This is especially important in large endeavors consisting of a significant amount of resources in which performance measures such as productivity can result in delays and cost overruns. Some examples of performance management techniques are the balanced scorecard, benchmarking, key performance indicators (KPIs) and metrics, performance appraisals, management by objectives (MBO), and personal development plans (PDP).

(*continued*)

Table 9.1 (Continued)   Program Management Skills

#	Skills	Description
80	Phase gate reviews	The phase gate review process is a technique in which the project or program of developing new products, enhancing business processes, etc. is separated into stages demarcated by tollgates. Each of the tollgates shows an important point of decision to either proceed or not. At these tollgates, the governance team of the program reviews the importance-performance metrics and determines whether the endeavor is ready to proceed to the next phase.
81	Planning theory, techniques, and procedures	Planning theory is a set of theoretical principles, definitions, behavioral interactions, and conclusions that characterize the knowledge base of planning for projects, programs, and portfolios. Planning techniques are the approaches or procedures practiced by planners in designing or reviewing their structure ideas, initiatives, and policies. Planners have a wide variety of analytical methods within their reach. Cost-benefit evaluation, risk assessment, environmental evaluations, program assessment, participatory approaches, and many others can be considered in this context.
82	PMI Code of Ethics and Professional Conduct	The PMI Code of Ethics and Professional Conduct provides an ethical framework for the project management professional. It illustrates the values to which program managers should strive and the practices that are essential to this profession. This code aims to engender trust among the project stakeholders and inject a positive optimism for this profession. The four fundamental principles are accountability, respect, fairness, and integrity.
83	Portfolio management	The centralized streamlining of one or multiple portfolios for the achievement of strategic goals and objectives by incorporating the concepts of identifying, prioritizing, authorizing, monitoring, and controlling of the entirety of the portfolio.

(continued)

Table 9.1 (Continued)   Program Management Skills

#	Skills	Description
84	Presentation tools and techniques	For program management professionals, one of the key activities is communication, and presentation is an important form of communication. Common presentations include kick-off meetings, performance reports, and discussion of important topics and decisions. Presentation techniques include using visual aids and maintaining focus. It is also important for the presenter to know the audience, rehearse the key messages, and deliver the right message.
85	Prioritizing	This is the process of determining the relative importance of requirements, processes, tasks, skills, and other activities. Depending on the purpose of prioritization, project and program managers should develop quantitative or qualitative evaluation schema to facilitate the prioritization process.
86	Problem-solving	In program management, problem-solving is a fundamental element. It is a method for the creation and implementation of a solution to obstacles and challenges that have arisen. There are four common steps in problem-solving: (1) determining the current status and the root cause of the problem; (2) identifying and analyzing options; (3) applying solutions; and (4) monitoring and adjusting the solution if required.

(continued)

Table 9.1 (Continued)   Program Management Skills

#	Skills	Description
87	Problem-solving tools and techniques	These are specific means, devices, or ways of addressing problems. Selective problem-solving tools and techniques include: 1. A Pareto chart is a bar chart paired with a line graph that displays their comparative importance by grouping the occurrence or cost of various issues. 2. The 5 Why's is a technique that drills down through successive layers of an issue using a set of questions. The main concept is that the answer serves as the foundation of the next why. 3. A Fishbone diagram separates potential causes into different divisions that split from the main problem. 4. Scatter plots utilize sets of data points to uncover correlations between variables. 5. Failure mode and effects analysis (FMEA) is a tool used to investigate possible defects or faults in the course of designing a product or process.
88	Procurement management	Procurement management is a systematic approach to maximizing the value of external purchases. Through the program life cycle, the goal of procurement management is to acquire the right products or services at a competitive price. For strategic procurements, it is important to develop and sustain partnerships with suppliers of products and services.

(continued)

Table 9.1 (Continued) Program Management Skills

#	Skills	Description
89	Product / service development phases	This refers to the various steps of product and service development. Common phases include: 1. Idea generation: The method of generating possible concepts for a novel product or service, or ideas about how a current product can be enhanced. 2. Filtering and screening: How to pick the best concept to move ahead to development. 3. Concept development: Trying out the concept with clients. 4. Commercial and market analysis (optional): The feasibility of the introduction of this concept commercially by analyzing cost and market demand. 5. Development: The technological phase that determines the cycle of production or service delivery. 6. Testing: Place the model product or service in the possession of consumers to obtain reviews and modify the product. 7. Marketing and pricing: How the latest or enhanced product or service will be priced and advertised. Depending on the situation, this phase may occur earlier than testing. 8. Go to market: The approach and strategy that the project or program manager would use to bring the latest product on sale accessible to and available for customers.

(continued)

Table 9.1 (Continued)   Program Management Skills

#	Skills	Description
90	Program and constituent project charter development	A charter is a structured agreement early in the life cycle, and it serves as a contract between the parties. On programs, program charters are generally between the program team performing the implementation and the sponsor who is providing the fund. Depending on the type of program, the program components are often projects. These constituent projects may also have specific project charters in which one party is the project team performing the project work, and the other party is the program manager who is responsible for providing funding and resources. As a contract, the main purpose of the charter is to gain the authorization of the funds and resources while agreeing to the scope and schedule of the work. Typical sections of the charter include program or project name; purpose and objective; broad statement of scope; budget; deliverables or outputs; risks and issues; timeframe and milestones; key stakeholders and other resource needs; team roles and responsibilities; and success criteria.
91	Program and project change requests	Program and project change requests are plans to change one or more parameters of a project or program after achieving agreement. This can occur during a project or program whenever changes occur. For example, a client may wish to change or modify the deliverables after an agreement. Most program changes are multifaceted, often impacting schedule, scope, resources, and cost.
92	Program initiation plan	This is a comprehensive description of the standard program start-up document whose objective is to gather and document the essential details required for the program. The program initiation plan should build on the program business case and explain what the program is striving for and preparing to accomplish and the justification for the significance of achieving these objectives. It may also include a list of individuals who have been involved in the development of the program.

(continued)

Table 9.1 (Continued)   Program Management Skills

#	Skills	Description
93	Program management plans	A program management plan is a unified, structured, and detailed document describing how the program is to be handled, implemented, and monitored. It includes the ultimate governance of the program, component details, the recognition of benefits, relevant management strategies and processes, schedules, and approaches used to organize, track, and manage the program as it proceeds. This document is developed early in the program life cycle and be revised as necessary to represent any changes during the implementation of the project.
94	Program mission and vision	A program mission statement is the concise overview of the basic purpose and primary goals of a program. A program vision statement outlines a program's future direction, and it explains what the organization would ideally like to accomplish with the program.
95	Program transition strategies	A program transition strategy is a document detailing the shifting of the program deliverables toward continual operation, which is essential to sustain program benefits. The transition strategy establishes the responsibility of the team, the requisite instruments, strategies, and methodologies for an effective transition. It also involves preparation for contingency and mitigation of risk.
96	Program management information systems (PMIS)	PMIS is an information framework that contains tools and methods used to compile, incorporate, and propagate program management process outcomes and new knowledge developed during the implementation. It is employed to support every part of the endeavor from start to closure and can involve both manual and computerized processes. Different types of PMIS software exist, but the majority have component sets like scheduling tools, content approval, collection and dissemination of information, and long-term storage.

(continued)

Table 9.1 (Continued)   Program Management Skills

#	Skills	Description
97	Public relations	Public relations are a way to gather and maintain support from the user community or the general public. Public relationships involve the effective marketing of information to informed people of the work, presenting critical information to develop trust, building momentum, and enabling a favorable view of the program.
98	Quality control and management tools and techniques	Quality control and management tools and techniques are implemented to achieve a high quality of program deliverables and outcomes. There are many quality management techniques involved in quality control. Selective tools include Cause-and-Effect Diagrams, Flowcharts, Check Sheets, Pareto Charts or Diagrams, Histograms, Control Charts, Scatter Diagrams, and Benchmarking.
99	Reporting tools and techniques	Reporting tools play a vital part in the communication of progress and performance. These can include EVA, timesheet report of key resources, vendor progress reports, budget and expense reports, project status reports, and resource workload. There are various techniques in gathering the reports. On programs, program managers generally establish a standard method of reporting and gathering information. Component managers then follow the program manager's guidelines in their reports. Regularly, the program managers compile an overall program report from the constituent report and share it with the key program stakeholders.

(*continued*)

Table 9.1 (Continued)   Program Management Skills

#	Skills	Description
100	Requirement analysis techniques	The requirement analysis emphasizes the activities that define the needs or criteria for fulfilling the new or updated product or project, considering the potentially overlapping requirements of the different stakeholders, evaluating, recording, validating, and maintaining the requirements for the project or program. Requirement analysis is essential for projects or programs to succeed or fail. Requirements should be recorded, adopted, observable, quantifiable, predictable, relevant to business needs or advantages recognized, and specified with the appropriate description for a detailed design. Common techniques include: 1. Eliciting Requirements (such as project charter or description): It has the details of the business operations and interactions with stakeholders. It can also be referred to as the *requirements gathering*. 2. Recording Requirements: Requirements must be recorded in several formats, typically with a summary list, which may consist of natural-language records, use cases, user reports, process details, and some structured data models. 3. Analyzing Requirements: To decide if the requirements set out are straightforward, full, unduplicated, succinct, true, consistent, and to resolve any obvious conflicts.

(continued)

Table 9.1 (Continued)   Program Management Skills

#	Skills	Description
101	Resource estimation (human and material)	Resources include personnel, equipment, locations, or funds that a project or program requires for implementation. The purpose of the resource estimate is to assign the required resources to every task on the list. The five common tools and techniques for estimating activity resources include: 1. Judgment of experts: This refers to engaging professionals who have already carried out the task of interest in the past and seeking feedback about what services are required to complete the task. 2. Alternative analysis: This involves exploring various strategies for the distribution of resources. This involves the change in the number of resources and the form of resources used. Oftentimes, there are several ways to execute a task, and alternative analysis allows the project or program manager to distinguish between different options. 3. Published estimation data: In certain industries, there may be published data on commodity products and services. 4. Detailed or bottom-up estimate: This involves separating complex operations into easier tasks and calculating the resources required for every small task. The requirement or expense of the resources of the specific task is then summed together to achieve an aggregate estimate. For larger projects, it is common to utilize software for estimating resources and costs.

(*continued*)

Table 9.1 (Continued)   Program Management Skills

#	*Skills*	*Description*
102	Resource leveling techniques	Resource leveling is a resource management strategy in which start and end dates are modified based on resource constraints to match the requirement for resources with the existing supply. The challenge of resource leveling may be conceived as an optimization challenge. The challenge can be overcome by various optimization algorithms, like accurate algorithms or meta-heuristic techniques. When carrying out project and program preparation tasks, the manager may try to coordinate tasks at the same time. For instance, if there is a need for more resources like equipment or personnel than allocated, or if a single individual is required for both tasks, the tasks would have to be deferred concurrently or successively to handle the challenge.
103	Risk analysis techniques	Risk analysis is a method that helps project and program managers recognize and manage possible challenges that could disrupt progress. To conduct a risk analysis, a project or program manager should first recognize the potential events that could occur. Then, there would be an assessment of the probability and impact. Risk analysis can be complicated, as one may have to rely on comprehensive details like detailed plans, financial records, safety procedures, marketing predictions, competitive shifts, and other related details. It is an important preparation tool that could conserve time, funds, and prestige. Risk analysis techniques include brainstorming, sensitivity analysis, probability analysis, Delphi method, Monte Carlo method, decision tree analysis, utility theory, and decision theory.
104	Risk management	Project and program risk management is the method of identifying or detecting, assessing, and reacting to uncertainties that occur during the life cycle of a project or program. The goal is to minimize the negative effects. Risks are uncertainties, and when they become real, they become "issues" that need to be resolved.

(continued)

Table 9.1 (Continued)   Program Management Skills

#	Skills	Description
105	Risk mitigation and opportunities strategies	Risk mitigation techniques are designed to minimize or reduce the negative effects of identified threats inherent to a particular situation before any damage or failure occurs. On opportunities, the goal is to exploit, enhance, or share a positive risk.
106	Root cause analysis	Root cause analysis (RCA) is a method of uncovering the deeper causes that initiated the problem or incident. RCA is predicated on the fundamental premise that good management involves dealing with both emerging issues and preventative measures. When applied correctly, the RCA approach furnishes the program manager with the opportunity to identify and eradicate a problem that has adversely affected the endeavor once it is discovered.
107	Safety standards and procedures	Standard safety and procedures are a collection of guidelines established to describe or optimize the security and well-being of the team members working on projects, programs, and portfolios. Standard safety procedures include conducting performance assessments, incorporating work design safety protocols, defining hazard management measures, and ensuring proper reporting and timely warning.
108	Scenario analysis	Scenario analysis is a method of assessing future events by evaluating different probable outcomes. Scenario analysis seeks to recognize potential changes and key events that can only be linked to the precedent.
109	Schedule management, techniques, and tools	Schedule management is a mechanism involving the establishment of guidelines and records for maintenance, development, coordination, and monitoring of schedules for duration and resources required for the completion of the program. Schedule management techniques include Mathematical Analysis, Critical Path Method (CPM), Program Evaluation and Review Technique (PERT), Duration Compression (fast-tracking and crashing), Simulation, Resource-Leveling Heuristics, Task List, and Gantt Chart for graphical representation.

(continued)

Table 9.1 (Continued)   Program Management Skills

#	Skills	Description
110	Scope management	Scope management is the method of determining what task is needed and whether the entirety of a task needs to be executed. Scope management plan is expected to offer a comprehensive procedure for assessing, managing, and monitoring the scope. A detailed scope should be obtained from the key stakeholders to develop and properly assess the scope. The scope should be prepared ahead of time, and the program manager has the responsibility to obtain proper approval before implementation.
111	Service level agreements	A service-level agreement (SLA) is a contract between a service provider and a customer. Service providers and the customer negotiate on basic elements of service – standard, availability, and commitments. SLA's most vital element is the provision of the services to the clients according to the contract terms. This may be a formally binding contract or not (e.g., corporate departmental relations). To guarantee effective compliance, these contracts are often structured with some boundary lines, with the stakeholders required to meet periodically to create a proper channel for communication. Incentives and penalties for the provider are spelled out in the contract. Most SLAs allow for a frequent (yearly) redesign for modification.
112	Social responsibility	Social responsibility implies that organizations must operate in a way that maximizes shareholder capital and benefits the public. Social responsibility is becoming increasingly relevant for investors and customers seeking projects and programs that support and enhance individuals and society. Social responsibility means that people and organizations have a responsibility to function in a way that will improve society. In this manner, the equilibrium between economic development and social and environmental welfare should be achieved. If this balance is achieved, social responsibility will be accomplished.

(*continued*)

Table 9.1 (Continued)   Program Management Skills

#	Skills	Description
113	Stakeholder analysis and management	Stakeholder analysis is the method of identifying stakeholders, determining their preferences, evaluating their impact, and assessing their influence. Program managers should conduct a stakeholder analysis early in the life cycle to enhance understanding and develop a stakeholder engagement plan that can be utilized during implementation.
114	Statistical analysis	Statistical analysis is an aspect of data analytics that deals with the gathering and assessment of data to discover patterns and order. Statistical analysis is applied in contexts such as compilation of empirical findings, data simulation, or development of polls and research. There are two major statistical methods employed to analyze data – descriptive and inferential statistics. Descriptive statistics quantify data from a subset of a population through some measures of central tendency like standard deviation, mode, mean, median, etc. Inferential statistics deduce the characteristics of a population. It also opines that the data collection observed is believed to be a subset from a broader population, thus making generalized conclusions on the population.
115	Strategic planning and analysis	Strategic planning is the method of creating a common vision concerning the future of an organization and determining the significant actions that will drive it. Strategic analysis is a method that entails examining the operational and business environment of an organization. Strategic analysis is one of the vital stages and an essential component in developing a strategic plan. One outcome of strategic planning and analysis is the identification of projects, programs, and portfolios.

(*continued*)

Table 9.1 (Continued)   Program Management Skills

#	Skills	Description
116	Succession planning	Succession planning is a method for recognizing and developing prospective leaders who can function as replacements for existing leaders who may leave the position due to attrition, retirement, resignation, or even death. Succession planning facilitates the availability of competent and trained personnel who are ready to undertake these positions when declared vacant. Succession planning is an integral component of the talent management system. It offers an opportunity to recognize vital roles, employees with the required skills and abilities, and vacancies that will need to be filled in short period.
117	Sustainability and environmental issues	Environmental sustainability is focused on how environmental resources can be safeguarded and preserved for posterity. Environmental issues reflect the adverse impacts of human operations on the biophysical world. Environmental conservation is a process of preserving the environment on a personal, corporate, or governmental basis, for the advantage of both the people and the environment. Sustainability is the answer to the preservation or reduction of the impact of environmental issues. Sustainability is essential for various reasons, such as environmental quality. For example, unpolluted air and a non-toxic climate are needed to have a safe society.
118	SWOT analysis	A SWOT analysis is an effective analytical method for the evaluation of an organization. SWOT is an acronym for strengths, weaknesses, opportunities, and threats. Strengths and weaknesses are intrinsic to an organization — factors that the organization can influence. opportunities and threats are extrinsic — events that are occurring outside the organization, that is, in the industry or broader economy. A SWOT analysis arranges an ordered list of organizational strengths, weaknesses, opportunities, as well as threats and is typically displayed in a 2×2 matrix.

(*continued*)

Table 9.1 (Continued) Program Management Skills

#	Skills	Description
119	System implementation models and methodologies	System Development Life Cycle (SDLC) is a common system implementation model and methodology, but there can be many variations. Originally developed for predictive development, such as waterfall, SDLC has been evolving. Today, in addition to waterfall, SDLC can be agile, lean, iterative, prototyping, and most recently DevOps models. The goal of each of these system implementation models and methodologies is to provide a uniform set of processes and procedures that enables the consistent progression of work with predictable and repeatable results.
120	Talent evaluation	Talent evaluation helps employers examine individuals' capabilities and determine their fit for certain roles. Talent evaluation is a vital component of a recruitment process on projects, programs, and/or portfolios, and it allows managers to determine which person to include, train, or promote.
121	Team competency assessment techniques	Conducting team competency assessments helps to discover a team's vulnerabilities so that new or extra team members with the appropriate abilities can be recruited. It helps to establish a checklist for both soft and hard skills required for a program.
122	Team development and dynamics	Team development is the process of encouraging and preparing a group of people assembled to function as a unified team to achieve the desired result. There are five phases of developing a team: forming, storming, norming, performing, and adjourning. Team dynamics are the subconscious, psychological factors that affect the course of the action and success of a team. Team dynamics are generated by the quality of the tasks of the team, the characteristics of individuals in the team, the working interactions among team members, and the setting where the team operates.

(continued)

Table 9.1 (Continued) Program Management Skills

#	Skills	Description
123	Time management	Time management is a technique to schedule time and to monitor the time spent on particular tasks so that individuals can function more effectively. Some individuals have better time management than others, but everyone should cultivate practices to enhance their abilities in time management. A person's well-being can decline without effective time management. Poor time management can also result in poor delivery of projects, exceeding deadlines, poorly coordinated operations, etc.
124	Training methodologies	The training methodology is concerned with strategies for the planning and execution of the training. Training methodology can be described as a body of methods, procedures, and guidelines employed by professionals. It is vital to choose a methodology that will be most suitable for training conditions. Variables to be considered include the culture of the environment, resources, duration, affordability, and desired outcome.
125	Trend analysis	Trend analysis is a methodology employed in a technical evaluation that aims to forecast future developments based on the current trend data. Trend analysis is predicated on the notion that what has occurred previously offers professionals an assumption of what is going to take place in the future.
126	Vendor management	Vendor management is the process of examining and sourcing suppliers, collecting price quotations, assessing capabilities and capacities, negotiating contracts, building relationships, allocating work, evaluating performance, and monitoring and control work performed. Programs managers are often responsible for locating acceptable suppliers, negotiating with suppliers to obtain the best prices for goods and services, and making sure that suppliers meet their contract agreements.

Chapter 10

Full Practice Tests

This book contains two practice tests of 170 questions each, which is the same number of questions as the actual exam. To maximize the experience of actual test taking, readers should secure the following before tackling the sample tests:

1. Quiet space free of clutter and distractions
2. Countdown timer
3. Few pieces of clean paper and pencils

Remember, in the actual test, the four-hour time limit is all-inclusive, including any breaks. Furthermore, if you plan to recreate any cheat sheets, the time required to create them should be within the four hours. Before tackling the test, it is also a good idea to review your test strategy. Lastly, the answer key is at the end of this chapter.

Are you ready?

10.1 Practice Test One

Question 1: Zhenzhen is the program manager for his organization. He is now working to define roles and responsibilities for required program-level quality assurance and quality control activities. On which of the following program activities is Zhenzhen working on?

A.   Program change monitoring and controlling
B.   Program information management
C.   Program risk management transition
D.   Program governance practices

Question 2: As it relates to stakeholder engagement, which of the following is not likely an area that is impacted by stakeholder issues and concerns?

A. Scope
B. Benefits
C. Risks
D. Governance

Question 3: The two distinct subphases of the program definition phase are:

A. Program formulation and program planning
B. Program initiation and program delivery
C. Program formulation and program closure
D. Program formulation and project planning

Question 4: Customers are who?

A. The past and future customers who will be watching intently to see how well the program delivers the stated benefits
B. Those who perceive that they will receive less benefit from or be disadvantaged by the program's activities
C. Product or service providers who are often affected by changing policies and procedures
D. The individual or organization that will use the new capabilities delivered by the program and derive anticipated benefits

Question 5: You are the program manager for your organization, and you and your team are considering the organizational culture and acceptance of change for each stakeholder. Which of the following planning activities are you currently working on?

A. Risk management planning
B. Resources management planning
C. Stakeholder analysis and engagement planning
D. Program management planning

Question 6: Primary metrics for stakeholder engagement include all of the following except:

A. Frequency or rate of communication with the project team
B. Positive contributions to the realization of the program's benefits
C. Stakeholder participation
D. Frequency or rate of communication with the program team

Question 7: Ella is the program manager for an agricultural company. She is working with her team to design some kind of supporting structure that may be able to provide practices for effective decision-making that can ensure the program is managed appropriately. Which is Elia and her team working on?

A. Program governance rules
B. Program governance policies
C. Program governance framework
D. Program governance processes

Question 8: Randy is a program manager. He is currently intending to modify the information distribution methods and processes so that an outside company handles this task. What is the potential issue with Randy's intentions?

A. The information should remain within the program's control in order to ensure the appropriate message is delivered to each audience
B. There is not a potential issue
C. The information should remain in the program's control and must be assigned to a full-time communication manager
D. Randy needs to be responsible for all program communication. It should be delegated to internal or external parties.

Question 9: You are the program manager for your organization, and you and your team are considering the degree of support or opposition to the program benefits for each stakeholder. Which of the following planning activities are you currently working on?

A. Stakeholder analysis and engagement planning
B. Risk management planning
C. Resources management planning
D. Program management planning

Question 10: Katie is a program manager. Recently, Katie was approached by a stakeholder who was concerned that preventive action was approved at the component level when he felt it should have been approved at the program level. How should Katie respond?

A. Katie should explain that preventive action can be approved only at the project level
B. Katie should explain that preventive action can be approved only at the component level
C. Katie should explain that preventive action can be approved at the component or program level
D. Katie should explain that preventive action can be approved only at the program level

Question 11: The program management office may support the program manager by all except:

A. Supporting program communications
B. Defining standard program management processes and procedures that will be followed
C. Supporting project-level change management activities
D. Supporting effective resource management

Question 12: After the program management plan is reviewed and formally approved, what phase begins?

A. Program benefits delivery
B. Program preparation
C. Program formulation
D. Component planning and authorization

Question 13: Ms. Fernandez is the new program manager for a digital art company. She just had a meeting with her main stakeholders, and one of them comes to her attention as problematic and keeps questioning and raising many concerns and negative aspects about the program and its intended benefits. Ms. Fernandez may have a lot of resistance from this particular stakeholder, who is part of the key stakeholders for the program since most of the program objectives will impact directly on his area. From the options below, which one is the FIRST thing Ms. Fernandez should do with this particular stakeholder, in order to guarantee program success?

A. Ask Human Resources department to fire this stakeholder from the organization
B. Ask the program sponsor to remove this stakeholder from the program
C. Understand the motivations of this particular stakeholder for opposing the program
D. Engage stakeholder in the whole program

Question 14: Dave is a program manager. He is currently going through the process of creating a resource plan which describes the use of scarce resources and the priority for which each component can plan for that resource. What activity is Dave performing?

A. Resource prioritization
B. Program risk management
C. Resource planning
D. Resource interdependency management

Question 15: Which one is the performance domain that manages program activities required to facilitate effective program definition, program delivery, and program closure?

A. Program stakeholder engagement
B. Program strategy alignment
C. Program life cycle management
D. Program benefits management

Question 16: Which program delivery management activity provides program managers with the data necessary to determine the program's state and trends and may point to areas in need of adjustment or realignment?

A. Component transition
B. Program performance monitoring and control
C. Program transition and benefits sustainment
D. Program performance reporting

Question 17: David is a program manager. He has currently just completed the program financial monitoring and control activity in which approved program changes were incorporated into the appropriate budget. Additionally, some financial forecasts were prepared for the program. As a result of these activities, what will David have to update?

A. Component payment schedules
B. Program management plan
C. Program payment schedules
D. Program budget baseline

Question 18: Adam is the program manager for a sport accessories company and he wants to analyze the potential impact of planned program changes on the expected advantages and outcomes. Which performance domain should Adam focus on?

A. Program benefits management
B. Program strategy alignment
C. Program life cycle management
D. Program stakeholder engagement

Question 19: Julian is the program manager for his organization, who is currently working on ensuring the communication of critical component-related information to key stakeholders. Which one of the following activities is Julian working on?

A. The phase closure process
B. The approval of the initiation of a new program component
C. The execution of a new program strategic plan
D. The presentation of a different strategy within the organization objectives

Question 20: Ms. Wilson is program manager for an entertainment and media industry company. She is currently working within the program definition phase and needs to get the formal approval of two documents. Which documents does she need to deliver for approval?

A. Program transition and closure and program governance plan
B. Program stakeholder engagement plan and program management plan
C. Program management plan and program roadmap
D. Program charter and program business case

Question 21: Paige is a program manager and one of her major milestones has been delayed. She wants to find a document which shows key dependencies between these major milestones. What should Paige be looking for?

A. Program management plan
B. Program roadmap
C. Program business case
D. Program charter

Question 22: ABC company is launching a new program. They are currently going through the process of assigning a program sponsor to oversee all program activity. What part of the program definition phase are they in?

A. Program formulation
B. Program benefits delivery
C. Program preparation
D. Program initiation

Question 23: During program controlling, the outputs of program change monitoring and controlling are all of the following except?

A. Approved change requests
B. Customer feedback requests
C. Updates to the program change log
D. Customer feedback requests and approved change requests

Question 24: What is the best definition of a portfolio?

A. Temporary endeavors undertaken to create a unique product, service, or result
B. Related projects, subsidiary programs, and program activities managed in a coordinated manner to obtain benefits not available from managing them individually
C. A collection of projects, programs, subsidiary portfolios, and operations managed as a group to achieve strategic objectives
D. A collection of projects, programs, subsidiary portfolios, and operations managed in a coordinated manner to obtain benefits not available from managing them individually

Question 25: Which of the following statements BEST describes why which one is more common – the concept of stakeholder engagement, rather than stakeholder management?

A. Because stakeholders do not manage the program, they are engaged into what the program benefits will produce
B. Because of the need to promulgate a direct management without a hierarchical affiliation between the stakeholders and the team
C. Because stakeholders need to be engaged to the objectives of the program, rather than to managing them
D. Because stakeholders do not need to be managed by the program manager. They need to be engaged to the program

Question 26: The Standard for Program Management is intended to provide a common understanding of the role of a program manager in general, especially when interacting with all except:

A. Project managers whose projects are part of the program
B. Portfolio managers whose portfolios do not include the program or its components
C. program beneficiaries
D. Portfolio managers whose portfolios include the program or its components

Question 27: Kathy is a program manager. She is currently in the process of performing detailed stakeholder analysis, including identifying stakeholders and categorizing their relationship to the program. What is Kathy creating?

A. Risk management plan
B. Stakeholder register
C. Stakeholder engagement plan
D. Stakeholder management plan

Question 28: Project team members are who?

A. Groups representing consumer, environmental, or other interests
B. The individuals performing program activities
C. The individuals performing constituent component activities
D. A group of participants representing various program-related interests with the purpose of supporting the program under its authority by providing governance practices

Question 29: During program planning, the outputs of the program scope management planning are all of the following except?

A. Program scope statement
B. Program scope management plan
C. Program work breakdown structure
D. Program schedule management plan

Question 30: Which one of the following options best describes what the program stakeholder engagement is?

A. A non-sense program activity
B. An individual program activity
C. A continuous program activity
D. A one-time program activity

Question 31: Which of the following options, best describes the following statement: "When defining stakeholders to a program, you, as a program manager, have to be very careful to select them so they all have the same level of influence within the whole program."

A. The statement is completely TRUE
B. The statement is completely FALSE
C. The statement is partially TRUE
D. The statement is partially FALSE

Question 32: Olivia is a program manager for a software distribution company. Olivia is currently working to monitor components for her program. On which of the following program benefits management is Olivia working on?

A. Benefits analysis and planning
B. Benefits identification
C. Benefits delivery
D. Benefits transition

Question 33: Joan is a program manager. She is currently in the process of setting procurement standards for program components. What activity is Joan performing?

A. Program procurement management plan development
B. Program procurement
C. Program procurement planning
D. Program procurement closure

Question 34: What is the best definition of a project?

A.　A collection of projects, programs, subsidiary portfolios, and operations managed as a group to achieve strategic objectives

B.　Related projects, subsidiary programs, and program activities managed in a coordinated manner to obtain benefits not available from managing them individually

C.　Temporary endeavors undertaken to achieve strategic benefits

D.　Temporary endeavors undertaken to create a unique product, service, or result

Question 35: Beth is a program manager. She is currently in the process of monitoring trigger conditions and contingency plans. What activity is Beth performing?

A.　Program risk monitoring and control

B.　Program quality control

C.　Program risk analysis

D.　Program risk response planning

Question 36: The project, or component manager, is who?

A.　The individual authorized by the performing organization to lead the team responsible for achieving program objectives

B.　The person assigned by the performing organization to lead the team that is responsible for achieving project objectives

C.　The person who provides resources and support for the program and is accountable for enabling success

D.　The person assigned by the performing organization to establish, balance, monitor, and control portfolio components to achieve strategic business objectives

Question 37: The program definition phase is what?

A.　Comprises the program activities performed to produce the intended results of each component in accordance with the program management plan

B.　Includes the program activities necessary to transition the program benefits to the sustaining organization and formally close the program in a controlled manner

C.　Consists of program activities conducted to authorize the program and develop the program roadmap required to achieve the expected results

D.　Involves the development of the program business case which states the overall expected benefits to be addressed by the program in support of the strategic initiatives

Question 38: Lewis is a program manager for a company dedicated to fashion jewelry elaboration and distribution. Lewis is currently working to define, create, maximize, and deliver the benefits provided by the program. On which of the following program management performance domains is Lewis currently working on?

A.   Program risk management
B.   Program benefits management
C.   Program governance
D.   Program life cycle management

Question 39: Who should continually monitor changes and update stakeholder engagement activities and deliverables as needed?

A.   Component managers
B.   Program management office
C.   Portfolio manager
D.   Program manager

Question 40: With regard to scope, programs:

A.   Have progressively elaborated throughout the project life cycle
B.   Have a scope that encompasses the scopes of its program components
C.   Have an organizational scope that changes with the strategic objectives of the organization
D.   Are progressively elaborated throughout the program life cycle

Question 41: Jeff is a program manager. He is currently in the process of ensuring that an environment conducive to effective risk management of components is provided. As part of the process, he is currently gathering and storing all information on projects and stakeholders. Which of the five crucial factors is Jeff working on?

A.   Availability of resources
B.   Control
C.   Budget and schedule activities
D.   Availability of information

Question 42: Joan is a program manager. She is currently working on stakeholder engagement activities. She has received a number of stakeholder concerns and issues and wants to document them to ensure they are tracked and addressed. Where should Joan document the concerns?

A.   Issues log
B.   Stakeholder management plan
C.   Stakeholder engagement plan
D.   Stakeholder register

Question 43: Isabella is the program manager for a garden company and she wants to monitor the interdependencies among the outputs being delivered by the various components within the program. Which performance domain should Isabella focus on?

A. Program benefits management
B. Program strategy alignment
C. Program life cycle management
D. Program stakeholder engagement

Question 44: Will is a program manager. He has just finished an activity which has yielded an output of quality change requests. Which activity has Will just completed?

A. Program quality control
B. Program quality assurance
C. Change management
D. Program quality planning

Question 45: George is a program manager. He has just finished analyzing program trends, which have revealed to George that there are two key areas of adjustment. Which activity has George performed?

A. Component transition
B. Program performance monitoring and control
C. Forecasts
D. Program performance reporting

Question 46: Sandy is a program manager. She is currently in the process of negotiating objectives, seeking agreement on sought after benefits, gaining commitment to resources, and seeking ongoing support throughout the program. What activity is Sandy working on?

A. Stakeholder interaction
B. Stakeholder communication
C. Stakeholder management
D. Stakeholder engagement

Question 47: Who is the one responsible to ensure all stakeholders are adequately and appropriately engaged throughout the duration of the program?

A. The program sponsor
B. The program manager
C. The program team
D. The program stakeholders

Question 48: From the following options, which one facilitates the governance practices?

A. The program manager
B. The program management office
C. The program sponsor
D. The program steering committee

Question 49: Through the five program management performance domains, the program manager oversees and analyzes component interdependencies to determine the optimal approach to managing program components. Actions related to these interdependencies include all except:

A. Align program efforts with the organizational strategy and the program's business case
B. Proactively assess and respond to risks spanning multiple components of the program
C. Lead and coordinate project activities for all projects within the program
D. Monitor benefits realization of program components to ensure they remain strategically aligned to the organization's goals

Question 50: The program closure phase includes activities necessary to do what?

A. Transition program benefits to the sustaining organization and formal close the program in a controlled manner
B. Transition project benefits to the sustaining organization and formal close the program in a controlled manner
C. Transition program benefits to the sustaining organization and formal close the project in a controlled manner
D. Transition component benefits to the sustaining organization and formal close the component in a controlled manner

Question 51: Ella is the program manager for a sales company, and she is now performing several activities in order to produce the intended results of each component in accordance with the program management plan. On which of the following program life cycle phases is Ella working on?

A. Program execution phase
B. Program definition phase
C. Program delivery phase
D. Program closure phase

Question 52: _____ is often expressed as direct and indirect communication among the stakeholders and the program's leader teams?

A. Program management
B. Program communication plan
C. Stakeholder engagement
D. Stakeholder management

Question 53: The outputs of program information archiving and transition are what?

A. Resources released to other organizational elements and lessons learned report to organizational governance bodies
B. Resources released to other organizational elements and contract closeout reports
C. Inputs to organizational archives and lessons learned report to organizational governance bodies
D. Inputs to organizational archives and contract closeout reports

Question 54: During program execution, cost is typically higher than the benefits realized in the program definition phase. During what phase do you expect the benefits delivered to outweigh the cost?

A. None of the above
B. Program closure
C. Program definition
D. Program delivery

Question 55: During the program schedule control activity, which of the following is something that should be reviewed to assess the impact of component-level changes on other components and on the program itself?

A. Program schedule standards
B. Program roadmap
C. Program resource schedule
D. Program master schedule

Question 56: Camila is a program manager for a women's clothing design and manufacturing company, who is establishing new design strategies to increase business income. Camila is dedicating full-time to link component outputs to the planned program outcomes. On which of the following documents is Camila currently working on?

A. Program charter
B. Benefits management plan
C. Program information management plan
D. Program management plan

Question 57: Successful program managers have strong leadership skills. These include all of the following except:

A. Not providing program resources and support for the change
B. Obtaining and evaluating the stakeholders' feedback on the program's progress
C. Facilitating or negotiating the approach to implement change
D. Engaging stakeholders to assess their readiness for change

Question 58: A key member of the program steering committee is who?

A. Component managers
B. Project team
C. Sponsor
D. Customers

Question 59: Program activities and integration management are concerned with collectively using resources, knowledge, and skills to execute the program. This process also involves making decisions about all of the following except which one?

A. Competing demands and priorities
B. Risks
C. Benefit strategy
D. Resource allocation

Question 60: Megan is a program manager. She is currently working on stakeholder identification. She has identified the funding organization, performing organization, program management office, and potential customers as stakeholders. What term would Megan use to describe these stakeholders?

A. External stakeholders
B. Primary stakeholders
C. Key program stakeholders
D. Secondary stakeholders

Question 61: Rick is a program manager. He is currently performing an activity which determines which risks might affect the program, documents their characteristics, and prepares for their successful management. What activity is Rick performing?

A. Program risk identification
B. Program risk response planning
C. Program risk analysis
D. Program risk management planning

Question 62: As defined by Project Management Institute (PMI), all five program management performance domains interact with each other throughout the course of the program. From the options below, which one describes how this interaction is given?

A. With varying degrees of intensity
B. With a fixed degree of intensity, established by PMI
C. With a variable intensity which depends upon the program resources and experience of the program manager
D. Interaction depends upon the complexity of the program

Question 63: Which of the following statement best describes how an operational activity may be part of a program?

A.　When the operational activity related to the program may be considered as program-related activities

B.　When the operational activity is related to the portfolio on which the program is part of

C.　When the operational activity is related to an administrative process on which the program is part of

D.　When the operational activity is related to project-related activities on which the program is part of

Question 64: Effective program governance includes all of the following except:

A.　Ensure that the goals of the program remain aligned with the strategic vision, operational capabilities, and resource commitments of the sponsoring organization

B.　Enabling the organization to assess the viability of the organization's strategic plan and the level of support required to achieve it

C.　Facilitating the engagement of program stakeholders by establishing clear expectations for program interaction with key stakeholders

D.　Establishment of processes for measuring progress against the benefits plan

Question 65: What is the majority of a program's cost attributed to?

A.　Overarching program initiatives

B.　Contract expenditures

C.　Program infrastructure

D.　Individual components

Question 66: Who needs to provide approval prior to advancing to the program transition?

A.　Program champion

B.　Governance board

C.　Program sponsor

D.　Program manager

Question 67: Sam is currently working on the program charter. He is currently defining why the program is important as well as what the program is trying to achieve. What is Sam providing?

A.　Strategic fit

B.　Vision

C.　Scope

D.　Justification

Question 68: Jesse is a program manager. He has just finished an activity which has yielded an output of financial closing statements and a closed program budget. Which activity has Jesse just completed?

A. Component cost estimation
B. Program cost budgeting
C. Program financial closure
D. Program financial monitoring and control

Question 69: Emily is a program manager. She has just completed an activity which has yielded outputs of corrective actions, approved change requests, and contract payments. What activity has Emily just completed?

A. Component cost estimation
B. Program financial closure
C. Program cost budgeting
D. Program financial monitoring and control

Question 70: You are the program manager for your company, and currently you are executing a strategic program that will increase business financial benefits by 10% in comparison with the last year's Q1.

As the program execution requires the engagement of most stakeholders and a proper governance, you often need to perform an escalation process between component teams, the program management team, and the program steering committee.

What type of escalation process is this?

A. Transversal escalation process
B. Team escalation process
C. Within the program
D. Outside the program

Question 71: You are the program manager for your organization, and you are currently working on the program charter's different sections.

You are working to describe why the program is important and what does it achieve. On which of the following sections, should you include this information, in order to achieve a well-structured program charter document?

A. Vision
B. Strategic alignment
C. Justification
D. Benefits

Question 72: If a request for correction action exceeds program-level thresholds, what can happen to the request?

A. It can be taken to the program manager for approval
B. It can be taken to the program champion for approval
C. It can be taken to the program governance board for approval
D. It can be taken to the program sponsor for approval

Question 73: Jana is a program manager for a visual entertainment corporation. Jana is currently working to report benefits for her program. On which of the following program benefits management is Jana working on?

A. Benefits transition
B. Benefits delivery
C. Benefits identification
D. Benefits analysis and planning

Question 74: Cristina is a program manager for a telecommunication equipment and sales company. Cristina is currently working to monitor the performance of benefits for her program. On which of the following program benefits management is Cristina working on?

A. Benefits delivery
B. Benefits transition
C. Benefits identification
D. Benefits sustainment

Question 75: The output to program resource transition is what?

A. Updates to the program roadmap
B. Resources released to other organizational elements
C. Program resource prioritization decisions
D. Updates to the program resource management plan

Question 76: The tools used for stakeholder engagement by the program manger and program team that should be updated as needed include all of the following except?

A. Stakeholder register
B. Stakeholder map
C. Stakeholder management plan
D. Stakeholder engagement plan

Question 77: The document that contains the detailed strategy for effective stakeholder engagement is called a?

A. Stakeholder risk register
B. Stakeholder engagement plan
C. Stakeholder monitor and action plan
D. Stakeholder management plan

Question 78: What does it mean that program and portfolio management functions are collaborative?

A. That both, program and portfolio managers collaborate together to the success of the projects, on which their respective instances belong to
B. That program manager works for the success of his program activities, and so it ensures the success of the portfolio
C. That portfolio manager's success is guaranteed by the success of program activities
D. That program and portfolio managers work together to ensure that benefits required by the organization are delivered

Question 79: During which phase do program initiation activities generally occur?

A. Program definition
B. Initial risk assessment
C. Program integration management
D. Program infrastructure development

Question 80: The application of knowledge, skills, tools, and techniques to project activities to meet the project requirements is:

A. Portfolio management
B. Program management
C. Project management
D. Project execution

Question 81: Alexander is program manager for Kira, an online games distribution company, which main business area is the entertainment and media industry. The company is working on the development of a new online game championship that will integrate gamers from all over the world, but Kira's top executives need to define and perform several changes in the program's initial goals and objectives. The changes that Kira's executives are proposing may have or may not have some associated risk in the program, which may be acceptable or desirable. What will be Alexander's responsibility over this?

A. Alexander will be solely responsible for program success
B. Alexander will have to recommend changes
C. Alexander will have to assess
D. Alexander will have to reject changes

Question 82: Laura is a program manager for a security and surveillance company, which is actually running a program to enhance technologically and methodologically all surveillance processes and policies. At the moment Laura and the project sponsor are evaluating together in order to establish a framework that will help the program to define the roles and responsibilities required to manage the benefits. On which of the following documents is Laura currently working on?

A. Program charter
B. Program management plan
C. Benefits management plan
D. Program roadmap

Question 83: Laura is currently working within the program definition phase. She is deploying the initial program organization and developing the program management plan. What subphase is Laura working on?

A. Program benefits delivery
B. Program formulation
C. Component planning and authorization
D. Program preparation

Question 84: Fernando is a program manager for an advanced technology consultancy firm. Fernando is currently working to establish a benefits management plan for her program. On which of the following program benefits management is Fernando working on?

A. Benefits sustainment
B. Benefits delivery
C. Benefits analysis and planning
D. Benefits transition

Question 85: Identifying the program's financial sources and resources, integrating the budgets of the program components, developing the overall budget for the program, and controlling the costs during the program are all activities related to:

A. Program cost estimation
B. Program change management planning
C. Program communications management planning
D. Program financial management planning

Question 86: Ron is a program manager who is establishing the program infrastructure in the early stages of the program. He is currently consulting with a group of key stakeholders to determine the program's infrastructure requirements. What is the term used to describe these key stakeholders?

A. Program management consultants
B. Program management team
C. PMO
D. Governance board

Question 87: Kevin is a program manager. He is currently working on stakeholder identification. As part of that process, interviews and focus groups have been completed. However, Kevin would like to solicit feedback from a greater number of stakeholders. What tool could Kevin use to accomplish his goal?

A. Knowledge repositories
B. Historical information
C. Additional individual interviews
D. Questionnaires

Question 88: As it relates to stakeholder engagement, which of the following is reviewed regularly to identify risks arising from lack of stakeholders participating?

A. Stakeholder management plan
B. Stakeholder engagement plan
C. Stakeholder register
D. Stakeholder metrics

Question 89: In some cases, the stewardship of sustaining benefits may need to transition all except which one of the following?

A. Another organization
B. Another entity
C. A subsequent program
D. A new component within the program

Question 90: Effective program governance includes all of the following except:

A. Creating an environment for communicating and addressing program risks and uncertainties to the organization
B. Providing a framework that is aligned with portfolio and corporate governance policies and processes for assessing and ensuring the program is compliant
C. Designing and authorizing the assurance process and executing reviews and health checks of the program progress in delivering its expected benefits
D. Developing the target dates and milestones for benefits achievement

Question 91: For large programs, what might a program manager do to develop in order, and to visually represent the interaction of all stakeholders' current and desired support and influence?

A. Stakeholder roadmap
B. Stakeholder map
C. Stakeholder engagement plan
D. Stakeholder register

Question 92: You are the new program manager in your organization, just certified a few weeks ago, and currently you are working with Gilmar, an experienced program manager who has managed many different programs for several organizations worldwide, but Gilmar is not PMI certified.

You are having a discussion with Gilmar on the way you want to prepare the Program governance plan. Gilmar is angrily arguing with you to prepare a stand-alone document for the governance plan, but you don't want to make different and separate documents, instead you are planning to include the governance plan as a subsection of the program management plan. Which of the following options is true regarding this scenario?

A. Gilmar is an experienced professional, so his opinion is always right
B. Gilmar is not PMI certified and you are, so Gilmar's opinion is worthless
C. You can prepare the governance management plan as a stand-alone document or as a subsection of the program management plan, both options are correct
D. The only way to prepare the program governance plan is as a subsection of the program management plan

Question 93: Which of the following statements best describes the scope definition for programs, according to its established definition?

A. Have a defined objective and is progressively elaborated throughout its life cycle
B. Have an organizational scope that changes with the strategic objectives of the organization
C. Encompasses the scope of its components
D. Cannot be modified according to the portfolio that covers the respective program, when there is a change in portfolio strategic objectives

Question 94: Greg is a program manager. He has decided to use a system which will allow access to engineering drawings, design specifications, and test plans. He feels that this will be an effective communication and information tool. What activity is Greg performing?

A. Information gathering and retrieval systems
B. Lessons learned database
C. Information distribution methods
D. Program communication considerations

Question 95: Renee is a program manager. She has just completed an activity which has yielded outputs of awarded contracts and request for proposal. What activity has Renee just completed?

A. Program procurement planning
B. Program procurement
C. Program procurement administration
D. Program procurement closure

Question 96: All of the following applies to program stakeholders except which one?

A. Defined as an individual or group that may be effected by, or perceived to be affected by, the program
B. May be internal or external to the program
C. May have a positive or negative impact on the outcome of the program
D. Should be identified, analyzed, categorized, monitored, and managed

Question 97: As it relates to stakeholder engagement, what type of analysis is done to understand the urgency and probability of stakeholder issues and determine which issues may turn into program risks?

A. Impact analysis
B. Communication analysis
C. Stakeholder engagement analysis
D. Risk analysis

Question 98: What begins when the program components have delivered all outputs and the program is delivering benefits?

A. Program closure phase activities
B. Program delivery phase activities
C. Program definition phase activities
D. Program transition phase activities

Question 99: All the following documents are created during program planning and are included in the program management plan except which one?

A. Benefits management plan
B. Stakeholder engagement plan
C. Project management plan
D. Governance plan

Question 100: Programs and projects are conducted to produce the outputs and outcomes required to support an organization's strategic objectives, and are significant elements of an organization's:

A. Governance board
B. Steering committee
C. Portfolio
D. Program management office

Question 101: From the following statements, which one is NOT a purpose of the program definition phase?

A. Evaluate the program risks
B. To progressively elaborate the goals and objectives to be addressed by the program
C. Define the expected program outcomes and benefits
D. Seek approval for the program

Question 102: During program planning, the outputs of the program communications management planning are all of the following except which one?

A. Business case updates
B. Program communication management plan
C. Communication requirements inputs to the stakeholder register
D. Business case updates and program communication management plan

Question 103: You are a program manager who had just finished with a critical activity on your program benefits management. Now you are arranging some workshops with critical stakeholders to review, define, and get approval from them on the key performance indicators (KPIs) and other measures that will be used to monitor program performance. What is the critical activity you had just finished?

A. Program closure
B. Benefits register update
C. Benefits analysis and planning
D. Benefits delivery

Question 104: Jen's program is progressing nicely, and she is ready to begin the program transition phase. Jen has reviewed the program work and is satisfied with it. Therefore, Jen gives the okay for the program transition phase to begin. What mistake has Jen made?

A. Jen has failed to get the approval of the governance board
B. Jen has not made a mistake
C. Jen needs to get the approval of the program champion
D. Jen needs to get the approval of the program sponsor

Question 105: Cindy is a program manager. She is currently working on program financial management. She is in the process of developing a document which dictates how and when contractors are paid in accordance with the contract provisions. What is Cindy developing?

A.   Program benefits reports
B.   Component payment schedules
C.   Program funding schedules
D.   Program budget

Question 106: You are a program manager for your company, and you just received a meeting request from your portfolio manager to review if the program you are leading is still being aligned to the organization's strategy.
    Why do you think your portfolio manager is asking for this meeting?

A.   Because the portfolio manager is not aware of what you are doing
B.   Because the portfolio manager may want to justify a slippage of the portfolio strategic objectives
C.   Because this is one of your main responsibilities as program manager
D.   Because the portfolio manager is performing a portfolio review process

Question 107: Mr. Kumar is program manager for a variety store company. Mr. Kumar is developing a communication strategy approach to enhance stakeholders in the program. Mr. Kumar needs to involve particular stakeholders in making the right decisions at the right time, so Mr. Kumar can move the program forward.
    From the options below, which factor should Mr Kumar need to consider?

A.   Assure decision-making stakeholders are provided with adequate information
B.   Ask the program sponsor to approve your program management plan
C.   Mitigate all risks
D.   Involve all stakeholders at the program level

Question 108: Organizations employ program management to:

A.   Reduce the staffing levels of the organization
B.   Pursue complex initiatives that support organizational strategy
C.   Pursue the efficient delivery of project outputs and outcomes
D.   Pursue complex initiatives that support individual outcomes

Question 109: During program execution, the output of program interdependency management is what?

A.   Program component prioritization decisions
B.   Proposal evaluation criteria
C.   Updates to the program resource management plan
D.   Quality test reports or measurement results

Question 110: What is performed to investigate, assess, and plan the support structure that will assist the program in achieving its goals?

A. Program communications management
B. Program stakeholder engagement
C. Component infrastructure development
D. Program infrastructure development

Question 111: Programs function similarly to projects in that the benefits are _____?

A. Approved
B. Delivered
C. Defined
D. Closed

Question 112: Seth is a program manager. He is currently working on stakeholder engagement and is performing an analysis to better understand the urgency and probability of stakeholder issues and determine which issues may turn into program risks. What type of analysis is Seth performing?

A. Impact analysis
B. Communication analysis
C. Stakeholder engagement analysis
D. Risk analysis

Question 113: Mr. Sato is the program manager for his organization, who just had a meeting with a stakeholder whose responsibility is to provide capable governance resources to oversee and monitor program uncertainty and complexity related to achieving benefits delivery. According to this responsibility description, what is the main role of this stakeholder?

A. Project manager
B. Member of the program steering committee
C. Member of the program management office
D. Program sponsor

Question 114: You are the program manager for your organization, and currently you are preparing yourself for a meeting you will have today with him. In your stakeholder register, you found this stakeholder has a high level of authority and low level of concern. From the options below, which one is the best strategy you can use with this stakeholder in order to engage him?

A. Monitor
B. Keep satisfied
C. Keep informed
D. Manage closely

Question 115: From the following statements, which one BEST explains what information can be retrieved from the milestones on a program roadmap?

A.   The point in time when the benefit is delivered to the program
B.   The point in time when the output is generated
C.   The completion of a defined program output
D.   The achievement and delivery of incremental benefits

Question 116: All the following documents are created during program planning and are included in the program management plan except which one?

A.   Organizational management plan
B.   Scope management plan
C.   Program roadmap
D.   Change management plan

Question 117: What is the relationship between program benefits management and program roadmap?

A.   The program benefits management defines the structure of the program components by identifying the relationships among the components and the rules that govern their inclusion; while the program roadmap establishes the architecture that maps how the components will deliver the capabilities and outcomes that are intended to achieve the program benefits
B.   The program benefits management establishes the architecture that maps how the components will deliver the capabilities and outcomes that are intended to achieve the program benefits; while the program roadmap defines the structure of the program components by identifying the relationships among the components and the rules that govern their inclusion
C.   The program benefits management establishes the architecture that maps how the components will deliver the capabilities and outcomes that are intended to achieve the program benefits; while the program roadmap describes the complexity arising from the different levels of impact the change potentially can cause in an organization
D.   The program benefits management establishes the architecture that maps how the components will deliver the capabilities and outcomes that are intended to achieve the program benefits; while the program roadmap describes the complexity arising from the different levels of impact the change potentially can cause in an organization

Question 118: During program closeout, a final program report is produced that may include all of the following except:

A. Financial performance assessments
B. Lessons learned
C. Successes and failures
D. List of current program stakeholders

Question 119: Lucy is the program manager for her organization, who is currently working for the assessment of the program resource needs and organizational commitments in addition to capabilities to fulfilling them. On which of the following program activities is Lucy working on?

A. Program governance practices
B. Program quality governance
C. Program governance reviews
D. Program closure

Question 120: Holly is a program manager. She has just completed an activity which has yielded outputs of awarded contracts and requests for proposals. What activity has Holly just completed?

A. Program procurement
B. Program procurement planning
C. Program procurement administration
D. Program procurement closure

Question 121: The program management office is what?

A. A public authority or government agency responsible for setting and managing regulatory and legal boundaries of their local or national governments
B. Organization whose personnel are the most directly involved in doing work of the project or program
C. A management structure that standardizes the program-related governance processes and facilitates the sharing of resources, tools, and techniques
D. The part of the organization or the external organization providing funding for the program

Question 122: Charlotte is the new program manager for a digital art company. She just had a meeting with main stakeholders, but especially one of them comes to mind since he seems to be problematic and keeps questioning and raising many concerns and negative aspects about the program and its intended benefits.

Charlotte may have a lot of resistance from this particular stakeholder, who is part of the key stakeholders for the program since most of the program objectives will affect directly on his area. Which one of the following strategies should Charlotte use with this particular stakeholder, in order to guarantee program success?

A. Ask Human Resources department to fire this stakeholder from the organization
B. Engage stakeholder to the whole program
C. Ask the program sponsor to remove this stakeholder from the program
D. Don't pay attention to what this stakeholder's opinion is. He is scared because of the impact the program will have to the corporate strategy

Question 123: Jeff is a program manager. He is currently in the process of utilizing historical information and interviews to gather information from stakeholders. What is Jeff doing?

A. Stakeholder analysis
B. Risk management
C. Stakeholder identification
D. Stakeholder engagement

Question 124: Nathan is the program manager for his organization, who just had a meeting with a stakeholder whose responsibility is to remove barriers and obstacles to program success. According to this responsibility description, what is the main role of this stakeholder?

A. Program sponsor
B. Removal manager
C. Project manager
D. Portfolio manager

Question 125: In order to help on program stakeholder engagement, what should you, as a program manager, need to do with the organization's current state and the intended benefits on the program's outcomes?

A. The program manager should understand the organization's current state and how the program benefits will move the organization to the future state
B. The program manager should not pay attention anymore to the organization's current state and just focus on the organization's future state
C. The program manager should keep the organization's current state invariable and adapt the program to this state
D. The program manager should only focus his efforts on the intended benefits on the program's outcomes and forget about a current state that will soon be obsolete

Question 126: Mr Ahmed is the program manager for a pool cleaning company and he wants to assign responsibility and accountability for the realization of program advantages provided by the program. Which performance domain should Mr Ahmed focus on?

A. Program strategy alignment
B. Program life cycle management
C. Program benefits engagement
D. Program stakeholder engagement

Question 127: You are the program manager for your organization, and you are currently starting with a new program within your organization, so you need to ensure that your program has a clear vision and goals, so you need to make sure that those effectively do support the organization vision and goals. What program performance domain do you need to focus on, in order to achieve this requirement?

A. Program stakeholder engagement
B. Program governance
C. Program life cycle management
D. Program strategic alignment

Question 128: Jane is a program manager. She is currently working on the resource interdependency management activity. She is working with component managers to ensure that a certain tool accounts for the timed use of interdependent resources as it relates to scheduling scarce program resources. What tool is Jane using?

A. Program charter
B. Program resource management plan
C. Program work breakdown structure
D. Program roadmap

Question 129: Which term best describes an individual or group of individuals who have an interest in the program and can influence or be influenced by its process or outcomes?

A. Program manager
B. Stakeholder
C. Champion
D. Sponsor

Question 130: Alexandra is a program manager for a fuel distribution company. Alexandra is currently working to derive and prioritize benefits for her program. On which of the following program benefits management is Alexandra working on?

A. Benefits transition
B. Benefits sustainment
C. Benefits delivery
D. Benefits analysis and planning

Question 131: The fundamental differences that are found in the way programs and projects are managed are all of the following except:

A. Uncertainty
B. Change
C. Complexity
D. Reporting

Question 132: In projects, change management is employed to help monitor and control the amount of variance from the planned cost and schedule for all of the following except:

A. Project manager
B. Project team
C. Supply management
D. Stakeholders

Question 133: You are the program manager for your company and now your are making a stakeholder analysis. You want to get feedback from a large number of stakeholders in the shortest time possible. What tool or technique will you use to achieve this objective?

A. Questionnaires and survey
B. Individual interviews
C. Focus groups
D. Meetings

Question 134: Carla is a program manager and is working within the early stages of a program. She is going through the process of identifying threats and opportunities to determine the probability of the program's successful delivery of organizational benefits. What is Carla doing?

A. Program sponsor selection and financing
B. Program Initiation
C. Initial risk assessment
D. Estimating scope, resources, and cost

Question 135: During program execution, the outputs of program contract administration are all of the following except?

A. Performance/earned value reports
B. Ongoing progress reports
C. Vendor/contract performance reports
D. Program management team performance reports

Question 136: Who are the ones uniquely positioned to monitor the progress of programs in their pursuit of organizational goals?

A. Program team
B. Program manager
C. Program stakeholders
D. Program governance participants

Question 137: Thomas is the program manager for his organization. He is now working to define minimum quality criteria and standards to be applied to all components of the program. On which of the following program activities is Thomas working on?

A. Program governance practices
B. Program change monitoring and controlling
C. Program information management
D. Program risk management transition

Question 138: Brittany is a program manager. She is currently in the process of reviewing program-level reports which contain a summation of the progress of the program's components, as well as the program's status relative to benefits. What type of report is Brittany reviewing?

A. Project status updates
B. Program forecast reports
C. Program benefits reports
D. Program performance reports

Question 139: Which of the following statements is NOT TRUE about program stakeholders?

A. Stakeholders have a positive impact on the outcome of a program
B. Stakeholders may be internal or external to the program
C. Stakeholder is an individual, group, or organization that may be affected by or perceive itself to be affected by a decision, activity, or outcome of a program
D. Stakeholders should be identified, analyzed, categorized, and monitored

Question 140: Chris is a program manager. He is currently considering various aspects for each stakeholder including their attitudes about the program and its sponsors as well as expectation of program benefits delivery. As a result of this effort, what is Chris likely to produce?

A. Stakeholder register
B. Stakeholder engagement plan
C. Risk management plan
D. Stakeholder management plan

Question 141: Craig is a program manager and is in the process of developing financial metrics by which the program's benefits will be measured. What activity is Craig performing?

A. Program financial analysis
B. Program financial management plan development
C. Program financial benchmarking
D. Program funding schedule development

Question 142: Reports that provide updated program status by tracking accomplishments at milestones and phase gates are called?

A. Project performance reports
B. Program financial management reports
C. Program risk management reports
D. Program performance reports

Question 143: Program financial management activities include all of the following except:

A. Informal communication such as emails, small group conversations, and staff meetings
B. Implementing earned value management (schedule performance index, cost performance index)
C. Monitoring contract expenditures to ensure funds are disbursed according to the contract
D. Monitoring costs reallocation impact and results among components

Question 144: Jan is the program manager for a large enterprise. Jan is currently working to retrieve data regarding the known program risks, their response plans, and escalation criteria. Which one of the following activities is Jan currently working on?

A. Program monitoring, reporting, and controlling
B. Program planning
C. Program execution
D. Program definition

Question 145: What consists of tools used to collect, integrate, and communicate critical information?

A. Program management office
B. Project management information system
C. Program management information system
D. Risk register

Question 146: Todd is a program manager. He made estimates some time ago for component costs which have proven to be high and have left some money in the program budget. Todd's program sponsor is very interested in hearing about the funds that are now available. Why is the sponsor interested?

A. It does not have any bearing on the sponsor
B. It means that program work was over-funded and the budget should be re-visited for all program components
C. It means that program work was not completed to the level of completion the sponsor had expected
D. It presents an opportunity for the sponsor to add additional products to the program

Question 147: Program planning subphase begins once the steering committee approves the program _____?

A. Charter
B. Roadmap
C. Risk management plan
D. Stakeholder engagement plan

Question 148: Denise is a program manager. She has just completed an activity which has yielded outputs of a contract management plan and invitation for bid. What activity has Denise just completed?

A. Program procurement planning
B. Program procurement administration
C. Program procurement closure
D. Program procurement

Question 149: Beth is a program manager and is currently documenting the program justification, strategic fit, and vision. What document is Beth working on?

A. Program charter
B. Program risk assessment
C. Program business case
D. Program roadmap

Question 150: A tool that can be used to rank stakeholders that includes the ability of a stakeholder to influence a program and the interest that each stakeholder has in the program is called:

A.   Cost-benefit analysis chart
B.   Power/interest grid
C.   SWOT analysis
D.   KPI chart

Question 151: How often is it recommended to perform program periodic health checks?

A.   Periodically to assure the realization and sustainment of program benefits
B.   Never since this practice is a waste of time and resources
C.   Once per program
D.   After extended decision-point periods and between every three decision-point periods

Question 152: The three phases of the program life cycle are:

A.   Program definition, program delivery, program closure
B.   Program formulation, program delivery, program closure
C.   Program definition, project delivery, program closure
D.   Program definition, program initiation, program closure

Question 153: Michaella is a program manager for a company dedicated to telephone cards manufacturing. Michaella is currently working to manage program activities required to facilitate effective program definition, program delivery, and program closure. On which of the following program management performance domains is she currently working on?

A.   Program risk management
B.   Program strategy alignment
C.   Program governance
D.   Program life cycle management

Question 154: Suppliers are who?

A.   Product or service providers who are often affected by changing policies and procedures
B.   The individual or organization that will use the new capabilities delivered by the program and derive anticipated benefits
C.   The past and future customers who will be watching intently to see how well the program delivers the stated benefits
D.   Those who perceive that they will have less benefit from or be disadvantaged by the program's activities

Question 155: Jian Li is the CEO for a large enterprise, who wants to achieve complex initiatives in order to support organizational strategies. Which of the following alternatives should Jian Li need to get support from, so he can achieve this?

A. Program management
B. Operational management
C. Project management
D. Portfolio management

Question 156: What should happen when a program is not authorized?

A. All work should cease immediately and the event should be recorded in the program definition records
B. It should be documented in the program management plan and stored in the lessons learned
C. It should be documented in the charter and stored in lessons learned
D. The event should be recorded on the program roadmap

Question 157: During the program financial monitoring and control activity, payments are made in accordance with all of the following except which one?

A. Component budgets
B. Contracts
C. Financial infrastructure of the program
D. Status of the contract deliverables

Question 158: Which one of the following statements its NOT FALSE about program benefits management?

A. Comprises a number of elements that are central to program success
B. Is the process that defines, creates, maximizes, and delivers the benefits provided to the program
C. Includes policies to clarify the program's planned benefits
D. Includes processes to monitor the program's capacity and capability

Question 159: Why is it important to get all stakeholders engaged into the program?

A. Because stakeholders will approve, at the end, the execution of the program in the organization
B. Because it is a means in which the program manager supports the achievement of the intended program benefits
C. Because engaged stakeholders will help remove any obstacles that the program execution may encounter on the road
D. Engaging stakeholders is the end objective of the activities and approaches described by Program stakeholder engagement

Question 160: A program stakeholder register is a tool used by the program manager and program management team. It is a reference document for the program team to use in all of the following except:

A.   Reporting
B.   Distributing program deliverables
C.   Documenting changes in program risks
D.   Providing formal and informal communications

Question 161: Walter is a program manager and is seeking your advice. One of his key stakeholders asked Walter about including something in the program scope that Walter believed was out of scope. The stakeholder disagreed and was unhappy with Walter's response. Where can Walter look to see if the stakeholder request is in scope?

A.   Initial requirements
B.   Work breakdown structure
C.   Program roadmap
D.   Program charter

Question 162: Keith is a program manager. One of the project managers has reported to Keith that a program component has been finished early. The project manager is surprised that Keith is not thrilled by this development. Why is Keith concerned?

A.   Keith should not be concerned. This situation should only be viewed as a positive
B.   It can cause a program scheduling challenge which will require Keith to address and resolve the gap between expected and actual completion of the component as well as its impact on other components
C.   Keith is concerned because by some components being finished early other dependent components now will definitely be late
D.   Keith should be not concerned. All other components can typically be very easily accelerated as most components only normally require minimal coordinator

Question 163: You are the program manager for your organization, and you and your team are considering the relevant phases applicable to stakeholders' specific engagement for each stakeholder. Which of the following planning activities are you currently working on?

A.   Risk management planning
B.   Resources management planning
C.   Program management planning
D.   Stakeholder analysis and engagement planning

Question 164: Kate is a program manager. She is currently working on the program schedule management activity. During this time, several project managers have provided Kate with their component detailed schedules. As a result, what might Kate need to be updated?

A. Program roadmap
B. Program schedule management plan
C. Program master schedule
D. Program management plan

Question 165: You are the program manager for your organization, and currently you are preparing yourself for a meeting you will have today with him. On your stakeholder register, you found this stakeholder has a low level of authority and low level of concern.

From the options below, which one is the best strategy you can use with this stakeholder in order to engage him?

A. Keep informed
B. Keep satisfied
C. Manage closely
D. Monitor

Question 166: Meilin is program manager for a Cable TV company, which is currently deploying a new video technology broadcasting system for corporate customers. Mellin's stakeholders' register list is quite long, strong, and detailed. It has the most influenced executives and teams within the company.

A few weeks ago, Mellin's strategy against some particular stakeholders has changed. Now she is more focused on providing daily reports for a particular set of stakeholders, and she is spending many working sessions and meetings negotiating and setting particular agreements with them, enhancing particular conflict resolution techniques, through self-courses she is taking at night. Why is Mellin behaving this way?

A. Mellin has detected some stakeholders' opposition to the program
B. Mellin wants to show the power she has and her complete authority
C. Mellin has got an ultimatum from the program governance board, because the objectives will not be achieved
D. Mellin is a facilitator, and she feels comfortable in meetings and self-training courses

Question 167: As part of stakeholder analysis and engagement planning, which of the following is not an aspect which is considered for each stakeholder?

A. Political culture
B. Ability to influence the outcome of the program
C. Expectation of program benefits delivery
D. Degree of support or opposition to the program benefits

Question 168: Which one of the following roles has the responsibility to ensure that the program team understands and abides by the governance procedures and the underlying governance principles?

A. The training manager
B. The program sponsor
C. The program manager
D. The program team

Question 169: All the following documents are created during program planning and are included in the program management plan except?

A. Lessons learned management plan
B. Information management plan
C. Procurement management plan
D. Quality management plan

Question 170: Dr. Garcia is a program governance executive who usually oversees program conformance to governance policies and processes. Which of the following is the main role Dr. Garcia has in the program?

A. Program manager
B. Project manager
C. Program risk manager
D. Program sponsor

10.2 Practice Test Two

Question 1: How often is communication between program managers and stakeholders to take place?

A. Never
B. Frequently
C. Monthly
D. Weekly

Question 2: Sophie is a program manager for a shipping and packing company. Sophie has been working on her program deliverables as a legacy program from a previous program manager who left the company a week ago.

As soon as Sophie started working on the benefits management, she noticed the team is not working to deliver the intended benefits over a structured planning, and every team member and each project manager are working independently, initiating and closing their corresponding components as they needed.

From the following possible options, stated below, which one best explains the expected impact that Sophie may have for this way of working schema into the program?

A. The program will not be impacted, since every project manager has the authority to run its project as they want

B. When the program closes, all benefits will be reflected as an overall benefit

C. Each benefit will reflect a particular project deliverable, and the program will reflect the overall benefit

D. The whole program will not reflect the overall benefits

Question 3: Jake is a relatively new program manager. In evaluating program components, he is concerned that some components are not producing immediate benefits. What would you tell Jake?

A. I would tell Jake that components which are not producing immediate benefits should be reviewed by the governance board

B. I would tell Jake that components which are not producing immediate benefits should be reviewed and re-evaluated by the program sponsor

C. I would tell Jake that some components may produce benefits immediately while other components are integrated with others before the associated benefits may be realized

D. I would tell Jake that typically most components must be integrated with others before the associated benefits may be realized

Question 4: What is the main purpose established for program benefits management?

A. The centralized management of one or more portfolios to achieve strategic objectives

B. Program activities performed to produce the intended results of each component in accordance with the program management plan

C. Program activities related to actively identifying, monitoring, analyzing, accepting, mitigating, avoiding, or retiring program risks

D. Maps how the components will deliver the capabilities and outcomes that are intended to achieve the program benefits

Question 5: During which activity are payments made in accordance with the contracts, with the financial infrastructure of the program, and with the status of the contract deliverables?

A. Program financial monitoring and control
B. Component cost estimation
C. Program cost budgeting
D. Program financial closure

Question 6: Who is the one who effectively guides the program formulation activity and facilitates the development of the required outputs?

A. The program manager
B. The project team
C. The program sponsor
D. The steering committee

Question 7: You are the program manager for your organization, and you are currently working on the program charter different sections.

You are working to describe what is the end state and how will it benefit the organization. On which of the following sections should you include this information, in order to achieve a well-structured program charter document?

A. Vision
B. Strategic alignment
C. Benefits
D. Scope

Question 8: What is the activity of determining the information and communication needs of program stakeholders?

A. Stakeholder engagement
B. Information distribution
C. Stakeholder engagement
D. Communications planning

Question 9: Yong is the program manager for his organization. He is now working to define any required program-level quality assurance or quality control activities. On which of the following program activities is Yong working on?

A. Program change monitoring and controlling
B. Program information management
C. Program governance practices
D. Program risk management transition

Question 10: You are the program manager for your company and you just finished preparing a document file which details the names of the major people within your organization, which may be affected by the outcomes of your program. This list contains the complete names, the organizational position with the organization, the role he or she will have in your program, the support level, the influence level in the organization, and other relevant information for the program. Now you have started to categorize this list. After this activity, what will be the next step you will need to do?

A.   Ask for vacations since you've been working hard until today
B.   Analyze the stakeholder register
C.   Categorize stakeholder register
D.   Prioritize stakeholder register

Question 11: The heart of stakeholder engagement is in what?

A.   Stakeholder communication
B.   Stakeholder analysis
C.   Risk management
D.   Quality control

Question 12: Programs function similarly to projects in that the program is _____?

A.   Approved
B.   Delivered
C.   Defined
D.   Closed

Question 13: Which of the following statement DOES NOT describe how the program manager interacts with stakeholders?

A.   Engages stakeholders by assessing their attitudes and interests
B.   Includes stakeholders in program activities and uses communications targeted to their needs
C.   Monitor stakeholder feedback within the context and understanding of the relationship to the program
D.   Provides training when needed within the context of the program

Question 14: Ethan is a program manager for an equipment rental company. Actually he and his team is working together with project managers, portfolio managers, and top executives on the organization's strategic planning. They are all evaluating and setting priorities on budget investments, so it should be aligned to organization's operational strategies. From the following options, which one best describes on what activity is Ethan and his team working on?

A. Project's program closure
B. Program closure
C. Program initiation
D. Program definition

Question 15: In what phase of the benefits program management is the benefits register most frequently updated?

A. Benefits analysis and planning
B. Benefits sustainment
C. Benefits identification
D. Benefits closure

Question 16: Components conducted to support a program include all except:

A. Projects
B. Subsidiary programs
C. Operations
D. Subsidiary portfolios

Question 17: Effective program governance includes all of the following except:

A. Establishment of KPIs and thresholds for evaluation
B. Establishing clear, well-understood agreements as to how the sponsoring organization will oversee the program and the degree of autonomy that the program will be given
C. Approving, endorsing, and initiating the program and securing funding from the sponsoring organization
D. Selecting, endorsing, and enabling the pursuit of program components, including projects, subsidiary programs, and other program activities

Question 18: What kind of relationship is the most appropriate one, when establishing a relationship between individuals responsible for program governance and program management?

A. A collaborative relationship
B. Individual and selfish
C. Competitive
D. Friendly

Question 19: The program management plan is created using all of the following documents except this one:

A.   Organization's strategic plan
B.   Business case
C.   Project charter
D.   Program charter

Question 20: Considering you are a program manager for your company, who is responsible for focusing on delivering the program's organizational benefits aligned with the organization's strategic plan?

A.   The program manager
B.   The project manager
C.   The portfolio manager
D.   The program sponsor

Question 21: All the following documents are created during program planning and are included in the program management plan except:

A.   Change management plan
B.   Communications management plan
C.   Component management plan
D.   Financial management plan

Question 22: Rich is a program manager. He has just finished an activity which has yielded an output of program performance reports. Which activity has Rich just completed?

A.   Component transition
B.   Forecasts
C.   Program performance monitoring and control
D.   Program performance reporting

Question 23: You are program manager and according to the definition established for program management, what tools can you apply in order to achieve your program objectives?

A.   Project management software, project processes, and program policies
B.   Knowledge, skills, and principles
C.   Project processes, project principles, and program manager
D.   Skills, program manager's experience, and team's experience

Question 24: The program governance plan does all of the following except:

A. Facilitates the design and implementation of effective governance
B. Is always included in the program management plan
C. Contains governance frameworks, functions, and processes
D. Stands alone as a document or subsection of the program management plan

Question 25: One of the primary roles of the program manager is to ensure that which of the following takes place?

A. All stakeholders are provided daily updates on program status
B. All stakeholders are provided daily updates on project status
C. All stakeholders are adequately and appropriately engaged
D. All stakeholders are adequately and appropriately managed

Question 26: What is the relationship between the vision and goals of the organization within the program?

A. It provides the basis for strategic mandates that drive the definition of most programs
B. They don't have any relationship since they are disconnected to each other
C. They refer to the same strategic planning roadmap
D. They provide a guide of what the program should accomplish as deliverables

Question 27: During program closeout, what is documented and shared with the organization?

A. Supplier contract details
B. Lessons learned
C. Individual team member performance reports
D. Project risk register

Question 28: Joshua is the program manager for his organization, who is currently working on ensuring the availability of resources to perform the component. Which one of the following activities is Joshua working on?

A. The phase closure process
B. The execution of a new program strategic plan
C. The approval of the initiation of a new program component
D. The presentation of a different strategy within the organization objectives

Question 29: The success of a program is measured by which one of the following:

A. Product and project quality, timeliness, budget compliance, and degree of customer satisfaction
B. The program's ability to deliver its intended benefits to the organization
C. The aggregate investment performance and benefit realization of the portfolio
D. The aggregate investment performance and benefit realization of the program

Question 30: During program controlling, the outputs of program scope monitoring and controlling are all of the following except?

A. Updated program scope statement
B. Updates to the project work breakdown structure
C. Updates to the program management plan
D. Updates to the program work breakdown structure

Question 31: Grace is a program manager and is planning to change the current information distribution method for particular parties to a web interface where all relevant program information will be posted. Is there an issue with Grace's plan?

A. Yes, information distribution should be done via fax, phone, and e-mail only
B. No, utilizing a web interface is an acceptable information distribution method
C. Yes, information distribution should be conducted primarily through memorandums and e-mails
D. Yes, utilizing a web interface is not an acceptable information distribution method

Question 32: Rebecca has just completed the process of assessing the feasibility of forming a program to achieve certain benefits as defined by senior leaders. As a result of the process, what might Rebecca have to update or create?

A. Statement of work
B. Roadmap
C. Business case
D. Charter

Question 33: The progressive elaboration of the goals and objectives to be addressed by the program is conducted in?

A. The program definition pages
B. The program closure phase
C. The program delivery phase
D. The program initiation phase

Question 34: The management, oversight, integration, and optimization of the program components that will deliver program benefits are called?

A. Program definition management
B. Program closure management
C. Program formulation management
D. Program delivery management

Question 35: At what level should the impact of threats and opportunities as they relate to the achievement of benefits be examined?

A. Governance level
B. Project level
C. Program level
D. Component level

Question 36: As part of the program financial closure activity and as a program nears completion, what type of reports are communicated in accordance with the stakeholder engagement plan?

A. Program budget
B. Final financial reports
C. Financial closing statements
D. Program financial management plan

Question 37: Valentina is a program manager for a satellite TV company. Currently Valentina is looking to get the approval within the designated executives in the company on the document which authorizes the program management team to use organizational resources to pursue the program's objectives; also she and her team are working to get approval on the document that contains formal projection of the benefits that the program is expected to deliver. In what program phase is Valentina's program currently being developed?

A. Program closing phase
B. Program execution phase
C. Program planning phase
D. Program definition phase

Question 38: You are the program manager for your organization, and you want to identify and assess the value and impact of program advantage against other options. Which performance domain should you focus on?

A. Program strategy alignment
B. Program life cycle management
C. Program benefits management
D. Program stakeholder engagement

Question 39: During program execution, the outputs of program information management are all of the following except:

A. Updates to the program information repository
B. Inputs to information distribution reporting
C. Lessons learned reports
D. Inputs to program reporting

Question 40: How is the program scope typically described?

A.   According to the impact on the areas that are included in the scope
B.   In the form of priorities established by the governance board
C.   In the form of expected benefits
D.   In the form of priorities established by key stakeholders

Question 41: Program funding models may include all of the following except:

A.   Funded entirely within the organization
B.   Managed within the organization but funded separately
C.   Fixed and cannot change after program formulation
D.   Funded and managed entirely from outside the organization

Question 42: Mike is a program manager and is currently in the process of compiling all available financial information and listing all income and payment schedules in sufficient detail so that the program's costs can be tracked. What is Mike developing?

A.   Component payment schedules
B.   Program funding schedules
C.   Program cost estimation
D.   Program budget

Question 43: The person authorized by the performing organization to lead the team and teams responsible for achieving program objectives is:

A.   Program manager
B.   Project manager
C.   Portfolio manager
D.   Program sponsor

Question 44: Changes to a project are generally local to the project and related to the:

A.   Tactical level
B.   Strategic level
C.   Operational level
D.   Executive level

Question 45: Jack is the program manager for a large enterprise. Jack is currently working to retrieve data regarding the operational status and progress of programs, components, and related activities. On which one of the following activities is Jack currently working on?

A.   Program planning
B.   Program monitoring, reporting, and controlling
C.   Program execution
D.   Program definition

Question 46: During program execution, the outputs of program communications management are all of the following except?

A. Notification of program change requests to the program and component teams, and the corresponding response to the change requests
B. Program financial reports for internal or external stakeholders or for the purpose of public disclosure
C. External filings with government and regulatory bodies as prescribed by laws and regulations
D. Design of reports required by program sponsors or program agreements, including formats and reporting frequency

Question 47: Matt is a program manager. He has just completed an activity which has yielded outputs that include audit findings and change requests. Which quality process has Matt just completed?

A. Quality assurance
B. Quality delivery
C. Quality planning
D. Quality control

Question 48: You are the program manager for your organization, and you and your team are considering the attitudes about the program and its sponsors for each stakeholder. Which of the following planning activities are you currently working on?

A. Risk management planning
B. Resources management planning
C. Program management planning
D. Stakeholder analysis and engagement planning

Question 49: Hannah is a program manager for a Variety store company. Hannah has detected the stakeholders for her program are starting to support other programs more actively, and decided to apply different communications strategies for each stakeholder in order to re-engage them efficiently. Which document should Hannah review in order to evaluate the most efficient communication and approach strategy for each of her stakeholders?

A. Stakeholder management plan
B. Risk management plan
C. Stakeholder engagement plan
D. Stakeholder register

Question 50: As it relates to resource interdependency management, what should account for the time use of interdependent resources when developing a schedule for scarce program resources?

A. Program charter
B. Program resource management plan
C. Program work breakdown structure
D. Program roadmap

Question 51: What establishes consistent policy, standards, and training for programs in the organization?

A. Program manager
B. Program management office
C. Component manager
D. Steering committee

Question 52: Mark is a program manager. He has just completed an activity which has yielded outputs that include standard reports and change requests. Which quality process has Mark just completed?

A. Quality delivery
B. Quality assurance
C. Quality planning
D. Quality control

Question 53: All the following documents are created during program planning and are included in the program management plan except which one?

A. Resource management plan
B. Risk management plan
C. Staff management plan
D. Schedule management plan

Question 54: Program manager stakeholder interaction includes all of the following except:

A. Monitors stakeholder feedback within the context and understanding of the relationship to the project
B. Engage stakeholders by assessing their attitudes and interests toward the program and their change readiness
C. Supports training initiatives as needed within the context of the program or related organizational structure of the program component
D. Includes stakeholders in program activities and used communications targeted to their needs, interests, requirements, expectations, and wants, according to their change readiness

Question 55: Diego is a program manager for a corporate business consultancy firm. Diego is currently working to derive benefits metrics for her program. On which of the following program benefits management is Diego working on?

A. Benefits identification
B. Benefits analysis and planning
C. Benefits delivery
D. Benefits transition

Question 56: Sophie is a program manager for a financial and investment advisory firm. Sophie is currently working to ensure continued realization of benefits for her program. On which of the following program benefits management is Sophie working on?

A. Benefits transition
B. Benefits delivery
C. Benefits sustainment
D. Benefits analysis and planning

Question 57: Dr. Diaz is a program manager for a vocational and trade schools institution. Currently Dr. Diaz and his team are arranging workshop sessions with the main stakeholders to define the metrics and procedures to measure benefits. To accomplish this the team will propose several KPIs for the stakeholders to evaluate and analyze. On which of the following documents is Dr. Diaz currently working on?

A. Benefits management plan
B. Procurement management plan
C. Program management plan
D. Program governance plan

Question 58: The program stakeholder engagement planning activity does what?

A. Determines the best way to manage program communications
B. Determines the best way to manage program risks
C. Outlines how all program stakeholders will be engaged throughout the duration of the program
D. Outlines how all program stakeholders will be managed throughout the duration of the program

Question 59: By using effective communications, a bridge can be created between all of the following except?

A. Diverse stakeholders who may have different cultural and organizational backgrounds
B. Stakeholders who cannot impact or influence the delivery of benefits by the program
C. Stakeholders with different levels of expertise
D. Stakeholders with different perspectives and interests

Question 60: Program team members are who?

A.   Groups representing consumer, environmental, or other interests
B.   The individuals performing constituent component activities
C.   The individuals performing program activities
D.   A group of participants representing various program-related interests with the purpose of supporting the program under its authority by providing governance practices

Question 61: The program sponsor, or champion, is who?

A.   The individual authorized by the performing organization to lead the team responsible for achieving program objectives
B.   The person assigned by the performing organization to establish, balance, monitor, and control portfolio components to achieve strategic business objectives
C.   The person assigned by the performing organization to lead the team that is responsible for achieving project objectives
D.   The person who provides resources and support for the program and is accountable for enabling success

Question 62: Felipe is a program manager for a finance investment institution. Felipe is currently working to map benefits into a program management plan for her program. On which of the following program benefits management is Felipe working on?

A.   Benefits sustainment
B.   Benefits identification
C.   Benefits analysis and planning
D.   Benefits delivery

Question 63: Kate is a relatively new program manager and has been approached by a few concerned stakeholders who have indicated that they are not receiving status updates as often as they expected. Kate was unaware of these requirements. Where should Kate look to see what the requirements are?

A.   Stakeholder engagement plan
B.   Communication plan
C.   Stakeholder management plan
D.   Information distribution

Question 64: Ross is a program manager. He is currently in the process of collecting and measuring performance information. What is Ross doing?

A.   Component transition
B.   Forecasts
C.   Program performance reporting
D.   Program performance monitoring and control

Question 65: Scott is a program manager and has received reports that a vendor is not living up to the defined standards for vendor performance. Scott is unsure on how to best handle the situation and wants to get more information on what the standards are. Where can Scott find this information?

A. Program charter
B. Program procurement plan
C. Program vendor management plan
D. Program financial management plan

Question 66: Beth is a program manager. She is currently training Bob, a new program manager. They are working on the program schedule management activity. Beth points out to Bob that one particular aspect of program components has a significant impact on the program schedule. What aspect is Beth explaining to Bob?

A. Timeline
B. Dependencies
C. Scope
D. Budget

Question 67: The centralized management of one or more portfolios to achieve strategic objectives is:

A. Project management
B. Portfolio management
C. Program management
D. Portfolio monitoring

Question 68: What is the main purpose of program periodic health checks?

A. To determine if the program manager will require some medicine
B. To recommend any changes in the current program, according to program sponsor's experience
C. To recommend changes in the program's performance and progress to assure program success
D. To assess a program's ongoing performance and progress toward the realization and sustainment of benefits

Question 69: Tim is a program manager and the company CEO approaches him and asks to see the primary document that was reviewed by the governance board when determining if the program would be authorized. What is the CEO asking Tim for?

A. Program charter
B. Program risk assessment
C. Program business case
D. Program roadmap

Question 70: Sandra is the program manager for her organization, who is currently working on the assessment of the strategic alignment of the program and its components within the intended goals of both the program and the organization. On which of the following program activities is Sandra working on?

A. Program governance reviews
B. Program governance practices
C. Program quality governance
D. Program closure

Question 71: As defined by PMI, all five program management performance domains interact with each other throughout the course of the program. What happens in some particular cases, on which you, as program manager, found that the interactions among the performance domains are similar and repetitive, between two separate programs?

A. The program sponsor has copied the scope and objectives of the other program
B. This cannot happen for any reason, so one of the programs must be canceled
C. The organization pursues similar programs
D. The organization is using the same strategic objectives for all its programs

Question 72: Mike is a program manager. He is currently working on stakeholder identification. As part of that process, interviews and focus groups have been completed. However, Mike would like to solicit feedback from a greater number of stakeholders. What tool could Mike use to accomplish his goal?

A. Surveys
B. Knowledge repositories
C. Historical information
D. Nominal group techniques

Question 73: Olivia is a program manager for a company dedicated to printing services. Olivia is currently working to identify and analyze stakeholder needs and manages expectations and communications to foster stakeholder support. On which of the following program management performance domains is Olivia currently working on?

A. Program risk management
B. Program strategy alignment
C. Program life cycle management
D. Program stakeholder engagement

Question 74: Regarding the organization program impact and its vulnerability to change, what should be the program managers' role within the organization?

A. Reject any organization changes
B. Prepare the organization to changes
C. Be a change motivator
D. As the champion for change

Question 75: Christopher is currently working on the program charter. He is currently describing what is going to be included in the program, and what is not part of the program. What is Christopher defining?

A. Assumptions
B. Timeline
C. Resources
D. Scope

Question 76: You are the program manager for your company, and currently you are executing a strategic program that will increase business financial benefits by 10% in comparison with the last year's Q1.

As the program execution requires the engagement of most stakeholders and a proper governance, you often need to perform an escalation process between the program management team, the program's steering committee, and other stakeholders. What type of escalation process is this?

A. Transversal escalation process
B. Team escalation process
C. Outside the program
D. Within the program

Question 77: All of the following skills and competences are commonly required by program managers except:

A. Integration skills
B. Stakeholder management skills
C. Communication skills
D. Stakeholder engagement skills

Question 78: Kevin is a program manager, who has been asked to develop a program which will improve culture at the company. He is currently conducting various activities which demonstrate how the program will deliver the desired organizational benefits. What phase is Kevin working within?

A. Program manager assignment
B. Program sponsor selection and financing
C. Program management plan development
D. Program initiation

Question 79: As it relates to stakeholder engagement, the program manager needs to bridge what gap in order to move the organization forward?

A. Stakeholder expectations and the benefits the program can provide
B. "As-is" state to "to be" state
C. Sponsor expectations and the benefits that the program can provide
D. "To-be" state to "as is" state

Question 80: Genghis is a program manager for a pet accessories company, who is currently working to identify and analyze stakeholder needs and manage expectations and communications to foster stakeholder support. On which domain should Genghis focus on?

A. Program stakeholder engagement
B. Portfolio stakeholder engagement
C. Project stakeholder management
D. Program stakeholder engagement

Question 81: During program execution, the outputs of program quality control are all of the following except:

A. Quality assurance audit findings
B. Quality control completed checklists and inspection reports
C. Quality change requests
D. Quality test reports or measurement results

Question 82: Stakeholder engagement can be expressed as what?

A. Direct and indirect communication between stakeholders and the corporate executives
B. Direct and indirect communication between stakeholders and the program team
C. Direct communication between the program manager and the program sponsor
D. Direct and indirect communication between stakeholders and the project team

Question 83: Sarah is a program manager. She is currently working on an activity to ensure that her program is producing the required capabilities and benefits on time. What activity is Sarah working on?

A. Program schedule management plan development
B. Program schedule planning
C. Program schedule control
D. Program master schedule development

Question 84: Jim is a program manager and is currently developing a plan to document funding schedules, the initial program budget, and contract payments. What is Jim working on?

A. Program management plan
B. Program financial monitoring
C. Program financial management plan
D. Program budget plan

Question 85: Potential customers are who?

A. The individual or organization that will use the new capabilities delivered by the program and derive anticipated benefits
B. The past and future customers who will be watching intently to see how well the program delivers the stated benefits
C. Those who perceive that they will achieve less benefit from or be disadvantaged by the program's activities
D. Product or service providers who are often affected by changing policies and procedures

Question 86: Kyle is a program manager. He is currently in the process of reviewing reports which contain high-level information on risks, changes, and changes under consideration. What type of report is Kyle reviewing?

A. Project status updates
B. Program forecast reports
C. Program benefits reports
D. Program performance reports

Question 87: Which one of the following roles has the responsibility to ensure that the program is run within the governance framework while managing the day-to-day program activities?

A. The program sponsor
B. The program manager
C. The program governance board
D. The program team

Question 88: As it relates to program quality control, who should determine the fitness for use of the benefits, product, or service delivered by the program?

A. Program management team
B. Program sponsor
C. Program manager
D. Those who receive it

Question 89: Ms Ivanov is a program manager for an agricultural company. Miss Ivanov is working hard to facilitate the design and implementation of effective governance to prepare documented descriptions of each program's governance frameworks, functions, and processes. On which deliverable is Ms Ivanov working on?

A. Program roadmap
B. Program governance plan
C. Program budget
D. Program stakeholder engagement plan

Question 90: The individual responsible to ensure that the program is run within the governance framework while managing day-to-day activities is who?

A. Program champion
B. Project manager
C. Program sponsor
D. Program manager

Question 91: Sarah is a program manager. She is currently in the process of tracking, monitoring, and controlling the program's funds and expenditures. What activity is Sarah conducting?

A. Component cost estimation
B. Program financial monitoring and control
C. Program financial closure
D. Program cost budgeting

Question 92: Joan is a program manager. One of Joan's program components is managed by Jill. Jill has asked Joan about the status of a vendor payment and believes it was due two weeks ago. Joan believes Jill is mistaken. Where can Joan find this information?

A. Program management plan
B. Program financial management plan
C. Program budget plan
D. Program charter

Question 93: Silvie is a program manager for a student training counselor firm. Silvie is currently working to consolidate coordinated benefits for her program. On which of the following program benefits management is Silvie working on?

A. Benefits delivery
B. Benefits transition
C. Benefits analysis and planning
D. Benefits identification

Question 94: The program delivery phase begins after what document is reviewed and formally approved?

A. Program management plan
B. Project management plan
C. Component management plan
D. Program plan

Question 95: Matías is a program manager for Performance Utility, an utility company. Recently, Performance Utility's top management was focused on making several changes to the organization's strategic plan, which impacted Marías' program directly.

In addition to this, Matías had to modify his whole program management plan and the benefits management plan. In order to complete the updates to reflect these changes, what is the next document Matías needs to update, in order to reflect the changes in the program management plan, and in consequence to align the new organization's strategic plan?

A. Program roadmap
B. Project roadmap
C. Program schedule
D. Project schedule

Question 96: The group or person who can formally close the program once all transitioning activities are complete is who?

A. Program sponsor or sponsoring organization
B. Program manager
C. Project manager
D. Operations

Question 97: Stacy is a program manager of a large program with diverse stakeholder groups. She is currently working with a group of stakeholders who are opposed to some recent program decisions. Stacy has been trying to diffuse the situation. Which of the following is a technique that Stacy might use with this stakeholder group?

A. Confrontation
B. Interviews
C. Questionnaires
D. Facilitated negotiation sessions

Question 98: The portfolio manager is who?

A. The person assigned by the performing organization to establish, balance, monitor, and control portfolio components to achieve strategic business objectives
B. The individual authorized by the performing organization to lead the team responsible for achieving program objectives
C. The person who provides resources and support for the program and is accountable for enabling success
D. The person assigned by the performing organization to lead the team that is responsible for achieving project objectives

Question 99: Why is it important to consider stakeholders who have a negative influence on the program?

A. Because they will need to be engaged as well in order to help them accept the benefits of the program
B. Stakeholders who have a negative influence on the program should not be considered
C. Only stakeholders who have a positive influence on the program should be considered, to help the program achieve the objectives earlier
D. Because when considering them, the program manager gives a sign of respect and can get benefits from them, as a return favor

Question 100: Ms Jones is a program manager for a telecommunication company. Ms Jones' team has recently found there is a new regulation promoted by the Senate that will have huge consequences on her current program. She has been notified that next week the Senate will vote for the new regulatory law. As part of the identified program stakeholders, she has the following stakeholder register:

■ Jennifer Cole: program sponsor: is the company Finance VP
■ Mario Minetti: external stakeholder, close friend of the President of Senate

From the options below, to whom, should she escalate this issue?

A. Mario Minetti
B. She should not escalate and solve the issue by herself
C. The President of Senate
D. Jennifer Cole

Question 101: Laura is a program manager for her company. Laura is currently working to identify and qualify benefits for her program. On which of the following program benefits management is Laura working on?

A. Benefits sustainment
B. Benefits delivery
C. Benefits identification
D. Benefits analysis and planning

Question 102: As it relates to stakeholder identification, what type of questions are recommended in order to best solicit stakeholder feedback?

A. Open ended questions
B. Multiple choice questions
C. True or false questions
D. Interview questions

Question 103: Managing projects, subsidiary programs, and program activities as a program to enhance the delivery of benefits by ensuring that the strategies and work plans of program components are responsively adapted to component outcomes, or to changes in the direction or strategies of the sponsoring organization is best defined as a:

A. Project
B. Program
C. Process
D. Portfolio

Question 104: Sarah is a program manager. She has developed a visual tool which identifies stakeholder needs, expectations, and influences. This visual tool contains information on interest level and power as well. What has Sarah created?

A. Stakeholder roadmap
B. Stakeholder engagement plan
C. Stakeholder register
D. Stakeholder map

Question 105: Ms. Wilson is program manager for an entertainment and media industry company. As part of her program management governance practices, she is ensuring that key risks and issues are escalated appropriately and resolved in a timely manner. Which one of the following practices best describes what Ms. Wilson is working on?

A. Effective risk and issue management
B. Program management
C. Stakeholder engagement
D. Escalation management

Question 106: Who is considered a core part of the program infrastructure and is responsible for supporting the management and coordination of the program and component work?

A. Program manager
B. Program sponsor
C. Program management office
D. Governance board

Question 107: Stakeholder engagement is conducted when?

A. Throughout the program life cycle
B. During program definition
C. During program benefits delivery
D. During program closure

Question 108: Paul is a program manager and is currently working on a deliverables-oriented hierarchical decomposition which encompasses the total scope of the program. What is Paul working on?

A. Program management plan
B. Program charter
C. Work breakdown structure
D. Program roadmap

Question 109: The program manager is selected during which subphase?

A. Program formulation
B. Program initiation
C. Program planning
D. Program definition

Question 110: Why is it often said that stakeholder engagement at the program level may be challenging?

A. Because not all stakeholders are often committed to the program
B. Because some stakeholders may view the program benefits as change
C. Because many stakeholders are not involved into the program
D. Because program managers do not communicate with stakeholders

Question 111: The output of program risk management transition is what?

A. Inputs to other organizational risk registers
B. Program risk register updates
C. Change requests
D. Contingency reserve and management reserve

Question 112: Organizational project management provides a framework:

A. In which portfolios are executed independently of other corporate activities
B. To how a program is structured and executed
C. In which portfolio, program, and project management practices are conducted independently to achieve strategic objectives
D. In which portfolio, program, and project management practices are integrated to achieve strategic objectives

Question 113: In order for a program manager to bridge the gap between the current state of the organization and the desired future state, the program manager should be familiar with which one of the following?

A. Operational standard operating procedures
B. Corporate communication strategies
C. Corporate organizational chart
D. Organizational change management

Question 114: Which of the following statements is TRUE about stakeholder engagement?

A. Stakeholder engagement can be only expressed as direct communication between program leaders
B. Engagement with the program team may be performed by people with different roles in the program and project teams
C. Stakeholder engagement can be only expressed as indirect communication between program leaders
D. Stakeholder engagement is only related to effective communication

Question 115: All of the following statements regarding change are correct except:

A. Project managers expect change and implement processes to keep change managed and controlled
B. Program managers expect change and implement processes to keep change managed and controlled
C. Programs are managed in a manner that accepts and adapts to change as necessary to optimize the delivery of benefits as the program's components deliver outcomes and/or outputs
D. Portfolio managers continuously monitor change in the broader internal and external environments

Question 116: Mary Ann is a program manager. She is currently in the process of collecting, measuring, and disseminating performance information and assessing overall program trends. What program delivery management activity is Mary Ann performing?

A. Program transition and benefits sustainment
B. Resource disposition
C. Program performance monitoring and control
D. Component transition

Question 117: Bill is in the early stages of a program and is working with his team and is asking them a series of questions including: What is the total length of the program? What will the end state look like and how will it benefit the organization? Based on Bill's line of questioning, what would you say Bill is working on?

A. Program management plan
B. Program business case
C. Program roadmap
D. Program charter

Question 118: Ms Dillon is the program manager for her organization, who just had a meeting with a stakeholder whose responsibility is to ensure program goals and planned benefits align with organizational strategic and operational goals.

According to this responsibility description, what is the main role of this stakeholder?

A. Project manager
B. Member of the program steering committee
C. Member of the program management office
D. Program sponsor

Question 119: Mary is a program manager. She is about to start the program stakeholder engagement process. Which of the following is not something Mary would need to do?

A. Track only internal stakeholders
B. Identify stakeholders
C. Study stakeholders
D. Categorize stakeholders

Question 120: Linda is a program manager. She is currently working on stakeholder identification. She has identified the program sponsor, program governance board, program team members, and herself. What term would Linda use to describe these stakeholders?

A. External stakeholders
B. Key program stakeholders
C. Primary stakeholders
D. Secondary stakeholders

Question 121: Danielle is a program manager. She has just completed an activity which has yielded outputs of component budget closures, program budget baseline updates, and corrective actions. What activity has Danielle just completed?

A. Component cost estimation
B. Program financial closure
C. Program cost budgeting
D. Program financial monitoring and control

Question 122: Programs use change management in what manner to adapt to the evolving environment?

A. Rearward-looking, proactive
B. Rearward-looking, reactive
C. Forward-looking, proactive
D. Forward-looking, reactive

Question 123: Program managers are likely to interact with many roles. Which of the following is the least likely?

A. Program team
B. External stakeholders
C. CEO
D. Sponsors

Question 124: When does stakeholder engagement occur during a program?

A. During program definition only
B. During fixed intervals such as the stakeholder management activity
C. Only during program strategy alignment
D. Continuously and throughout the duration of the program

Question 125: During program planning, the outputs of the program financial management planning are all of the following except?

A. Program cost estimation assumptions
B. Program financial management plan
C. Initial program budget
D. Program funding schedules

Question 126: Program information archiving and transition is what?

A. Collection and archiving of program and component records and documentation for use by other elements of the organization
B. Important to release resources as the program is being closed
C. Formally closes out each agreement of the program after ensuring compliance
D. Collection and archiving of portfolio and component records and documentation for use by other elements of the organization

Question 127: Jana is the program manager for his organization, who just had a meeting with a stakeholder whose responsibility is to provide governance support for the program to include oversight, control, integration, and decision-making functions.

According to this responsibility description, what is the main role of this stakeholder?

A. Project manager
B. Member of the program management office
C. Program sponsor
D. Member of the program steering committee

Question 128: Which of the following phases includes program activities required for coordinating and managing the actual delivery of the program?

A. Program definition phase
B. Program delivery phase
C. Program closure phase
D. Program benefits management phase

Question 129: During program benefits delivery, value delivery focuses on:

A. Ensuring programs and projects are selected, prioritized, and staffed according to the organization's strategic plan for realizing desired organizational value
B. Ensuring the stakeholder engagement plan is synchronized with the program communication management plan
C. Ensuring the linkage of enterprise and program plans, defining, maintaining, and validating the program value proposition, and aligning program and enterprise operations management
D. Ensuring that the program delivers the intended benefits

Question 130: During which of the following program initiation activities are response strategies and plans developed?

A. Program sponsor selection and financing
B. Program manager assignment
C. Initial risk assessment
D. Program budget development

Question 131: Paul is a program manager. He has just finished an activity which has yielded an output of quality control completed checklists. Which activity has Paul just completed?

A. Program quality control
B. Program quality assurance
C. Change management
D. Program quality planning

Question 132: As it relates to stakeholder engagement, which of the following is not an area that is impacted by stakeholder issues and concerns?

A. Costs
B. Schedules
C. Assumptions
D. Priorities

Question 133: What does it mean that program and project management functions are collaborative?

A. That both program and project managers work together for the success of the portfolio on which their respective components belongs to
B. That program manager works for the success of his program activities, and so it ensures the success of the related projects
C. That project managers work for the program success and program managers work for project success
D. That both program and project managers work together to define strategies for pursuing program goals

Question 134: You are the program manager for your organization, and you want to align the expected program advantages with the organization's goals and objectives. Which performance domain should you focus on?

A. Program strategy alignment
B. Program life cycle management
C. Program benefits engaement
D. Program stakeholder engagement

Question 135: Tyler is a program manager. Recently, he received some feedback from the program sponsor that he felt his risk management process wasn't leading to the type of increase in opportunities he would expect to see. Tyler didn't feel that this was his responsibility. What would you tell Tyler?

A. I would tell Tyler that the program is not responsible for generating opportunities
B. I would tell Tyler that the responsibility of generating opportunities is at the project level
C. I would tell Tyler that the program is responsible for managing threats, but that opportunities don't increase over the length of the program
D. I would tell Tyler that the program should generate opportunities over time by using common innovative management methods

Question 136: Which program initiation activity involves comparing the candidate program to other organizational initiatives to determine the priority of the program?

A. Program sponsor selection and financing
B. Program manager assignment
C. Initial risk assessment
D. Estimating scope, resources, and cost

Question 137: Emma is the program manager for an entertainment company, who had recently changed the organizational strategy and now, her program is not aligned with it, so she is now performing several activities in order to get the program terminated earlier or transitioned to another program. On which of the following program life cycle phases is Emma working on?

A. Program execution phase
B. Program closure phase
C. Program definition phase
D. Program delivery phase

Question 138: You are the program manager for your company and you've just been notified that your major stakeholder has been replaced by a new Operational Manager, who is deeply involved into your program and previously performed as a major consultant during the initiating and planning phases. This new stakeholder is also proposing additional deliverables. Which one of the following documents, MAY YOU NOT NEED to update, regarding the program stakeholder engagement deliverables?

A. Stakeholder management plan
B. Stakeholder register
C. Stakeholder map
D. Stakeholder engagement plan

Question 139: Program activities and integration management are concerned with collectively using resources, knowledge, and skills to execute the program. This process also involves making decisions about all of the following except which one?

A. Changes due to uncertainty and complexity of the program scope
B. Interdependencies among components
C. Stakeholder considerations
D. Coordination of work to meet the program objectives

Question 140: Christine is a program manager. She is currently considering the stakeholders ability to influence the outcome of the program as well as the degree of support or opposition to the program benefits. As a result of this effort, what is Christine likely to produce?

A. Stakeholder register
B. Risk management plan
C. Stakeholder management plan
D. Stakeholder engagement plan

Question 141: Beth is a program manager. She has just completed an activity which has yielded outputs of proposal evaluation criteria and request for quote. What activity has Beth just completed?

A. Program procurement planning
B. Program procurement
C. Program procurement administration
D. Program procurement closure

Question 142: As it relates to program risk analysis, what type of techniques are useful to support program management decisions?

A. Neither qualitative nor quantitative
B. Qualitative only
C. Both qualitative and quantitative
D. Quantitative only

Question 143: Kevin is a program manager. He is currently in the process of disseminating performance information and assessing overall program trends. What is Kevin doing?

A. Program performance monitoring and control
B. Component transition
C. Forecasts
D. Program performance reporting

Question 144: During program formulation, the sponsoring organization will assign someone to what role to oversee the program?

A. Project stakeholder
B. Program stakeholder
C. Program champion
D. Program sponsor

Question 145: Mrs. Rodriguez is a program manager for a rugs and carpets manufacturing company, who is working with several highly trained experienced professionals who are providing their expertise in applying program governance practices to provide oversight, support, and decision-making capability to Mrs. Rodriguez's program.

From the following options, these professionals are part of which program governance group?

A. The program stakeholders
B. The program governance board
C. The steering committee
D. The program management office

Question 146: Program steering committee is consulted to determine if the program can be all of the following except which one?

A.   If the program will remain open to support operational management of the resulting benefits
B.   A program has met all desired benefits and that all transition work has been completed within the component transition
C.   There is another program or sustaining activity that will oversee the ongoing benefits
D.   There may be work required to transition the resources, responsibilities, knowledge, and lessons learned to another sustaining entity

Question 147: Barry is a program manager and is currently documenting program governance, risks and issues, and program components. What document is Barry working on?

A.   Program risk assessment
B.   Program charter
C.   Program business case
D.   Program roadmap

Question 148: There are multiple ways to collect information related to stakeholders, including all of the following except:

A.   Historical information
B.   Individual interviews, questionnaires, and surveys
C.   Focus groups
D.   Looking up the individual on social media

Question 149: Beth is a program manager. She is currently working on stakeholder identification. She has identified suppliers, competitors, governmental regulatory agencies, and affected organizations as stakeholders. What term would Beth use to describe these stakeholders?

A.   External stakeholders
B.   Primary stakeholders
C.   Key program stakeholders
D.   Secondary stakeholders

Question 150: You are the program manager for your organization, and you and your team are considering the expectation of program benefits delivery for each stakeholder. Which of the following planning activities are you currently working on?

A.   Risk management planning
B.   Resources management planning
C.   Program management planning
D.   Stakeholder analysis and engagement planning

Question 151: Santiago is a program manager for a specialty or rare pets company, which now is focusing to develop a new inventory software suite with several functionalities for sales, veterinarian, inventory, financial and research.

Santiago has just identified its major stakeholders for the program, and he had already listed her in the stakeholder register. Before Santiago can start analyzing the stakeholder register, what does he need to do first?

A. Analyze stakeholder register
B. Review stakeholder register
C. Categorize stakeholder register
D. Prioritize stakeholder register

Question 152: Why is it often said that relatedness in programs differs from portfolios?

A. Programs are related directly with projects but portfolios are not directly related with projects
B. In programs the achievement of the intended benefits is dependent on the delivery of all components in the scope of the program. In a portfolio the work included depends on the portfolio owner
C. Programs are related to portfolios, but portfolios cannot be related to programs
D. Different programs are related to each other in the same portfolio, but there are no relatedness that can be established between different portfolios within the same organization

Question 153: Program procurement closure outputs do not include:

A. Contract closeout reports
B. Inputs to other organizational risk registers
C. Updates to lessons learned
D. Closed contracts

Question 154: You are the program manager for your organization, and you and your team are considering the ability to influence the outcome of the program for each stakeholder. Which of the following planning activities are you currently working on?

A. Stakeholder analysis and engagement planning
B. Risk management planning
C. Resources management planning
D. Program management planning

Question 155: Stephanie is a program manager and has decided that it is necessary to initiate a new program component in order to conduct the integration efforts of several components. Stephanie believes that if she doesn't do this that the components will not produce the expected benefits. How would you advise Stephanie?

A. I would tell Stephanie that what she is doing is correct. Sometimes it is necessary to initiate a new program to integrate multiple components

B. I would tell Stephanie that what she is doing is incorrect. If she is trying to integrate multiple components, she needs to initiate multiple components

C. I would tell Stephanie that what she is doing is correct. It is always necessary to initiate a new component to integrate other components

D. I would tell Stephanie that what she is doing is incorrect. Another component should not be introduced

Question 156: Programs function similarly to projects in that the program is _____?

A. Approved
B. Delivered
C. Opened
D. Closed

Question 157: Tina is a program manager. She is currently in the process of evaluating stakeholder engagement. She is currently looking at each stakeholder's rate of communication with the program team. What type of stakeholder engagement metric is this considered?

A. Communication metric
B. Primary stakeholder engagement metric
C. Residual stakeholder engagement metric
D. Secondary stakeholder engagement metric

Question 158: Sandra is a program manager for a health research laboratory. Sandra is currently working to maintain a benefits register for her program. On which of the following program benefits management is Sandra working on?

A. Benefits sustainment
B. Benefits analysis and planning
C. Benefits transition
D. Benefits delivery

Question 159: Olivia is a program manager. A corrective action was recently presented, which exceeds program-level thresholds. What should Olivia do?

A. Olivia has the ultimate decision of rejecting or approving the corrective action
B. The request should be presented to the program governance board for approval
C. The request should be presented to the program champion for approval
D. The request should be presented to the program sponsor for approval

Question 160: Which of the following statement is NOT TRUE regarding the initiation of a program?

A. To pursue new goals, objectives, or strategies
B. To accomplish changes upon organizational strategic objectives
C. To group common new and ongoing projects related between each other
D. To hide failures and errors as a result of ongoing projects and deliverables

Question 161: Who should be responsible for defining the types of changes that a program manager would be independently authorized to approve?

A. The program steering committee
B. The program manager
C. The program team
D. The program sponsor

Question 162: You are the program manager for your organization, and currently you are preparing yourself for a meeting you will have today with him.

In your stakeholder register, you found this stakeholder has a high level of authority and high level of concern.

From the options below, which one is the best strategy you can use with this stakeholder in order to engage him?

A. Manage closely
B. Monitor
C. Keep satisfied
D. Keep informed

Question 163: You are the program manager for your company, and you are working on a state of the art technology program to develop a new inventory software solution for the company. Your main stakeholder and primary client who will directly be affected by the program, Juan Jose, is the operation manager for the company. He is angrily arguing with you, because you are asking him to provide you with new information you need to update your list of stakeholders and opinions of the programs.

According to Juan Jose's opinion, all stakeholders' engagement information was already provided and there is no need to update it. What will be your arguments opposed to Juan Jose's way of thinking?

A. Juan Jose is right, and you need to apologize
B. Juan Jose may be right, and you need to listen him
C. Juan Jose is completely wrong, and he needs to provide with an update
D. Juan Jose is partially wrong, and you need to negotiate with him

Question 164: Ms. Levi is the program manager for a flower exportation company and she wants to evaluate how the outputs delivered by the various components within the program contribute overall to the program's utility. Which performance domain should Ms. Levi focus on?

A. Program benefits management
B. Program strategy alignment
C. Program life cycle management
D. Program stakeholder engagement

Question 165: How is the program budgetary process usually being facilitated to a degree necessary to support the approved business case?

A. By the program governance
B. By the customers
C. By the program sponsor
D. By the financial department

Question 166: You are the program manager for your organization, and currently you are preparing yourself for a meeting you will have today with him.

In your stakeholder register, you found this stakeholder has a low level of authority and high level of concern.

From the options below, which one is the best strategy you can use with this stakeholder in order to engage him?

A. Monitor
B. Keep informed
C. Keep satisfied
D. Manage closely

Question 167: Tools used by the program manager to appropriately engage stakeholders include all of the following except:

A. Strong communication skills
B. Time management skills
C. Negotiation skills
D. Conflict resolution skills

Question 168: As part of stakeholder analysis and engagement planning, which of the following is not an aspect which is considered for each stakeholder?

A. Organizational culture and acceptance of change
B. Attitudes about the program and its sponsors
C. Governmental regulations
D. Degree of support or opposition to the program benefits

Question 169: John is a program manager. He is currently in the process of updating the program master schedule. As he is doing this, he is noticing that some individual project schedules need to be altered. Which should John do?

A. John should have the individual project managers manage their schedules independent of the program
B. John should only be concerned with the program schedule and doesn't have to worry about individual project schedules
C. John should direct the changes to the individual project schedules to maintain an accurate and up-to-date program master schedule
D. John should not make the individual project schedules change. He should adapt the program master schedule to best fit the project schedules.

Question 170: Will is a program manager. He is currently in the process of setting up pre-negotiated contracts, blanket purchase agreements, and qualified seller lists for program components. Which activity is Will performing?

A. Program procurement contract administration
B. Program procurement administration
C. Program procurement closure
D. Program procurement

10.3 Answer Key for Practice Test One

1. D. When working with roles and responsibilities for required program-level quality assurance and quality control activities, Zhenzhen is working with program quality governance, which is part of program governance practices. Refer to Section 6.1.7/Page 74 of the Standard.
2. D. Refer to Section 5.3 of the Standard.

3. A. Refer to Section 7.1.2 Program Definition Phase of the Standard.

4. D. Refer to Section 5.1 Program Stakeholder Identification of the Standard.

5. C. As part of the stakeholder analysis and engagement planning activities, organizational culture and acceptance of change for each stakeholder are taken into consideration. Refer to Section 5.3/Page 64 of the Standard.

6. A. Refer to Section 5.4 Program Stakeholder Engagement of the Standard.

7. C. A framework is a supporting structure, so the program governance framework may be able to provide practices for effective decision-making that can ensure the program is managed appropriately. Refer to Section 6.1/Page 67 of the Standard.

8. A. Refer to Section 8.2.2.1 of the Standard.

9. A. As part of the stakeholder analysis and engagement planning activities, degree of support or opposition to the program benefits for each stakeholder is taken into consideration. Refer to Section 5.3/Page 64 of the Standard.

10. C. Refer to Section 7.2.2.3 of the Standard.

11. C. Refer to Section 1.9 Role of the Program Management office of the Standard.

12. A. Refer to Section 7.1.3 of the Standard.

13. C. The program manager should understand the motivations of each stakeholder who could attempt to alter the course of the program. Refer to Section 5.1/Page 59 of the Standard.

14. A. Refer to Section 8.2.7 of the Standard.

15. C. Program life cycle management is the performance domain that manages program activities required to facilitate effective program definition, program delivery, and program closure. Refer to Section 7.1/Page 89 of the Standard.

16. B. Refer to Section 8.2.2.2 of the Standard.

17. B. Refer to Section 8.2.9 of the Standard.

18. A. On this question the word "benefit" has been replaced by a synonym. So program benefits alignments is the right option. Refer to Section 4.1/Page 43 of the Standard.

19. B. The approval of the initiation of a new program component generally includes ensuring the communication of critical component-related information to key stakeholders. Refer to Section 6.1.11/Page 77 of the Standard.

20. D. Program charter and program business case are developed and approved during the program definition phase. Refer to Section 6.1.3/Page 72 of the Standard.

21. B. Refer to Section 3.3 of the Standard.

22. A. Refer to Section 7.1.2.1 of the Standard.

23. B. Refer to Section 8.2.1 Program Change Monitoring and Controlling of the Standard.

24. C. Refer to Section 1.2.2 Portfolio Definition of the Standard.

25. B. This statement is the best description to differentiate both concepts. Refer to Section 5.1/Page 57 of the Standard.

26. B. Refer to Section 1.1 Purpose of the Standard.
27. B. Refer to Section 5.1 of the Standard.
28. C. Refer to Section 5.1 Program Stakeholder Identification of the Standard.
29. D. Refer to Section 8.1.2 Program Planning Phase Activities of the Standard.
30. C. Stakeholder engagement is a continuous program activity. Refer to Section 5.4/Page 64 of the Standard.
31. B. This option best describes the given statement. Refer to Section 5.1/Page 57 of the Standard.
32. C. When working to monitor components, Olivia is working on Benefits delivery phase. Refer to Section 4.3/Page 51 of the Standard.
33. B. Refer to Section 8.1.2.7 of the Standard.
34. D. Refer to Section 1.2.2 Project Definition of the Standard.
35. A. Refer to Section 8.2.8 of the Standard.
36. B. Refer to Section 5.1 Program Stakeholder Identification of the Standard.
37. C. Refer to Section 7.1.1 Program Life Cycle Phases Overview of the Standard.
38. B. Program benefits management defines, creates, maximizes, and delivers the benefits provided by the program. Refer to Section 2.1/Page 25 of the Standard.
39. D. Refer to Section 5.5 Program Stakeholder Communications of the Standard.
40. B. Refer to Section 1.4 The Relationship among Portfolio, Program, and Project Management of the Standard.
41. D. Refer to Section 8.2.8.2 of the Standard.
42. A. Refer to Section 5.3 of the Standard.
43. A. On this question the word "benefit" has been replaced by a synonym. So program benefits alignments is the right option. Refer to Section 4.1/Page 43 of the Standard.
44. A. Refer to Section 8.2.6.1 of the Standard.
45. B. Refer to Section 7.2.2.3 of the Standard.
46. D. Refer to Section 5.4 of the Standard.
47. B. This is one of the primary roles of the program manager. Refer to Section 5.4/Page 64 of the Standard.
48. B. The program management office facilitates the governance practices. Refer to Section 6.2.3/Page 82 of the Standard.
49. C. Refer to Section 1.3 What Is Program Management of the Standard.
50. A. Refer to Section 7.1.4 Program Closure Phase of the Standard.
51. C. Program delivery phase consists of program activities to produce the intended results of each component in accordance with the program management plan. Refer to Section 7.1.1/Page 90 of the Standard.
52. C. Stakeholder engagement is often expressed as direct and indirect communication among the stakeholders and the program's leader teams. Refer to Section 5.1/Page 57 of the Standard.
53. C. Refer to Section 8.3.2 Program Information Archiving and Transition of the Standard.
54. B. Refer to Section 4.2 Benefits Analysis and Planning of the Standard.

55. D. Refer to Section 8.2.9 of the Standard.
56. B. The actions described on the text correspond to the expected content of a document when preparing a benefits management plan. Refer to Section 4.2.1/Page 50 of the Standard.
57. A. Refer to Section 5.0 Program Stakeholder Engagement of the Standard.
58. C. Refer to Section 5.0 Program Stakeholder Engagement of the Standard.
59. C. Refer to Section 7.2 of the Standard.
60. C. Refer to Section 5.1 of the Standard.
61. A. Refer to Section 8.2.8.1 of the Standard.
62. A. All five domains interact with each other with varying degrees of intensity. Refer to Section 2.2/Page 25 of the Standard.
63. A. This is the best description possible on how an operational activity may be part of a program. Refer to Section 1.2.2/Page 7 of the Standard.
64. D. Refer to Section 6.0 Program Governance of the Standard.
65. D. Refer to Section 8.2.3.2 of the Standard.
66. B. Refer to Section 6 of the Standard.
67. D. Refer to Sections 3.2 and 3.3 of the Standard.
68. C. Refer to Section 8.3.1 of the Standard.
69. D. Refer to Section 8.2.3 of the Standard.
70. C. Escalation process within the program is performed between component teams, the program management team, and the program steering committee. Refer to Section 6.1.6/Page 73 of the Standard.
71. C. Justification describes why the program is important and what does it achieve. Refer to Section 7.1.2/Page 93 of the Standard.
72. C. Refer to Section 7.2.2.3 of the Standard.
73. B. When working to report benefits, Jana is working on Benefits delivery phase. Refer to Section 4.3/Page 51 of the Standard.
74. D. When working to monitor the performance of benefits, Cristina is working on Benefits sustainment phase. Refer to Section 4.5/Page 55 of the Standard.
75. B. Refer to Section 8.3.4 Program Resource Transition of the Standard.
76. C. Refer to Section 5.4 Program Stakeholder Engagement of the Standard.
77. B. Refer to Section 5.3 Program Stakeholder Engagement Planning of the Standard.
78. D. This is the best and accurate reason of collaborative work between program and portfolio management activities. Refer to Section 1.4.2/Page 12 of the Standard.
79. A. Refer to Section 8.1 of the Standard.
80. C. Refer to Section 1.4 The Relationship among Portfolio, Program, and Project Management of the Standard.
81. C. Since the program is facing some changes proposed by Kira's top executives, as a program manager Alexander cannot be solely responsible, and neither can recommend or reject the proposed changes. In this case, Alexander will have to assess whether the risks associated with potential changes are acceptable or desirable. Refer to Section 6.1.8/Page 74 of the Standard.

82. C. The actions described in the text correspond to the expected content of a document when preparing a benefits management plan. Refer to Section 4.2.1/Page 50 of the Standard.
83. D. Refer to Section 7.1.2 of the Standard.
84. C. When working to establish benefits management plan, Fernando is working on Benefits analysis and planning phase. Refer to Section 4.2/Page 48 of the Standard.
85. D. Refer to Section 8.1.2 Program Planning Phase Activities of the Standard.
86. B. Refer to Section 6.2.6 of the Standard.
87. D. Refer to Section 5.2 of the Standard.
88. D. Refer to Section 5.3 of the Standard.
89. D. Refer to Section 7.2.2 Program Integration Management of the Standard.
90. D. Refer to Section 6.0 Program Governance of the Standard.
91. B. Refer to Section 5.1 of the Standard.
92. C. The program governance plan may be a stand-alone document or a subsection of the program management plan. Refer to Section 6.1.1/Page 67 of the Standard.
93. C. This is the scope definition for a program. Refer to Section 1.4/Page 11 of the Standard.
94. A. Refer to Section 8.2.4 of the Standard.
95. B. Refer to Section 8.2.5 of the Standard.
96. D. Refer to Section 5.0 Program Stakeholder Engagement of the Standard.
97. A. Refer to Section 5.4 of the Standard.
98. A. Refer to Section 8.3 Program Closure Phase Activities of the Standard.
99. C. Refer to Section 7.1.2 Program Definition Phase of the Standard.
100. C. Refer to Section 1.2 What is a Program of the Standard.
101. A. To evaluate the program risks is not a purpose of the program definition phase. Refer to Section 7.1.2/Page 91 of the Standard.
102. A. Refer to Section 8.1.2 Program Planning Phase Activities of the Standard.
103. B. After benefits register update you may arrange some workshops with critical stakeholders to review, define, and get approval from them on the KPIs and other measures that will be used to monitor program performance. Refer to Section 4.2.3/Page 50 of the Standard.
104. A. Refer to Section 8.3.2 of the Standard.
105. B. Refer to Section 8.1.2.5 of the Standard.
106. D. On portfolio review processes, the program scope and objectives are evaluated to see if they are still aligned with the organization's strategy. Refer to Section 2.3/Page 26 of the Standard.
107. A. When decision-making stakeholders are provided with adequate information, they can involve particular stakeholders to help the program move forward. Refer to Section 5.5/Page 66 of the Standard.
108. B. Refer to Section 1.5 The Relationship among Organizational Strategy, Program Management, and Operations Management of the Standard.
109. C. Refer to Section 8.2.7.1 Program Resource Management of the Standard.

110. D. Refer to Section 7.2.2 Program Integration Management of the Standard.
111. B. Programs function similarly to projects in that the benefits are delivered. Refer to Section 7.1/Page 89 of the Standard.
112. A. Refer to Section 5.2 of the Standard.
113. B. Member of the program steering committee's typical responsibilities includes providing capable governance resources to oversee and monitor program uncertainty and complexity related to achieving benefits delivery. Refer to Section 6.2.2/Page 81 of the Standard.
114. B. When a stakeholder has a high level of authority and low level of concern, he needs to be kept satisfied. Refer to Section 5.2/Page 62 of the Standard.
115. D. The milestones signal the achievement and delivery of incremental benefits. Refer to Section 4.3.1/Page 52 of the Standard.
116. A. Refer to Section 7.1.2 Program Definition Phase of the Standard.
117. B. This is the correct relationship between program benefits management and program roadmap. Refer to Section 4.2.2/Page 50 of the Standard.
118. D. Refer to Section 7.2.2 Program Integration Management of the Standard.
119. C. When working with program resource needs and organizational commitments in addition to capabilities to fulfilling them, Lucy is working with Program governance reviews. Refer to Section 6.1.9/Page 75 of the Standard.
120. A. Refer to Section 8.1.2.7 of the Standard.
121. C. Refer to Section 5.1 Program Stakeholder Identification of the Standard.
122. B. This stakeholder feels threatened by the changes of the program, so it is better to work closely to engage him to the program, so he can soon start feeling comfortable. Refer to Section 5.1/Page 59 of the Standard.
123. A. Refer to Section 5.2 of the Standard.
124. A. Program sponsor's typical responsibilities include removing barriers and obstacles to program success. Refer to Section 6.2.1/Page 80 of the Standard.
125. A. The program manager needs to bridge the gap between the current state and the intended future state, driven by the intended benefits on the program's outcomes. Refer to Section 5.1/Page 59 of the Standard.
126. C. On this question the word "benefit" has been replaced by a synonym. So program benefits alignments is the right option. Refer to Section 4.1/Page 43 of the Standard.
127. B. Program governance ensures that any program within its area of authority defines its vision and goals in order to effectively support those of the organization. Refer to Section 6.1.2/Page 71 of the Standard.
128. C. Refer to Section 8.1.2.9 of the Standard.
129. B. Refer to Section 5 of the Standard.
130. D. When working to derive and prioritize benefits, Alexandra is working on Benefits analysis and planning phase. Refer to Section 4.2/Page 48 of the Standard.
131. D. Refer to Section 2.5 Program and Project Distinctions of the Standard.
132. C. Refer to Section 2.5 Program and Project Distinctions of the Standard.

133. A. Questionnaires and surveys help solicit feedback from a greater number of stakeholders. Refer to Section 5.2/Page 62 of the Standard.
134. C. Refer to Section 8.1.1.8 of the Standard.
135. D. Refer to Section 8.2.5 Program Procurement Management of the Standard.
136. D. The program governance participants are the ones uniquely positioned to monitor the progress of programs in their pursuit of organizational goals. Refer to Section 6.1.5/Page 72 of the Standard.
137. A. When working with minimum quality criteria and standards to be applied to all components of the program, Thomas is working with program quality governance, which is part of program governance practices. Refer to Section 6.1.7/Page 74 of the Standard.
138. D. Refer to Section 8.2.2.2 of the Standard.
139. A. Stakeholders have a positive or negative impact on the outcome of a program. Refer to Section 5.1/Page 57 of the Standard.
140. B. Refer to Section 5.3 of the Standard.
141. B. Refer to Section 8.1.2.5 of the Standard.
142. D. Refer to Section 7.2.2 Program Integration Management of the Standard.
143. A. Refer to Section 8.2.3 Program Financial Management of the Standard.
144. A. Program monitoring, reporting, and controlling is an activity related to known program risks, their response plans, and escalation criteria. Refer to Section 6.1.5/Page 72 of the Standard.
145. C. Refer to Section 7.2.2 Program Integration Management of the Standard.
146. D. Refer to Section 8.1.1.3 of the Standard.
147. A. Refer to Section 7.1.2 Program Definition Phase of the Standard.
148. D. Refer to Section 8.2.5 of the Standard.
149. A. Refer to Section 3.2 of the Standard.
150. B. Refer to Section 5.2 Program Stakeholder Analysis of the Standard.
151. A. It is recommended to perform program periodic health checks periodically to assure the realization and sustainment of program benefits. Refer to Section 6.1.10/Page 76 of the Standard.
152. A. Refer to Section 7.1.1 Program Life Cycle Phases Overview of the Standard.
153. D. Program life cycle management manages program activities required to facilitate effective program definition, program delivery, and program closure. Refer to Section 2.1/Page 25 of the Standard.
154. A. Refer to Section 5.1 Program Stakeholder Identification of the Standard.
155. A. Program management is what guarantees the achievement of complex initiatives to support organizational strategies. Refer to Section 1.5/Page 14 of the Standard.
156. C. Refer to Sections 3.2 and 3.3 of the Standard.
157. A. Refer to Section 8.1.2.5 of the Standard.
158. A. This statement is true. Refer to Section 4.1/Page 43 of the Standard.
159. B. This is the best description of program stakeholder engagement. Refer to Section 5.1/Page 57 of the Standard.

160. C. Refer to Section 5.1 Program Stakeholder Identification of the Standard.
161. B. Refer to Section 8.1.2.12 of the Standard.
162. B. Refer to Section 8.2.8.2 of the Standard.
163. D. As part of the stakeholder analysis and engagement planning activities, relevant phases applicable to stakeholders' specific engagement for each stakeholder are taken into consideration. Refer to Section 5.3/Page 64 of the Standard.
164. C. Refer to Section 8.2.9 of the Standard.
165. D. When a stakeholder has a low level of authority and low level of concern, he needs to be monitored. Refer to Section 5.2/Page 62 of the Standard.
166. A. These are the skills recommended to a program manager, to help defuse stakeholder opposition to the program. Refer to Section 5.4/Page 65 of the Standard.
167. A. Refer to Section 5.3 of the Standard.
168. C. The program manager is the one responsible to ensure that the program team understands and abides by the governance procedures and the underlying governance principles. Refer to Section 6.1/Page 67 of the Standard.
169. A. Refer to Section 7.1.2 Program Definition Phase of the Standard.
170. A. Program manager's typical responsibilities include overseeing program conformance to governance policies and processes. Refer to Section 6.2.4/Page 83 of the Standard.

10.4 Answer Key for Practice Test Two

1. B. Communications between program managers and stakeholders take place frequently. Refer to Section 5.1/Page 57 of the Standard.
2. D. All program outputs should be integrated to the program as a whole. Refer to Section 4.3.1/Page 52 of the Standard.
3. C. Refer to Section 7.1.3.2 of the Standard.
4. D. This is what the program benefits management establishes. Refer to Section 4.2.2/Page 50 of the Standard.
5. A. Refer to Section 8.2.3 of the Standard.
6. A. The program manager effectively guides the program formulation activity and facilitates the development of the required outputs. Refer to Section 7.1.2/Page 91 of the Standard.
7. A. Vision describes what is the end state and how will it benefit the organization. Refer to Section 7.1.2/Page 93 of the Standard.
8. D. Refer to Section 8.1.2.2 of the Standard.
9. C. When working with any required program-level quality assurance or quality control activities, Yong is working with program quality governance, which is part of program governance practices. Refer to Section 6.1.7/Page 74 of the Standard.

10. B. The listed activities are part of the stakeholder register activities, so, once all major stakeholders are listed in the stakeholder register, the program manager will categorize them in order to start analyzing them. Refer to Section 5.2/ Page 62 of the Standard.
11. A. Refer to Section 5.5 Program Stakeholder Communications of the Standard.
12. C. Programs function similarly to projects in that the program is defined. Refer to Section 7.1/Page 89 of the Standard.
13. D. The stakeholder "supports" training, they don't necessarily provide it. Refer to Section 5.1/Page 57 of the Standard.
14. D. Since Ethan and his team are working on prioritizing and evaluating investments aligned with organization's strategic planning, they are defining the scope and resources for the organization's program. Refer to Section 2.3/ Page 26 of the Standard.
15. A. The benefits register is updated during the benefits analysis and planning phase. Refer to Section 4.2.3/Page 50 of the Standard.
16. D. Refer to Section 1.2 What is a Program of the Standard.
17. A. Refer to Section 6.0 Program Governance of the Standard.
18. A. This means that both the individuals responsible for program governance and program management need to work together as a team to achieve the desired goals. Refer to Section 6.2/Page 78 of the Standard.
19. C. Refer to Section 7.1.2 Program Definition Phase of the Standard.
20. A. The program manager is the one responsible for the whole program success, and this includes that the program benefits are aligned with the organization's strategic plan. Refer to Section 1.4.1/Page 12 of the Standard.
21. C. Refer to Section 7.1.2 Program Definition Phase of the Standard.
22. C. Refer to Section 7.2.2.3 of the Standard.
23. B. These are the main tools used in program management. Refer to Section 1.3/Page 8 of the Standard.
24. B. Refer to Section 6.1.1 Program Governance Plan of the Standard.
25. C. Refer to Section 5.4 Program Stakeholder Engagement of the Standard.
26. A. The vision and goals of the organization provide the basis for strategic mandates that drive the definition of most programs. Refer to Section 6.1.2/ Page 71 of the Standard.
27. B. Refer to Section 7.2.2 Program Integration Management of the Standard.
28. C. The approval of the initiation of a new program component generally includes ensuring the availability of resources to perform the component. Refer to Section 6.1.11/Page 77 of the Standard.
29. B. Refer to Section 1.4 The Relationship among Portfolio, Program, and Project Management of the Standard.
30. B. Refer to Section 8.2.9 Program Schedule Monitoring and Controlling of the Standard.
31. B. Refer to Section 8.2.2.1 of the Standard.
32. C. Refer to Section 3.1 of the Standard.

33. A. Refer to Section 7.1.2 Program Definition Phase of the Standard.
34. D. Refer to Section 7.2.2 Program Integration Management of the Standard.
35. C. Refer to Section 8.2.8.2 of the Standard.
36. B. Refer to Section 8.3.1 of the Standard.
37. D. Since the documents described correspond to the program charter and the program business case, approval of the business case and program charter occur in the program definition. Refer to Section 6.1.3/Page 72 of the Standard.
38. C. On this question the word "benefit" has been replaced by a synonym. So program benefits alignments is the right option. Refer to Section 4.1/Page 43 of the Standard.
39. C. Refer to Section 8.2.4 Program Information Management of the Standard.
40. C. Refer to Section 8.1.2.12 of the Standard.
41. C. Refer to Section 8.1.2 Program Planning Phase Activities of the Standard.
42. D. Refer to Section 8.1.2.3 of the Standard.
43. A. Refer to Section 1.7 Role of the Program Manager of the Standard.
44. A. Refer to Section 2.5 Program and Project Distinctions of the Standard.
45. B. Program monitoring, reporting, and controlling is an activity related to operational status and progress of programs, components, and related activities. Refer to Section 6.1.5/Page 72 of the Standard.
46. D. Refer to Section 8.2.2 Program Communications Management of the Standard.
47. A. Refer to Section 8.2.6 of the Standard.
48. D. As part of the stakeholder analysis and engagement planning activities, attitudes about the program and its sponsors for each stakeholder are taken into consideration. Refer to Section 5.3/Page 64 of the Standard.
49. D. The stakeholder register has the information required to establish the communication and approach strategy for each stakeholder. Refer to Section 5.5/Page 66 of the Standard.
50. C. Refer to Section 8.2.7 of the Standard.
51. B. Refer to Section 7.2.2 Program Integration Management of the Standard.
52. B. Refer to Section 8.2.6 of the Standard.
53. C. Refer to Section 7.1.2 Program Definition Phase of the Standard.
54. A. Refer to Section 5.0 Program Stakeholder Engagement of the Standard.
55. B. When working to derive benefits metrics, Diego is working on Benefits analysis and planning phase. Refer to Section 4.2/Page 48 of the Standard.
56. C. When working to ensure continued realization of benefits, Sophie is working on Benefits sustainment phase. Refer to Section 4.5/Page 55 of the Standard.
57. A. The actions described on the text correspond to the expected content of a document when preparing a benefits management plan. Refer to Section 4.2.1/Page 50 of the Standard.
58. C. Refer to Section 5.3 Program Stakeholder Engagement Planning of the Standard.

59. B. Refer to Section 5.5 Program Stakeholder Communications of the Standard.
60. C. Refer to Section 5.1 Program Stakeholder Identification of the Standard.
61. D. Refer to Section 5.1 Program Stakeholder Identification of the Standard.
62. C. When working to map benefits into a program management plan, Felipe is working on Benefits analysis and planning phase. Refer to Section 4.2/Page 48 of the Standard.
63. B. Refer to Section 8.1.2.2 of the Standard.
64. D. Refer to Section 7.2.2.3 of the Standard.
65. B. Refer to Section 8.1.2.7 of the Standard.
66. B. Refer to Section 8.1.2.11 of the Standard.
67. B. Refer to Section 1.4 The Relationship among Portfolio, Program, and Project Management of the Standard.
68. D. Program health checks assess a program's ongoing performance and progress toward the realization and sustainment of benefits. Refer to Section 6.1.10/Page 76 of the Standard.
69. A. Refer to Section 3.2 of the Standard.
70. A. When working with strategic alignment of the program and its components with the intended goals of both the program and the organization, Sandra is working within Program governance reviews. Refer to Section 6.1.9/Page 75 of the Standard.
71. C. When the organization pursues similar programs, the interactions among the performance domains are similar and repetitive. Refer to Section 2.2/Page 25 of the Standard.
72. A. Refer to Section 5.1 of the Standard.
73. D. Program stakeholder engagement identifies and analyzes stakeholder needs and manages expectations and communications to foster stakeholder support. Refer to Section 2.1/Page 25 of the Standard.
74. D. The program manager should be the champion of change in the organization. Refer to Section 5.1/Page 59 of the Standard.
75. D. Refer to Section 8.1.2.12 of the Standard.
76. C. Escalation process outside the program is performed between the program management team, the program's steering committee, and other stakeholders. Refer to Section 6.1.6/Page 73 of the Standard.
77. B. Refer to Section 1.7 Role of the Program Manager of the Standard.
78. D. Refer to Section 8.1.1.3 of the Standard.
79. B. Refer to Section 5.4 of the Standard.
80. A. Program stakeholder engagement is the performance domain that identifies and analyzes stakeholder needs and manages expectations and communication to foster stakeholder support. Refer to Section 5.1/Page 57 of the Standard.
81. A. Refer to Section 8.2.6 Program Quality Assurance and Control of the Standard.
82. B. Refer to Section 5.0 Program Stakeholder Engagement of the Standard.

83. C. Refer to Section 8.2.9 of the Standard.
84. C. Refer to Section 8.1.2.5 of the Standard.
85. B. Refer to Section 5.1 Program Stakeholder Identification of the Standard.
86. D. Refer to Section 8.2.2.2 of the Standard.
87. B. The program manager is the main person responsible to ensure that the program is run within the governance framework while managing the day-to-day program activities. Refer to Section 6.1/Page 67 of the Standard.
88. D. Refer to Section 8.2.6.1 of the Standard.
89. B. On the program governance plan is the deliverable established to design and implement effective governance to prepare documented descriptions of each program's governance frameworks, functions, and processes. Refer to Section 6.1.1/Page 67 of the Standard.
90. D. Refer to Section 6.0 Program Governance of the Standard.
91. B. Refer to Section 8.2.3 of the Standard.
92. B. Refer to Section 8.1.2.5 of the Standard.
93. B. When working to consolidate coordinated benefits, Silvie is working on Benefits transition phase. Refer to Section 4.4/Page 53 of the Standard.
94. A. Refer to Section 7.1.2 Program Definition Phase of the Standard.
95. A. The program roadmap should be updated to reflect changes in the benefits management plan. Refer to Section 4.3.1/Page 52 of the Standard.
96. A. Refer to Section 7.1.4 Program Closure Phase of the Standard.
97. D. Refer to Section 5.4 of the Standard.
98. A. Refer to Section 5.1 Program Stakeholder Identification of the Standard.
99. A. This is the reason why it is important to consider stakeholders who have both positive and negative influence on the program. You, as a program manager, need to hear opinions from all sources. Refer to Section 5.2/Page 62 of the Standard.
100. A. As external stakeholder and close friend of the President of Senate, it may have more influence to solve the issue. Refer to Section 5.1/Page 57 of the Standard.
101. C. When working to identify and qualify benefits, Laura is working on Benefits identification phase. Refer to Section 4.1/Page 46 of the Standard.
102. A. Refer to Section 5.1 of the Standard.
103. B. Refer to Section 1.2 Program Definition of the Standard.
104. D. Refer to Section 5.1 of the Standard.
105. A. Effective risk and issue management ensures that key risks and issues are escalated appropriately and resolved in a timely manner. Refer to Section 6.1.6/Page 73 of the Standard.
106. C. Refer to Section 1.9 of the Standard.
107. A. Refer to Section 5.0 Program Stakeholder Engagement of the Standard.
108. C. Refer to Section 8.1.2.12 of the Standard.
109. A. Refer to Section 7.1.2 Program Definition Phase of the Standard.
110. B. This is the most often and accurate reason. Refer to Section 5.1/Page 57 of the Standard.

111. A. Refer to Section 8.3.5. Program Risk Management Transition of the Standard.
112. D. Refer to Section 1.4 The Relationship among Portfolio, Program, and Project Management of the Standard.
113. D. Refer to Section 5.0 Program Stakeholder Engagement of the Standard.
114. B. This statement is TRUE about stakeholder engagement. Refer to Section 5.1/Page 57 of the Standard.
115. B. Refer to Section 1.4 The Relationship among Portfolio, Program, and Project Management of the Standard.
116. C. Refer to Section 8.2 of the Standard.
117. D. Refer to Section 3.2 of the Standard.
118. B. Member of the program steering committee's typical responsibilities includes ensuring program goals and planned benefits align with organizational strategic and operational goals. Refer to Section 6.2.2/Page 81 of the Standard.
119. A. Refer to Section 5 of the Standard.
120. B. Refer to Section 5.1 of the Standard.
121. D. Refer to Section 8.1.2.5 of the Standard.
122. C. Refer to Section 2.5 Program and Project Distinctions of the Standard.
123. C. Refer to Section 1.1 Purpose of the Standard.
124. D. Refer to Section 5.4 of the Standard.
125. A. Refer to Section 8.1.2 Program Planning Phase Activities of the Standard.
126. A. Refer to Section 8.3.2 Program Information Archiving and Transition of the Standard.
127. D. Member of the program steering committee's typical responsibilities includes providing governance support for the program to include oversight, control, integration, and decision-making functions. Refer to Section 6.2.2/Page 81 of the Standard.
128. B. Refer to Section 8.2. Program Delivery Phase Activities of the Standard.
129. D. Refer to Section 4.3.2 Benefits and Program Governance of the Standard.
130. C. Refer to Section 3.5.3 of the Standard.
131. A. Refer to Section 8.2.6.1 of the Standard.
132. C. Refer to Section 5.3 of the Standard.
133. D. This is the best and accurate reason of collaborative work between program and project management activities. Refer to Section 1.4.3/Page 12 of the Standard.
134. C. On this question the word "benefit" has been replaced by a synonym. So program benefits alignments is the right option. Refer to Section 4.1/Page 43 of the Standard.
135. D. Refer to Section 8.2.8.2 of the Standard.
136. D. Refer to Sections 8.1.2.12 and 8.1.2.3 of the Standard.

137. B. Program closure phase consists of program activities to get the program terminated earlier or transitioned to another program. Refer to Section 7.1.1/ Page 90 of the Standard.

138. A. On program management, the focus is on engagement. Thus, the answer is stakeholder engagement plan. Refer to Section 5.4/Page 64 of the Standard.

139. C. Refer to Section 7.2.1 Program Activities Overview of the Standard.

140. D. Refer to Section 5.3 of the Standard.

141. B. Refer to Section 8.1.2.7 of the Standard.

142. C. Refer to Section 8.2.8.2 of the Standard.

143. A. Refer to Section 7.2.2.3 of the Standard.

144. D. Refer to Section 7.1.2.1 of the Standard.

145. D. The program management office is a management structure that provides professional expertise using staff highly trained in applying program governance practices to provide oversight, support, and decision-making capability to the program. Refer to Section 6.2.3/Page 82 of the Standard.

146. A. Refer to Section 7.1.4 Program Closure Phase of the Standard.

147. B. Refer to Section 3.2 of the Standard.

148. D. Refer to Section 5.2 Program Stakeholder Analysis of the Standard.

149. C. Refer to Section 5.1 of the Standard.

150. D. As part of the stakeholder analysis and engagement planning activities, expectation of program benefits delivery for each stakeholder is taken into consideration. Refer to Section 5.3/Page 64 of the Standard.

151. C. Once all major stakeholders are listed in the stakeholder register, the program manager will categorize them in order to start analyzing them. Refer to Section 5.2/Page 62 of the Standard.

152. B. One of the differences between programs and portfolio resides on relatedness as the difference between how the delivery of intended benefits depends upon its components or portfolio owner. Refer to Section 2.4/Page 27 of the Standard.

153. B. Refer to Section 8.3.3 Program Procurement Closure of the Standard.

154. A. As part of the stakeholder analysis and engagement planning activities, ability to influence the outcome of the program for each stakeholder is taken into consideration. Refer to Section 5.3/Page 64 of the Standard.

155. A. Refer to Section 7.1.3.2 of the Standard.

156. D. Programs function similarly to projects in that the program is closed. Refer to Section 7.1/Page 89 of the Standard.

157. B. Refer to Section 5.3 of the Standard.

158. D. When working to maintain a benefits register, Sandra is working on Benefits delivery phase. Refer to Section 4.3/Page 51 of the Standard.

159. B. Refer to Section 7.2.2.3 of the Standard.

160. D. A program initiation is not related to hide errors nor failures of any kind. Refer to Section 1.2.1/Page 6 of the Standard.

161. A. The program steering committee is responsible for defining the types of changes that a program manager would be independently authorized to approve. Refer to Section 6.1.8/Page 74 of the Standard.
162. A. When a stakeholder has a high level of authority and high level of concern, he needs to be managed closely. Refer to Section 5.2/Page 62 of the Standard.
163. C. Stakeholder engagement is a continuous activity and you frequently will need to update it, so Juan Jose is completely wrong on his way of thinking. Refer to Section 5.4/Page 64 of the Standard.
164. A. On this question, the word "benefit" has been replaced by a synonym. So program benefits alignments is the right option. Refer to Section 4.1/Page 43 of the Standard.
165. A. Program governance facilitates program funding to the degree necessary to support the approved business case. Refer to Section 6.1.3/Page 72 of the Standard.
166. B. When a stakeholder has a low level of authority and high level of concern, he needs to be kept informed. Refer to Section 5.2/Page 62 of the Standard.
167. B. Refer to Section 5.4 Program Stakeholder Engagement of the Standard.
168. C. Refer to Section 5.3 of the Standard.
169. C. Refer to Section 8.2.9 of the Standard.
170. D. Refer to Section 8.2.5 of the Standard.

For more test questions or inquiries about PgMP training, complete the product registration with author at www.pmoadvisory.com/product-registration.

Index

Note: Locators in *italics* represent figures and **bold** indicate tables in the text.

Printed in the United States
by Baker & Taylor Publisher Services